REAPING WHAT SHE SOWS

Also by Nancy Matsumoto

Exploring the World of Japanese Craft Sake

By the Shore of Lake Michigan

Unforgotten Voices From Heart Mountain

REAPING
WHAT
SHE SOWS

HOW WOMEN ARE
REBUILDING
OUR BROKEN FOOD
SYSTEM

NANCY
MATSUMOTO

MELVILLE HOUSE
BROOKLYN · LONDON

Reaping What She Sows

First published in 2025 by Melville House Publishing
Copyright © 2024 by Nancy Matsumoto
All rights reserved
First Melville House Printing: August 2025
Distributed by Penguin Random House LLC,
1745 Broadway, New York, NY 10019 USA.
www.penguinrandomhouse.com

Melville House Publishing
46 John Street
Brooklyn, NY 11201

and

Melville House UK
Suite 2000
16/18 Woodford Road
London E7 0HA

mhpbooks.com
@melvillehouse

ISBN: 978-1-68589-203-6
ISBN: 978-1-68589-204-3 (eBook)

Library of Congress Control Number: 2025939743

Designed by Beste M. Doğan

Printed in the United States of America
10 9 8 7 6 5 4 3 2 1

A catalog record for this book is available from the Library of Congress

The authorized representative in the EU for product safety and compliance is
Easy Access System Europe, Mustamäe tee 50, 10621 Tallinn, Estonia.
gpsr.requests@easproject.com

For all of those who feed the world—body and soul—and nourish the earth.

CONTENTS

INTRODUCTION

ON AN EARLY SEPTEMBER AFTERNOON, I stand with Noreen Thomas on the edge of the pancake-flat, twelve-hundred-acre Moorhead, Minnesota, farm that has been in the Thomas family for close to one hundred fifty years. Since being certified organic in 1997, it has produced high-quality organic grains, garden produce, and pasture-raised eggs. Thomas points to the bird habitat buffer she is encouraging with a late-August hay cutting, which will provide ample protection for ground-nesting meadowlarks.

The bright-yellow-bellied birds' numbers had for years been in steep decline due to loss of habitat and mortality caused by intensive single-crop farming of corn, soy, or sugar beets, and the chemical fertilizers and pesticides that mode of farming relies on. Today, the birds' resurgent presence on Doubting Thomas Farms is a sign of ecosystem health. Not only do they add beautiful color and song to the landscape, they are also the first defense against pests such as caterpillars and grasshoppers, keeping their numbers in check. In another part of the farm, Thomas shows me a trial field of perennial sunflowers, part of a set of practices that are making the surrounding land and waters healthier and more climate resilient, and filling a gap in the market after the Russia–Ukraine war made sunflower oil harder to come by.

Doubting Thomas is an outlier in Clay County and in Minnesota, where only one percent of farms are certified organic. It is a tiny island of biodiversity in a vast golden sea of genetically modified, chemically treated monocrops that ripple out as far as the eye can see. Going against the tide has not been easy, but Thomas says, "It's about providing really good food for my family, my grandchildren, and the community. If people didn't discern a difference in flavor, I wouldn't bother. But they do, and it's something we've forgotten, how food should taste."

Thomas is just one of the dozens of audacious women I met on my travels across North and Central America, from the Indigenous fishing grounds off Vancouver Island, British Columbia, to the lush tropical cacao forests of Belize, and the gently sloping mountains of Vermont, who are creating an alternative or "alt food system" that is shorter, more direct, transparent, and equitable than the broken food system run by the global monopolies of Big Food.

By "food system," I mean the processes and infrastructure involved in feeding a population, from sowing seeds, to growing and harvesting, to processing, packaging, distribution, and disposal. It may seem counterintuitive to talk of a broken food system. The shelves of our big box stores are stocked to the rafters with products, and we've come to take for granted their accessibility and low prices. What could be wrong with that? We are so comfortably ensconced in the world that industrial Big Food has constructed around us that we are unable to see that all this cheap and convenient food is eroding our health, our environment, the health and wellbeing of our laborers, and our choices.

It takes imagination to see that there is another way to live, another way to harvest our land and our seas, to feed the world equitably and with dignity, and to protect our planet. According to a report from the United Nations Food and Agriculture Organization (FAO), the hidden cost of our global food system in 2020 amounted to $12.7 trillion,[1] or about 10 percent of global GDP. Seventy-three percent of those hidden costs are related to unhealthy dietary patterns that our industrialized food system promotes. Developed countries, with their diets high in processed foods, refined carbohydrates, and saturated fats, and low in whole fruits, vegetables, and grains, bear the brunt of these costs, in the form of chronic diseases such as diabetes and heart disease. Costs to the environment—over half of which are due to food production–related nitrogen emissions and are a primary driver of biodiversity loss[2]—account for another 20 percent. And as ample evidence has shown, those costs are disproportionately borne by the poorest among us, who cannot afford to cocoon themselves in the protective swaddling of countries or neighborhoods where the air is cleaner, the waters less toxic, the grocery aisles filled with chemical-free food. Unless we change the way we produce food, continued destruction of ecosystems and habitats will threaten our ability to sustain human populations.

I have spent much of my career chronicling different aspects of "the good food movement" toward healthier and more sustainable growing practices. It is a subject matter that chose me. As someone who loves to eat and drink, and write about eating and drinking, reporting on the creations of top chefs and the sourcing of rare ingredients felt pleasurable yet incomplete. My love for these things was too closely tied to the impulse that drove me to write a junior high school report on global hunger: the belief that access to delicious and nourishing food is a basic human right.

My views have been shaped by my culture, too. As the third-generation daughter of Japanese immigrants, I felt the unspoken love that is best communicated through cooking and eating together around the dining room table; the delight taken in fresh, seasonal ingredients; the respect paid to nature, and those who farm, fish, forage, and hunt for our food; the concept of *mottainai*, of never wasting food that can feed a hungry mouth. Wasting food, as my father liked to say, "is a crime against nature."

Being the daughter of World War II US concentration camp survivors made me appreciate the forms of cooperative and mutual aid that my ancestors practiced when the government of their adoptive country was not on their side. So it was natural to want to tell similar stories in this book, of the importance of First Nations people and members of the African, Vietnamese, Palestinian, and Indian diasporas in creating and maintaining forms of mutual aid, and their work building more just and resilient food systems that helped them thrive on the margins of the dominant food system.

They are cultivating a modern hybrid form of land and water stewardship, combining the ancient wisdom of traditional food gathering and production with more than a half century of trial, error, and research into organic and regenerative (meaning replacing as much energy as you take from nature) methods. For these women who have dedicated their lives to forging a more democratic, healthy, and climate-resilient way of food production, the question has been: What will it take to hasten the dismantling of our broken food system?

In addition to the devastating loss of life the COVID-19 pandemic caused, it also revealed the cracks and flaws in our globalized industrial food system. Widespread shortages of basic foods and supplies were a shocking wake-up call to the fact that the highly processed foods and factory-farmed animals we've come to take for granted rely on very long, global supply chains that are fragile and increasingly vulnerable. The war between Ukraine and Russia created a supply chain disruption in grains and fertilizer. We witnessed the mass slaughter of animals and the dumping of milk due to interruptions to the global supply chain. Increasingly frequent episodes of climate instability, too, have underscored how vulnerable we are when any kind of global crisis disrupts the normal flow of goods around the globe. Food, we realized, was a form of national security, and we ignore local food production and resilience at our peril.

The good news is that people turned to shorter supply chains closer to home: the farmers, fishers, and ranchers we overlooked because going to the supermarket to buy inexpensive fruit from Peru or beef from Brazil was more convenient. We discovered that producers closer to home offer food that is fresher, more nutritious, and often more equitable, and that we can support local economies at the same time. We discovered, as paleontologist, ecologist, and food systems expert Catherine Badgley says, "that resilience is at the local scale, and not through enormous supply chains."

The industrialized Big Food system relies on those enormous chains, as well as economies of scale, large government agricultural subsidies, well-compensated lobbyists, and extractive farming practices, which determine what and how we eat. "Extractive," in the context of agriculture is the opposite of "regenerative," meaning taking out more biomass and fertility than is put back into the land. Usually it involves the use of chemical fertilizers to make up for the loss of native soil fertility, the clearing of big trees, and tilling the soil with machines. It is valuing the gains from this extraction, but not making up for the losses.[3] The growing interest in regenerative agricultural practices reflects a desire to reverse centuries of exploitative practices and restore balance to our ecosystem, and this interest was on full display during the tumult of the pandemic.

As I write this, Donald Trump has just begun his second term as president of the United States. The next four years will likely see the unraveling of gains made during the previous administration to fix our broken food system and make the lessons of this book—on the importance of mutual aid, cooperative assistance, and ancestral knowledge—all the more relevant. As I write this, in Canada, where I am living, society has been thrown into chaos by the 25 percent tariffs Trump has imposed on Canadian goods. With $70 billion USD in agricultural trade between two countries hanging in the balance, farmers on both sides of the border will suffer. Like the pandemic, this crisis will underscore the need for more local and regional food systems. You can make it a priority to fight for such systems over the corporate consolidation and lobbying power of Big Food. You can make it a priority to fight for the health, safety, and fair wages of migrant farm workers; for federal and state antidiscrimination policies; for practices that support soil conservation, clean water policies, and climate resilience.

As for my subjects, you may wonder, why the focus on women? Women have historically been important leaders of food production and distribution. But in the post-matriarchal societies of the modern age, male farmers gained better access to land ownership, credit, and agricultural education. In North America—with the exception of wartime shortages in male labor—that shift has occurred as the small family farm has given way to male-dominated mega-farms.

Yet it is because women have been relegated to the margins of food production that they are the early adopters of progressive food system change. Bu Nygrens, director of purchasing at the women-owned produce distribution company Veritable Vegetable, cites UN studies that have demonstrated "when women control the finances of a community they share the wealth. People do not go hungry, children are fed, and everyone gets a fair shake. It's about cooperation not about competition."

Finally, although I focus on alt food system producers and not on their much more numerous industrial-scale counterparts, this book is not about bashing large-scale, long-supply-chain producers, and lionizing the artisanal, the direct trade, and the small batch just for their own sake. I am arguing for systemwide change, bringing the two sides together so that one day they will become more similar than different. That is happening, and I have met the people who are on the ground and on the water building local food networks and pushing for grassroots change. Now it's time for you to meet them, too.

Nancy Matsumoto
Toronto, 2025

REAPING
WHAT
SHE SOWS

CHAPTER ONE

BLACK MUTUAL AID, FROM THE RURAL SOUTH TO THE URBAN NORTHEAST

IN A REMOTE, DENSELY WOODED corner of the New Communities land trust in Albany, Georgia, ancient bald cypresses drip with Spanish moss, insects buzz, and humidity oozes like oil from the lush green former plantation that surrounds me, a scene torn from the pages of a southern gothic novel. To start my journey through the alt food system, I have headed south, to trace the history and modern-day legacy of the African American agricultural cooperatives and mutual aid societies that could serve as a road map forward, an example of a more equitable and transparent way to produce and distribute food.

In *South to America*, the scholar of African American culture Imani Perry demonstrated how the creation of the institution of slavery set the pattern, the deep warp and weft of how life would be conducted in the United States. To understand our country, she asserted, you have to understand the South. My search is for the creative solutions that African slaves and their descendants came up with to combat centuries of systemic racism. To understand how we can free ourselves from the late-stage capitalism of Big Food oligarchies, I want to see how that system of cooperation can energize and unite today's efforts to forge an alternative food system.

I have come here to meet an icon and hero of Black rural farmers, Shirley Sherrod. Her history, as well as the land trust's, stretches back to the earliest days of the Civil Rights Movement and embodies the close connection between the blood-soaked days of Freedom Riders and lunch counter protests and the fight for Black farmers' access to land. New Communities draws on a rich history of Black cooperatives and mutual aid societies, an organizational model based on the sharing of resources, equipment, technical knowledge, and pooled savings.

America's earliest rice-, tobacco-, and cotton-growing empires were built on the backs and agricultural expertise of generations of kidnapped African slaves who toiled on this land and across the cotton- and rice-growing colonies. Some women survived the notoriously treacherous Middle Passage across the Atlantic with seeds braided into their hair to ensure they would have familiar crops to grow on the other end.[1]

By all rights, these skilled farmers' post–Civil War descendants should have been inheritors of their richly detailed agricultural know-how, free to amass land and wealth through that knowledge. But things didn't work out that way. The "Forty acres and a mule" idea of freedmen land ownership that can be traced back to the Confiscation Act of 1865, when Confederate lands were seized from owners for redistribution, never stood a chance. Within a year, the federal government began returning land to pardoned plantation owners. To protect themselves from the angry Black farmers trying to safeguard their newly acquired but tenuously held land, White landowners formed private militias that were the precursors to the Ku Klux Klan. Southern racism simply adopted new guises: discriminatory Black Codes and then Jim Crow laws.

Shockingly, the biggest loss of Black farmland has occurred since World War II, a period when nearly a million Black farmers have been driven off their land through means both legal and illegal.[2] Some of the most vitriolic and egregious examples of the systematic discrimination by the United States Department of Agriculture against Black farmers came during the Civil Rights Movement of the late 1950s and 1960s.[3] While demonstrators and freedom fighters picketed and staged sit-ins in the cities, the rural White agricultural elite, those in charge of doling out USDA credit to purchase land or equipment, farm loans, crop insurance, and scientific and technological guidance, withheld all of those things from Black farmers. Economic discrimination against these farmers went hand in hand with the routine intimidation and violence they endured.

The United States Department of Agriculture, by administrating a form of structural racism that denied Black farmers access to loans, credits, and other programs that allowed White farmers to build generational wealth, has overseen the loss of more than twelve million acres of farmland owned by Black farmers over the last century.[4] Today, Black people account for more than 13 percent of the US population but just 1.7 percent of its farmers. This robbing of land and livelihood was happening all around Shirley as she came of age in Georgia. Their losses, economists estimate, have amounted to hundreds of billions of dollars, perhaps even in the trillions. And it was not just Black wealth and a means of self-sufficiency that was foreclosed, it was generations of accumulated agricultural wisdom.

SHIRLEY SHERROD'S ENTRY INTO THE MOVEMENT

WHEN I BEGAN REACHING OUT to Black women agricultural leaders, I discovered a tight-knit group of women scattered throughout the South, connected through their efforts to preserve Black farm culture and protect and grow its land holdings. I also found that all roads led to Shirley Sherrod, who had mentored and guided so many of them.

I pull up to her sprawling Georgia farm in my gray rental car on this sweltering August day. Dressed in a navy blouse and pants, Shirley's hair is an attractively styled swirl of gray and black. She wears a mask indoors, a concession to the fact that COVID is still a threat, and that her longtime husband, Charles—a founding member of the Student Non-Violent Coordinating Committee and a civil rights icon in his own right—is at home and ailing. She looks tired, but her memory is as sharp as a sickle. I can still see traces of the glowing, beautiful seventeen-year-old she was in 1965. So beautiful that before even meeting her, the young Charles Sherrod, in town canvassing for Black voter registration, took one look at her photograph in the family home and declared, "I'm going to marry that girl."

Shirley was a high school senior in Baker County, Georgia, that year, the same year her father, Hosie Miller, was shot in the fields of his five-hundred-acre corn, cotton, and peanut farm by a White farmer named Cal Hall Jr. The two had argued in the past, usually over the way that Hall's cows wandered onto Miller's fields. This time, when Miller told Hall they could settle their dispute in court and turned around to go shut the gate, Hall shot Miller in the back, the bullet penetrating his chest, abdomen, and liver. Miller died ten days later in the hospital. Despite the presence of two eyewitnesses, an all-White grand jury refused to indict Hall, and a second attempt to bring murder charges against Hall was also unsuccessful.

Her father's killing marked a turning point in Shirley's life—she gave up her ambitions to move north and escape the limited prospects she faced at home in the Jim Crow south. She decided to stay in Baker County to fight for change.

SHIRLEY AND CHARLES SHERROD
AND NEW COMMUNITIES

THE SMALL OFFICE SPACE WE are sitting in is part of a reincarnated collaborative farm and nonprofit educational organization that Shirley, Charles, and a group of civil rights activists established in 1969:

New Communities. Its goal was to secure farmland for landless southern Black people, and its organizers took their inspiration from precolonial collectivist societies in Africa, the Americas, and China, as well as twentieth-century Jewish land settlements. Charles was among an idealistic group of organizers and dreamers that set off to tour kibbutzim in Israel in 1968, returning fired up and filled with plans to start their own collective farm.

They succeeded, but only after a fight; when racist governor Lester Maddox denied their bid for federal funds, Charles salvaged the project by touring the region to raise private funds. In 1969 New Communities became the largest Black-owned farm in the country, devoting 2,200 acres of its land to growing corn, peanuts, and soybeans, and in its huge greenhouse, new crops like muscadine grapes. Members sold produce and pork products from their smokehouse at roadside stands. At its height, New Communities covered 5,700 acres. But its display of self-sufficiency drew vitriolic opposition from neighbors.

Although five hundred families wanted to move in, White lenders talked them out of the long-term renewable leases, pointing out that they would never own land. Their buildings were shot at while cooperative members were inside them. Liquid fertilizer they ordered would arrive either highly diluted and ineffective, or tampered with to create uneven growth in the farm's cornfields. "They just came at us in every way to block us, to do anything to get that land from us," Sherrod recalls. While plantations owned by wealthy landowners received financing for irrigation, New Communities' application was denied. One USDA Farmer's Home Administration (FmHA) administrator told Shirley, "You'll get a loan here over my dead body."[5]

Severe drought in the early 1980s and the denial of an emergency loan from the FmHA led to the farm's foreclosure in 1985. Compensation for their suffering did not come until 2009, when New Communities received $12.8 million, plus $330,000 for the mental anguish incurred from the USDA.

This was just one piece of the landmark 1999 Pigford v. Glickman class-action lawsuit brought against the USDA by an impoverished North Carolina farmer named Timothy Pigford, joined by hundreds of Black farmers. The suit alleged racial discrimination against them and failure to properly investigate complaints between 1983 and 1997. When the decision was handed down, there were 18,000 Black farms in America, a fraction of the 925,000 in 1920.[6] In total, more than $1 billion was paid out to approximately 16,000 victims, with New Communities receiving the largest award of all. But it was too late for hundreds of thousands of Black farmers, and since the verdict, the number of Black farms has continued to dwindle.

The Sherrods eventually resurrected New Communities, purchasing Cypress Pond Plantation (a more recent name; during the Civil War it was known as The Homestead Place) for $4.5 million in 2011. This is the prime piece of property I am standing on today, which sprawls over sixteen hundred acres on the outskirts of Albany, one of nine plantations once owned by Hartwell Hill Tarver, one of Georgia's wealthiest citizens and owner of more than a thousand slaves.

The Sherrods envision this version of New Communities as a farm and home for progressive thought and action. In addition to growing muscadine grapes, Satsuma oranges, blueberries, and a variety of vegetables, two hundred acres are allotted to the land trust's pecan cooperative, which helps small growers in the area improve production and processing methods and get access to market. Through its allied nonprofit Southwest Georgia Project for Community Education, founded by the Sherrods in 1961, activities include farm field days for products such as beekeeping, truffle growing, and rice-growing trials done in collaboration with a Louisiana-based collective called Jubilee Justice (JJ).

Sherrod has three goals: to increase community access to fresh and affordable foods, deliver opportunities and resources to underserved farmers of color, and build a more equitable local food system. The project she hopes will deliver on these is a planned $20 million food hub centered on a former Winn Dixie grocery store in Albany, which will include a fresh food market, a grocery aggregation and distribution center, a wellness clinic, and a community kitchen for food and food truck entrepreneurs. It is the modern-day equivalent of the many mutual aid initiatives that nourished Black agricultural communities cut off from access to capital and public funds.

Amber Bell, project director for the food hub, grew up in Albany, Georgia, witnessing the high rates of hypertension and diabetes among her relatives and neighbors. To help combat the diet-related disease and the food deserts all around her, she earned undergraduate and graduate degrees in public health. But it wasn't until becoming Sherrod's assistant and then working for the Southwest Georgia Project that she saw the connection between these social ills and farming. "My grandparents' generation did everything in their power to give their children an education so my parents would not have to pick cotton. We lost a whole generation to agriculture, but my generation, we understand its value," she tells me.

For me, the story of overcoming racial and economic discrimination—situations where the deck is so stacked that conventional methods of seeking justice are not even on the table—through mutual aid and economic cooperation is a familiar one. My parents and their families were among the 120,000 people of Japanese descent who were unconstitutionally stripped of their land and rights during one of the most shameful chapters of US history: the forced World War II–era removal and imprisonment of all people of Japanese descent living on the West Coast. Two-thirds of those torn from their homes and communities were American-born citizens, and all of them were sent to remote World War II concentration camps. Scare-mongering politicians fanned the flames of race-hatred and hysteria in large part because it was a convenient justification for taking away the livelihood of Japanese farmers after the bombing of Pearl Harbor. Japanese residents in California controlled less than 2 percent of the farmland in the state before 1940 yet produced a third or more of its fruits and vegetables.[7]

When you are barred from purchasing land, or procuring farm loans and crop insurance, then robbed of your livelihood, the only avenue left is reliance on each other. So, like southern Black people, the Japanese prisoners pooled their business and organizational skills. In the prison camp where my father and his family were sent, they launched Manzanar Cooperative Enterprises, owned, operated, and managed entirely by prisoners. In addition to what goods they could source from outside the prison, the cooperative provided services ranging from shoe repair to barber and beauty shops. I am here to learn from the women applying the lessons of their forebears and mine to the present-day alt supply chains of the rural African American South.

THE NEW GUARD: KONDA MASON
AND JUBILEE JUSTICE

NOT LONG AFTER ANDREW JACKSON wrested this corner of southwest Georgia from the Muskogee Creek Nation in 1814, wealthy cotton planters from the central and eastern part of the state and the Carolinas moved in, assembling thousand-acre-plus parcels and importing slaves to work them. By 1840 enslaved Africans and African Americans outnumbered Whites, and by 1860, accounted for three-quarters of the population in Albany, Georgia.[8]

Spirits from the past still linger here in the New Communities' compound, where I, a visitor from the North, am a fish out of water, drifting through the algae-scented air that rests upon eerily still Rawls Pond. As I survey the profusion of bald cypress trees surrounding me, their lush green branches dripping with tassels of brown Spanish moss, and feel the weight of the humid air on my skin, I picture the sepia-toned photos of the era, fields of cotton as far as the eye can see, populated by African slaves and their children, dressed in long skirts and white work shirts, bent over to harvest, or balancing large woven baskets filled with fluffy white cotton bolls on their heads. The sight of an anachronistic, boxy white RV snaps me out of my unsettling reverie.

This is the vehicle that members of Jubilee Justice's Black Farmer's Rice Project have been living out of during their seventeen-day listening tour of southern, Black-owned farms. New Communities is the latest stop on the organization's tour, where they will view rice-growing trials and brainstorm on everything from growing practices to marketing plans. JJ is devoted to repairing wounds suffered by both Black people and the lands they worked; in addition to the rice trial plots, JJ plans to open a learning center on the New Communities site. Included in the group are founder Konda Mason and farmer Iriel Edwards.

Though not the literal descendants of the hundreds of slaves who once worked these grounds, JJ farmers are their spiritual successors, pulled back to the land by collective memories that transcend time. Using regenerative agricultural practices, they are building a vertically integrated— where one entity controls the entire chain of production—cooperative of

Black rice farmers throughout the South. In addition to planting, harvesting, cleaning, and storing grain, JJ will provide milling, packaging, and access to new markets.

Terms such as "agroecology," "climate-smart agriculture," "sustainable," and the broader term "permaculture" to varying degrees encompass the tenets of regenerative agriculture: tilling the soil as little as possible to leave topsoil and its dense network of microbes intact, planting "cover crops" to slow the process of erosion; enhancing soil health, water absorption and retention; reducing weeds, and helping control pests and disease with minimal use of chemical fertilizers and pesticides. Often poultry, livestock, and other animals and insects are incorporated into such landscapes to further increase biodiversity.

Mason, JJ's founder and president, is a slight woman with penetrating eyes and long black dreadlocks. She's dressed in a khaki shirt with sleeves rolled up to her elbows, faded blue jeans and a face mask, even in the scorching heat. Mostly, she listens. "I'm a starter, then I pass the organization on to the next person," she tells me. Her previous ventures include an Oakland coworking space, a microlending fund, and a conference on restorative economics and community capital.

In 2019, Mason attended a gathering of women CEOs of B Corps ("beneficial corporations" that prioritize not only profits, but also social and environmental good) in New York, where she met Caryl Levine, co-founder and co-CEO (along with her husband, Ken Lee) of the heirloom and organic rice company Lotus Foods. She learned about the couple's efforts to teach smallholders a method of farming known as Systemic Rice Intensification (SRI) that is far less water intensive, improves yields, and produces rice much higher in micronutrients than conventional rice-growing practices. Because it requires far fewer hours in the fields, the growing method results in a dramatic reduction in work-related injuries and conditions among the mostly women and girls involved in planting and harvesting rice.

Impressed with Lotus's work with smallholder women farmers, Mason, thinking of the generations of West African slaves who were expert growers of Carolina Gold rice and cotton, asked, "What about developing a supply chain of Black rice farmers?" This was the conversation that sparked the idea for Jubilee Justice, and the effort to convince Black southerners to consider farming as a livelihood. "After emancipation, many former slaves said, 'I'm not doing this anymore,'" Mason explains. "We're working toward the reinvigoration of the legacy of rice grown by Black folk and *owned* by Black folk."

But Mason's vision goes well beyond teaching African Americans to farm again; her goal is to reverse more than three centuries of extraction and exploitation and create spiritual healing through what she calls "reparative genealogy" or "restorative justice." Martin Luther King Jr. famously said, "The arc of the moral universe is long, but it bends toward justice." JJ wants it to bend a little harder, "toward justice, equity, and repair."

Some of that healing and reparations work has already begun. New Communities and JJ, along with the Decolonizing Wealth Project, have together redistributed $2 million to BIPOC (Black, Indigenous, and People of Color) farms, land justice, and food sovereignty organizations. Separately, Jubilee Justice and New Communities have distributed another $1 million using the services of the donor-advised fund Amalgamated Foundation.

After her eureka moment with Caryl Levine, Mason connected with Elisabeth Keller, a nurse-midwife turned president of her family's 3,600-

acre Inglewood Plantation in central Louisiana, the largest organic farm in the state. Although Keller's family made its fortune in oil, not the slave trade, she was looking to repair the historic wrongs that occurred on her land. With backing from Inglewood, Jubilee Justice purchased five acres of farmland in Alexandria, Louisiana. JJ's plans include training Black farmers in sustainable, regenerative land management practices and co-operative ownership, and securing financial security by controlling the entire rice value chain.

This means not only teaching farmers how to grow rice regeneratively but then building out its alt supply chain with transparent growing and labor practices, and cutting out the many middlemen that make commodity rice farming a race to the bottom in price, quality, and sustainability. The co-op has built a mill and plans to sell its threshed, dried, and milled rice through its website and under its own brand as a sub-label under Lotus Foods. So far Mason has recruited thirteen farming families in Louisiana, Mississippi, South Carolina, Georgia, North Carolina, Alabama, and Kentucky who are growing organic specialty rice varieties. For now, they are sharing a small Japanese Iseki combine harvester, transporting it from farm to farm on a trailer. Jubilee Justice is building an alt food chain.

Unlike this tight-knit, regenerative, regional rice-supply-chain-in-the-making, global commodity rice supply chains are highly complex, extremely long, and nontransparent. Rice accounts for nearly a fifth of the calories consumed by humans, and 90 percent of the world's supply is grown in Asia, although it is a staple consumed throughout the world.

Commodity rice growing has evolved to maximize yield, involving intensive use of water that has depleted aquifers. Heavy use of herbicides, chemical fertilizers, and pesticides has polluted groundwater. Rice cultivation is also a primary contributor to greenhouse gas emissions, responsible for a hefty 10 percent of global methane gas released.[9] All of these factors have taken a toll on rice-growing ecosystems and the laborers who toil in them. It is a system now being taxed further by rising temperatures and more frequent disruptive weather events.[10]

Once harvested, rice is sold by farmers to millers, who send the milled rice on to distribution centers, often through agents or traders, and then finally to international buyers and retailers. The biggest suppliers control as much of the supply chain as possible, including farms and milling facilities, and act as exporter and supplier. With little to no access to credit, training, financial services, or trading opportunities,[11] smallholder farmers are at the mercy of the fluctuating global commodities market.

Worldwide, there are more women engaged in rice growing—sowing seeds, transplanting seedlings, weeding, harvesting, threshing, winnowing, and cleaning—than any other livelihood, an estimated half billion women and girls,[12] most of whom live in poverty. They are the human capital the commodity system relies upon even as increasingly sophisticated and high-yielding seeds are developed in laboratories. This is why the high-yielding, water- and labor-saving SRI system of rice growing, developed in Madagascar in the early 1980s, is so important to both Lotus Foods' mostly women growers and Jubilee Justice.

The transparent, resilient local food system and cooperative enterprises that New Communities and JJ are building are the opposite of the opaque global industrial food system, in which it is almost impossible to trace a product to its original farmer or producer.

Yet it is too easy to say that buying direct from a local producer like New Communities or Jubilee Justice farmers is the only way to get ethically and regeneratively grown rice. One small rice-growing cooperative, COFE (Cambodian Organic Rice Farmers), sells the same certified organic and fair trade kha mali rice to both the fair trade, heirloom rice importer Lotus Foods and a subsidiary of the Madrid-based rice-producing giant Ebro. But it is only when buying through Lotus that you know who produced your rice and how it was farmed. When COFE's product enters the Ebro supply chain, that information is lost. In this case, the Ebro consumer is getting something better than they could hope for, but that is not usually true when dealing with the longer supply chain.

Sometimes a short, ethical supply chain product is hidden in plain sight in a big box store. Lotus's organic millet and brown rice ramen, for example, is a top seller in Costco stores across North America. The product stays stocked in Costco warehouses because it consistently meets the minimum of eight hundred units sold per week, per store—a threshold very few of the small or regional producers in this book can meet. The onus is on us, the consumer, to look for companies like Lotus that we know are part of the alt food system we want to support.

JESSICA GORDON NEMBHARD:
THE AFRICAN AMERICAN COOPERATIVE MOVEMENT

WHAT I HAVE WITNESSED IN Georgia, and learned through my conversations with Sherrod and Mason, is that the sharing of agricultural expertise, the efforts to address supply chain bottlenecks and to create self-run food and agriculture hubs to help give small farmers access to market all have roots in earlier African American cooperative ventures and can even be traced back to traditional African societal structures.

To learn more about those, I reach out to scholar Jessica Gordon Nembhard, who teaches community justice and social economic development at John Jay College of the City University of New York and is the author of *Collective Courage: A History of African American Cooperative Economic Thought and Practice*. In it, she traces the history of powerful African American social and business organizations that pooled members' skills and assets, made their communities self-sufficient, and gave them a fighting chance in the dominant White power structure that had shut them out. In researching her book, she found that "almost all African American leaders were involved in Black cooperatives in some manner; they either promoted or engaged in the practice of cooperative ownership, particularly in their early careers or as part of their vision for a prosperous future without discrimination. In many ways the cooperative history is a retelling of African American history in general."

I spoke to Gordon Nembhard hoping to learn more about these cooperatives, what made them successful, and how they continue to level the playing field for marginalized communities and products. In the post–Civil War south, community aid was often disseminated through mutual aid societies. "Very early on, Black women-led mutual aid societies outgrew their male-led counterparts. They skyrocketed in numbers in the 1700s and 1800s, notably in Philadelphia, and to a lesser degree in New York City. Every major city had a Black mutual aid society, and most had more women than men. Women were instrumental in organizing, fundraising, day-to-day operations and networking among different organizations." Activities ranged from pooling their money to help each member achieve her financial goals more quickly, to cooperative grocery stores and protecting fugitive slave and free African Americans from kidnapping.

These societies reflected updated patterns of social organization that Black slaves brought with them from Africa. "Early African civilization included all kinds of cooperatives and solidarity economics. In many civilizations, women were the agricultural leaders, while men did the hunting and gathering." When Southern colonialists kidnapped African slaves and transported them to North America, "They didn't realize that women were the agriculturalists; they were just importing Black men and forcing them to farm."

In the late nineteenth and early twentieth century, mutual aid societies gave way to Black cooperatives, which emerged in tandem with the Civil Rights Movement. Gordon Nembhard defines a cooperative as "a member-owned company formed to serve a social need, often to provide a quality good or service (one that the market is not adequately providing) at an affordable price." Cooperatives have also been a way to create a production or distribution system where the market has failed to do so. In post–Civil War southern Black communities, which lacked access to affordable goods and services or the ability to produce and distribute products, the cooperative—funded by pooled resources—was the best answer.

I thought about the co-op at Manzanar, the high desert California prison camp to which my father and his family were forcibly relocated during World War II. It became home to the second-largest consumer cooperative in the United States, in today's dollars doing a booming $14 million in business annually to help provision its eleven thousand inmates. And it was only one of nine such Japanese-run wartime prison cooperatives spread across the western United States, which did a total of, again in today's dollars, $130 million in commerce.[13]

Many of these prison co-ops worked with the Associated Cooperatives in Oakland, California, to source goods. There, the prisoners found co-op workers who were staunchly aligned with their belief in overcoming oppression through cooperative economics. In today's global agribusiness-dominated food system, local cooperatives are one time-tested method of creating a more regional, healthy, and equitable food system.

In the Jim Crow South, cooperatives drew on the networks of community organizations and churches that had served as training grounds for generations of Black women leaders. "Black cooperatives often put women in leadership positions, or if not, women were acknowledged as playing integral roles compared to men in figurehead positions. Women often took on the role of education, of making sure members understood the model, and they were often touted as the ones raising the money, rallying enthusiasm when things were tough," Gordon Nembhard explains.

One powerful example of the Black business and agricultural resistance Gordon Nembhard describes is the farm cooperative founded by Fannie Lou Hamer, the Black Mississippi sharecropper and activist. In 1969 Hamer launched Freedom Farms Cooperative in Sunflower County, Mississippi. Funded by donations from nonprofits, civil rights activists, and the National Council of Negro Women, it amassed 680 acres of land. Hamer's goals were to build affordable, clean, and safe housing; develop an entrepreneurial clearing house, a small-business incubator that would provide resources for new business owners and training for those with limited skills; and develop an agricultural cooperative that would meet the food and nutritional needs of the county's most vulnerable people. Hamer made it clear that this applied to people of all colors.[14]

THE FEDERATION OF SOUTHERN COOPERATIVES

IN 1967, TWO YEARS BEFORE Fannie Lou Hamer founded Freedom Farms, a group of African American farmers who had had enough of routine, discriminatory treatment launched the Federation of Southern Cooperatives (FSC). In 2009, speaking before a group of young Black FSC organizers in Epes, Alabama, Wendell Paris Sr., a founding member, described the organization's role of providing members "the heart and backbone" they needed to fight back. Quoting the legendary Ezra Cunningham, another FSC founding member, Paris said, "If they had given us the right to go in and eat in those restaurants (referring to the famous lunch counter sit-ins of the civil rights era), we wouldn't have had the money to pay for it. The Federation was set up so you would have some money in your pocket."[15]

FSC was conceived as a "coop of coops," an umbrella organization for state-level cooperatives whose members included farmworkers, credit unions, domestic workers, and fishermen. Their objective was to find a solution to rural Black extreme poverty through a combination of collective fundraising, education, jobs, technical advice, training, and public policy lobbying.

It put money in farmers' pockets by helping them purchase and hold on to land, providing education in basic skills, and most important, aggregating their strength and buying power to counter a system of federal loans and assistance that was determined to shut them out. Through these efforts, a decade after its launch, the FSC helped preside over one million acres of farmland across the South. It was determined to cut the middlemen out, bypass racist Farmers Home Administration practices, and maximize profits for impoverished Black farmers.

Like New Communities, the FSC was guided by the global ideals of the cooperative movement. While Charles Sherrod and partners had visited kibbutzim in Israel, the FSC was influenced by the Rochdale Society of Equitable Pioneers, a nineteenth-century British cooperative famous for the codification of the principles of the movement. They are voluntary, open membership; democratic control by members; member contribution and control of capital; autonomy and independence; the provision of information; education and training; cooperation among cooperatives; and a shared concern for community.

The FSC helped steward African American land and resources in low-income rural communities and encourage small, sustainable, and organic farms. Teaching farmers how to erect hoop houses to extend the growing system, create water catchment systems to capture runoff, and provide training in soil nutrient analysis were all part of its educational programs.

Predictably, these activities provoked a backlash from the White establishment. In 1965, Martin Luther King Jr. preached at the Pleasant Grove Baptist Church in Gee's Bend, Alabama, home to a woman-run FSC member cooperative, the Freedom Quilting Bee. He encouraged them to register to vote and take part in the planned march from Selma to Montgomery. Town officials retaliated by shutting down the ferry service that connected their small town to Campden, where they were to vote. They were jailed before they even made it to the ferry.

In short, the FSC was constantly challenged by White society; by the early 1980s it was forced to pull back its reach from eleven southern states to four: Mississippi, Alabama, Georgia, and South Carolina. In 1985 the FSC merged with the Land Assistance Fund to better focus on land retention for Black landowners and family farmers.

The fight continues to this day. About fifteen thousand farmers of color expected debt relief after the passage in 2021 of $4 billion of federal debt forgiveness, intended to make amends for decades of racial discrimination. But close to a dozen opposition lawsuits from banks and White supremacist groups (including one Texas lawsuit spearheaded by Stephen Miller, former advisor and speechwriter, and current deputy chief of policy to Donald Trump) tied up the money in the courts until lawmakers repealed the program and folded debt relief funds into a much more broadly defined program under the 2022 Inflation Reduction Act. The earlier legislation's debt relief—targeted specifically for Black farmers to right the wrongs of racial disparity—was replaced by payments earmarked for "economically distressed" farmers regardless of color.

SHIRLEY BLAKLEY AND THE FSC

WHILE THE FOUNDING FSC LEADERSHIP was mostly male dominated, today it is filled with powerful Black women leaders, as are New Communities, Jubilee Justice, and the National Black Food and Justice Alliance. One FSC leader, Shirley Blakley, is its board president. She gave me a brief history of her family on the land, as former sharecroppers, and before that, plantation slaves. She credits her mother, Johnnie B. Lagone Moore, for building the Mississippi family farm from the soil up. "My parents didn't have the resources to own their own farm, so Johnnie B., she worked other farms to make a dollar, then purchased a mule and a plow. As time went on, by selling the little yield she produced, she was able to buy farm equipment: some disc harrows, a tiller, and in later years a tractor. There really wasn't anybody to teach her, and she had only an eighth-grade education. But this was just instilled in her from the beginning, how to make the land flourish," Blakley says.

Since her farm income wasn't enough, Johnnie B. held off-farm jobs to make ends meet, as a domestic in households and cooking at restaurants. "And she fed the whole community. She was a great cook. I miss the peas, the corn, the okra and beans she used to cook," Blakley adds wistfully.

"My mother loved eating from the ground, and watching her crops grow. Cotton, corn, vegetables, you name it, she grew it. She would always say the land could make you a living, timber could make you a living." While other Black farmers had little luck navigating the federal agricultural bureaucracy, Johnnie B. was a savvy customer; she benefited from ASCS (Agricultural Stabilization and Conservation Services, which later became part of the Farm Services Agency) programs. "They offered seed, fertilizer, and she took advantage of whatever was available, she did whatever she had to do to meet the note," Blakley recalls. "She was twenty when she started, and she was eighty-six when she passed in 2009. 'With knowledge of the land, you can keep your head above water,' she always said."

Johnnie B. joined the cooperative movement in the 1980s, and when Blakley completed a tour of duty with the military in Panama in 1986, she returned to Noxubie County to help out with her mother's Mississippi V4 cooperative, one of the strongest in the Federation. She worked her way up to the position of president of the Mississippi Association of Cooperatives, and then became the FSC's first female board member and board president.

Blakley's primary mission now is to advocate for farm retention, to ensure that the Federation continues to "provide technical assistance and adequate financial resources to put boots on the ground to help develop them." To stay on their land, farmers have to understand estate planning, what it takes to hold on to land. "The biggest loss of land for people of color is not having an estate plan, not knowing when to pay taxes, or getting to the point where you have to trade with the general store to get your fertilizer. If you miss that note, they'll come back and get your farm, for just a twenty-something or hundred-dollar note," she says.

Blakley is part of an unbroken line of southern Black agriculturalists whose knowledge and love of the land is born of centuries of working it, first as slaves, then as sharecroppers. It may not be an unbroken line, but there is a rootedness, and they are trying to either retain or regain ownership of farmland. In the northeastern United States, the legacy of Black farming exists, but in smaller numbers. Perhaps this is why the two strong Black women leaders I'm about to meet both have roots in the South and are focused on shifting power and capital into new networks of Black farmers.

UPDATING THE MUTUAL AID MODEL FOR THE NORTHEAST: KAREN WASHINGTON AND OLIVIA WATKINS, BLACK FARMER FUND

KAREN WASHINGTON AND OLIVIA WATKINS' New York City–based Black Farmer Fund (BFF), founded in 2020, has made more than $600,000 in gifts and low-interest loans to Black food and farming businesses, and raised more than $12 million toward its $20 million nonprofit community investment fund. These transplanted southerners have assimilated the cooperative and Civil Rights lessons of the South but say their work is also rooted on the principles of the food sovereignty movement (which asserts the right of every community to control and distribute its own healthy, ecologically grown, culturally appropriate food).

Washington, a physical therapist whose family is from Georgia, was drawn back to the land when her fight to start a community garden in her South Bronx neighborhood in the late 1990s turned her into a community organizer and activist around food issues, and eventually one of the most powerful voices in Black agriculture. In 2010, she founded the annual Black Urban Growers (BUGS) conference, which draws upwards of six hundred people a year to build community and nurture collective Black agrarian leadership. Her long involvement in the food justice movement led her to coin the term "food apartheid," shorthand for the way racial discrimination shapes access to and control over food resources. And it was she who planted the seed for the idea of the Black Farmer Fund at a 2017 farming gathering at Stone Barns Center for Food and Agriculture in Westchester County, New York.

As usual, in a sea of White faces, "you could count on one hand" the number of BIPOC people in attendance, Washington recalls. In this case, there were five. She commandeered the center's library for the smaller group and exhorted its members to brainstorm ways to build the generational wealth they had been excluded from. In a country where black farmers only own 2 percent of all farmland, and in a state where only 139 of its 57,000 farmers were Black, her message to the group was, "We need to talk about land, about wealth, to think about financial education, investment, starting some sort of investment fund."

One person, Watkins, stood up to volunteer. Growing up in a family that has tended land in North Carolina since the 1890s, she had cultivated an agroforestry ecosystem with value-added[16] beekeeping and mushroom-growing enterprises, and led an effort to lower taxes on the family land and access capital for different projects while protecting it from development. To better address the structural inequalities that she and other Black agriculturists faced, Watkins told the Stone Barns group, she was interested in starting some sort of investment fund for Black food and farm businesses.

This joint project with Watkins would be about putting capital and land in the hands of Black farmers and creating an "ecosystem" of like-minded organizations. Watkins returned to school to earn an MBA; she wanted to learn more about finance and how to access capital to fund the food justice movement. She and Washington also began reaching out to find partners and donors, eventually settling on a community investment fund model that would empower community members to develop their own locally determined solutions with the help of network-wide engagement.

In addition to providing loans and grants, a priority is building networks—through technical assistance and mentorship—that will connect often isolated Black farmers. To build collective power and wealth, BFF has grown its ecosystem of allied organizations to include the policy, advocacy, and educational organization Black Farmers United NYS (New York State); Soul Fire Farm and training center, which has helped build a pipeline of new farmers; Corbin Hill Food Project, which builds food sovereignty in underserved neighborhoods in New York City through food distribution; and the Northeast Farmers of Color Land Trust, which is working to put more farmers of color on the land, equitably and securely.

On a crisp November day, I head to Argyle, New York, to visit one part of the Black Farmer Fund ecosystem and one of its initial ten investment cohort members—Ashanti Williams of the Black Yard Farm Collective. Though the farm started as a collective and she hopes to add members over time, for now she is in fact a solo operator, growing vegetables, herbs, poultry, and small ruminants for meat and wool on her forty-four-acre farm. Other members of the BFF—which represents a cross-section of farmers and businesses across the Northeast—include a Caribbean-produce specialist, an herbal apothecary, and a fruit orchardist.

The table in Williams's spacious farmhouse is decorated for next week's Thanksgiving holiday, with candles, dried corn, pinecones, and small pumpkins, their colors echoing the flaming reds, yellows, and oranges on her forty-four-acre farm. A stream runs through her property, skirting a stand of birch trees and connecting to a pond that anchors one end of the land. On the other stands a greenhouse holding the last remains of summer's bounty, a barn that Williams has just started cleaning out, and a pair of mangalitsa pigs. A black Spanish heritage turkey named Tom, now retired from breeding duties, will not be eaten for Thanksgiving but will instead continue his designated guard turkey duties.

A native of the Bronx, Williams, too, can trace her roots back to southern farmers. She grew up with parents who cleared out an unused lot near their apartment building and started a community garden, and a grandfather who grew up picking cotton with his sharecropping family in South Carolina. Her family started a youth garden when she was eleven, and she says, "I grew up with the idea instilled in me that community—in her neighborhood it was composed mostly of Black, Caribbean, and Latino people—was important. I didn't know we were poor because we could go to the garden and pick fresh tomatoes for tomato sandwiches, and collard greens," she says. Community garden members came back from fishing expeditions and threw community fish fries; one year, she tried grilled venison, a member's hunting bounty, for the first time. As fulfilling as these experiences were, she knew that there was something missing: Her family had always worked the land, she says, "but land ownership has always been missing. And this is important to me."

It was only after joining the BFF ecosystem that Williams was finally able to put that last piece in place. It was her fellow Bronx resident and farming mentor Karen Washington who first introduced her to BUGS, the Black Urban Growers conference, and then to BFF. In poor urban neighborhoods and communities of color like the one she grew up in, poverty, redlining,[17] environmental racism, and the epigenetic (how behaviors and environment can cause changes in gene expression over time) results[18] of generations of oppression have resulted in higher rates of chronic diseases and cancer, and shorter life expectancies. Add this to the systematic stripping of land from Black farmers, and you can see why access to nutritious, high-quality food is so important to Williams and the BFF and BUGS farmers.

When Black Yard Farm was accepted as part of BFF's first cohort in 2021, it was on a different property and Williams was farming with five others. With a $50,000 grant and the promise of another $50,000 loan, things looked promising. But a month in, three members departed over interpersonal friction, then their landlord decided he would not lease the land after all; the remaining three members had to scramble to find another property. When all the dust settled, Williams found herself a sole operator on the Argyle farm in March 2022. She knew enough to get an up-front lease. In early 2023, a second disbursement from the BFF loan, along with technical and budgeting assistance the organization provided, helped get her started.

Williams's lease gives her right of first refusal, but she must make an offer by March 2026. "It's amazing, but it's also scary," she says, as she'll have to come up with the rest of the funding to buy the land. Of her plans to restore the cooperative model, she says, "I'd like to build a community here," for the near future with mostly agriculturally based businesses such as beekeepers or mushroom growers, and eventually maybe with "folks doing land-based work, education, or creating healing spaces, or art-related events."

"WHY HAVE MY TRIALS FAILED?": IN THE FIELDS AT NEW COMMUNITIES

BACK AT NEW COMMUNITIES WITH Shirley Sherrod and Konda Mason of Jubilee Justice, I am standing in the experimental rice field, where JJ and New Communities farmers are sharing their experiences and rice-growing techniques. The group has spent the first part of the day in indoor talks, so it is 5 p.m. by the time we leave the New Communities' air-conditioned office to check out the farm's half-acre experimental rice field. Yet even at this late afternoon hour, the scorching hot sun beats down mercilessly on our faces. New Communities farmer Zel Taylor, dressed in a black T-shirt that reads POWER TO THE PEOPLE, leads the way. Sherrod follows us in her car, a choice dictated by both back troubles and her ongoing communications with a staff member who is trying to buy a tractor at auction.

Accompanying Mason are JJ farmer Iriel Edwards and Erika Styger, a Cornell agronomist who advises the team on the climate-smart System of Rice Intensification (SRI) rice-growing method the JJ farmers have adopted, the same one promulgated by Lotus Foods and increasingly used by smallholder farmers around the world.

Styger explains how in conventional rice production, continually flooded fields prevent oxygen from permeating the soil, resulting in anaerobic digestion, or the breakdown of organic matter, and the release of methane into the atmosphere. SRI, by contrast, calls for alternately wetting and drying the fields, with the dry spells preventing anaerobic digestion. This agroecological method of growing has been shown to reduce net greenhouse gas emissions by 30 percent compared to standard rice-growing practices, and reduce greenhouse gas emissions per kilogram of rice produced by more than 50 percent.[19]

To offset the higher incidence of weeds and pests that can result from not flooding the fields continually, farmers weed the fields and focus intensely on organic methods of weed suppression. In front of a small clump of Scarlett rice plants (a new red long grain rice created through a collaboration between Cornell and the USDA), New Communities farmer Taylor (who since my visit to New Communities has moved on to start her own farm and art collective) runs through the litany of threats she must battle, from climate extremes to weeds to pests, all while trying to remain chemical fertilizer–free and pesticide-free. She is eager to compare and discuss techniques with the JJ farmers to sharpen and expand the tools in their arsenal: organic neem oil, which causes predators to die off, but leaves beneficial pollinators and earthworms intact; corn grits and molasses to fight fire ants and other pests; or fish emulsion fertilizer.

Taylor has trialed a handful of rice varieties this season, just a small percentage of the twenty-four different specialty rice varieties Jubilee Justice has planted at its Alexandria, Louisiana, farm, and she wants to know why some of her trials have failed. The discussion that Styger facilitates in response ranges from the importance of soil exudates (molecules released through the plant's roots that act as messengers between plant, soil bacteria, and fungi, influencing nutrient availability and helping the soil adhere and clump), the transplanting of seedlings, and the use of the "biorational" (biologically derived, low-impact products) fungicide Trilogy to control the ever-present threat of mold in this hot and humid climate. This is exactly the kind of knowledge sharing—among researchers and food producers, between experienced farmers and novices, and across geographical boundaries—that will strengthen and help grow this fledgling alt food system. And it is one that I will see repeatedly in my alt food system travels, a sign of growing strength and resilience.

My visit with New Communities and Jubilee Justice, and my immersion into the history of African American agricultural cooperatives and mutual aid organizations such as the Federation of Southern Cooperatives and the Black Farmers Fund, has not only struck a chord with my own family's history, it has served as the basic training and road map for the rest of my alt food systems tour. Through their example of building self-reliant ecosystems of collective fundraising, financing, farmer education, and policy work on land access and reparations, they have shown how we can build a similar, self-reliant, values-driven alt food system. More than ever, we need one that stands outside Big Food, which, like the rest of the global economy, is being driven by an ever-increasing concentration of power among a small group of corporations. Ninety percent of the US economy is now dominated by the top one percent of companies,[20] which prioritize profits over the wellbeing of our bodies, our communities, our workers, and our planet.

Instead of remaining at the mercy of these monopolies, global commodity price fluctuations, and mergers and acquisitions that squeeze small- and mid-sized producers out of existence or subject them to limited access to capital based on race, we can create and support short, direct, regional, equitable, and regenerative supply chains. Armed with this primer on one alt food system model, I set off on the rest of my tour.

CHAPTER TWO

THE WHOLE GRAIN MAVERICKS WHO ARE REBUILDING OUR LOCAL GRAIN ECONOMY

BACK IN THE WINTER OF 2010, I noticed a new stall selling freshly milled New York State flour at Manhattan's Union Square Greenmarket. It was the first time I had seen locally milled whole wheat, rye, or spelt, and it was from a company called Farmer Ground, based in the Finger Lakes region of New York. Most of the grain came from nearby Oechsner Farms, where organic grains were grown in rotation with a mix of clover, grasses, and other legumes.

Eight summers later, in 2018, during a fellowship at the Stone Barns Center for Food and Agriculture that gathered nine women working at the intersection of agriculture and climate change, I met head baker Adam Tan, who made unbelievably airy, tender, and crusty sourdough whole wheat baguettes. Another Stone Barns baker, Trang Tran, had recently returned from a stint baking on the West Coast. There she had seen the local grain movement taking shape, led by a cadre of heritage grain devotees, including Nan Kohler of Grist & Toll, the first urban mill to return to Los Angeles in one hundred years. At The Rose Café in Venice, where she worked, her employer had purchased a small mock mill for bakers to experiment with local whole grains. Like those West Coast bakers, the Stone Barns' ethos prized regionally grown grain nurtured in cover-crop nourished, microbe-rich soil, milled on site on an Austrian-made Osttiroler mill.

At the on-site Blue Hill Grain Bar, where we loved lining up for tender, aromatic spelt or emmer scones, a wall-mounted illustration of "rotation grains" depicted a wheel whose spokes were thirteen different varieties of grains that enhanced soil health and produced delicious food.

Meanwhile, we fellows were receiving our own education on the revived local grain economy. During a grain discussion session with Blue Hill at Stone Barns chef Dan Barber, we tasted delicious loaves made with his eponymous Barber wheat, a hard red winter wheat that is a cross between a Spanish heritage wheat and a modern variety developed in collaboration with Dr. Stephen Jones, a wheat breeder, geneticist, and founder of the Washington State University Breadlab.

Later, I would realize that I was witnessing the re-localization of the Northeastern United States' former grain baskets, an alt food system movement that was spreading across the globe, from Japan to Israel. At the time, though, I was too busy absorbing how shockingly tasty bread made with locally grown and milled whole grain was compared to the industrial white bread most Americans have grown up on. Take a whiff of freshly milled, 100 percent whole wheat and you'll detect subtle grassy, nutty, even floral notes. Do the same with even organic white flour and it will be hard to detect anything.

The typical white bread loaf uses 72 percent extraction flour, meaning that less than 30 percent of the grains' original nutrients—its bran and germ—are retained while the rest is sifted out. To preserve the flour, bleaching agents are added, and loaves are loaded with preservatives, emulsifiers, conditioners, and additives (many of them poorly or barely regulated by the FDA[1]) found in ultra-processed foods. Ironically, makers may add iron, riboflavin, thiamine, and niacin to "enrich" the impoverished flour.

Beyond superior taste, a clear nutritional case can be made for whole grain breads: they are packed with all the B complex vitamins except B12,[2] are high in vitamin E, zinc, and magnesium, and replete with protein, healthy fats, oils, and fiber. Bread made with unsifted whole grain flour bears the same relationship to commercial commodity bread that a living human being, filled with personal quirks and constantly regenerating cells, does to their favorite digital avatar.

REPLACING COMMODITY FLOUR, CREATING A REVOLUTION: JUNE RUSSELL

IN 2004, THE EPICENTER AND origin of New York's soon-to-be-revitalized grain basket was June Russell and GrowNYC, the nonprofit organization that oversees the city's network of greenmarkets. That year, the market was feeling pressure to review its baker's rules; there was some tension around how much bakers were contributing to the mission of the greenmarkets, which was to support the revitalization of local agriculture and growers through direct market opportunities.[3]

Produce sold at the greenmarket had to be grown within a prescribed radius from New York City, yet bakers were selling banana bread made with commodity white flour, white sugar, and blatantly nonlocal bananas. How could these bakers, who were not saddled with the risks of catastrophic weather events that farmers face, do more to support local farmers? Incorporating local flour seemed the obvious answer, but where would that come from? At the time, most grain farming in New York consisted of soy and corn for animal feed.

Russell's role as manager of farm inspections gave her the opportunity to speak to farmers, processors, and agriculture experts in the field, and she began working toward a solution. By 2008 she had met small grain pioneers like Aurora Mills in Maine and La Milanese, an organic grain processor in Quebec, both of whom had revived the regional tradition of milling that had been lost over the last hundred years as it was unable to compete with the efficiencies and large scale of midwestern grain farms and giant milling facilities. It was Russell who in 2008 encouraged farmers Erick Smith and Thor Oechsner to start operating the mill Oechsner had purchased but was not yet running; she was looking for local flour to sell at the city's greenmarkets. "June was pivotal in those early years, giving us our foothold in the New York City food scene and introducing us to a lot of our early, foundational customers," recalls Greg Russo, one of the founders of Farmer Ground, the grain company whose presence I had noticed in 2010 at the Union Square Greenmarket.

Russell had identified contacts at the Northeast Organic Wheat Project and the Northeast Organic Farming Association chapters in New York, Vermont, and Massachusetts; she realized she could connect them to farmers market bakers and begin to develop not just a regional supply chain, but a new "grain value chain"—a term that emphasizes value added along the chain, both monetary and nonmonetary, including benefits to nature ("ecosystem services") and ethical values. That chain included plant breeders, farmers, millers, brewers, and distillers, as well as hard-to-find small-scale equipment ranging from combines to oat rollers.

Russell took on the additional and unofficial role of manager of GrowNYC Grains and would go on to spend more than a decade building up this new regional grainshed, which, like the broader term "foodshed," describes the region in which grain or food is grown and processed, the markets it passes through, and places where it is consumed.

Russell's early Northeastern organic farmer contacts were testing small grain varieties as a way to expand soil-building cover crops—many of which can "fix" nitrogen or, with the aid of symbiotic soil bacteria, convert inert nitrogen in the air to a form that plants can absorb. Incorporating cover crops builds soil, inhibits the growth of weeds, prevents water loss, and can reduce or eliminate a farmer's dependence on fossil fuel–based chemical fertilizers and pesticides. Ridding the land of chemical fertilizers and pesticides in turn eliminates toxic runoff water, allowing a resurgence of the ecosystem's insect, bird, pollinator, and wildlife populations. A revitalized local grain basket, Russell knew, would be good for the land, good for local economies, and good for the health of all of the urban and rural dwellers with access to its harvests.

But she soon discovered that you couldn't just hand a sack of whole grain heritage flour to white flour bakers and wait for delicious baked goods to emerge. "Multiple generations of baking practices had become so calibrated to commodity flour," she explains, that these bakers knew nothing about the difference between winter or spring wheat, or the protein or gluten content of different heritage grains. As wheat was commoditized, the American wheat breeding program had selected high-protein varieties that could withstand the rigors of mechanization. Bakers adapted to the new highly refined, roller milled, super white flour with an industrialized style of baking that relied on rapid fermentation, additives, and preservatives.

At a 2009 meeting between bakers and local millers, the latter were disappointed to land only one new customer. One baker said flatly to a miller, "Your flour doesn't work." Russell's job was that of facilitator, trying to figure out where knowledge gaps lay and how to fill them. It was a lesson in how much more complex wheat was to other agricultural products. "No one would hand an heirloom tomato back and say, "This doesn't work," she notes. "I don't think bakers knew where to start." They had to learn to handle the nuances and variations of whole grain flour, which could fluctuate widely from harvest to harvest.

"No bakers or chefs were working with local grains until June sought out growers and millers upstate and directed their products to the New York City marketplace. She brought regional farmers and city bakers together—a powerful lift in rebuilding our regional food and farm economy," says Mary Cleaver, a longtime Manhattan-based caterer and leader in food system change. Russell helped incubate a number of artisan bakeries that became important wholesale buyers of local heritage grain, including She Wolf Bakery and Lost Bread Co. It has been artisan bakers, whose values aligned with those of the regional grainshed movement and wrote their business plans around it, who have played a key role in growing the value chain and ushering in a whole new world of flavors, textures, and interpretation of heritage grains.

Yet Russell takes exception to characterization of this movement as simply a revival of an earlier, golden age of the regional breadbasket. "It was colonial agriculture, and from what I've seen, a mix of reckless practices. They exhausted the soil, which is part of why production had to move out of the Northeast," she says. The modern organics movement has a good half century of science-backed data behind it, so today's combination of traditional, pre-industrial techniques and modern tools and practices is a different form of agriculture—a reminder that the regenerative agriculture movement can get caught up in the romance of past and discount the advances of the present. What makes this style of farming so effective is the combination of the old and the cutting edge.

By the time she left GrowNYC in 2021, it was aggregating from fourteen regional mills and it represented another seven that did not become regular members; greenmarket bakers were purchasing 65,000 pounds of regional grains per month. In 2020 GrowNYC moved 150,000 pounds of local grains in retail sales at its farmers market grain stands throughout the city.

Sadly, when Russell left to become director of regional food programming at the Glynwood Center for Regional Food and Farming, GrowNYC discontinued its retail local grain stand, an important link in the supply chain she built. Looking back on what she achieved, Russell expresses a mix of grief over the cuts and pride in what she accomplished: "It took on a life of its own, and we were able to mobilize the assets of the greenmarkets and the good will of the community. I felt like we moved the needle, and that's amazing."

THE RENEGADE BAKER

SOUTHERN ONTARIO DOES NOT HAVE the most robust regional grainshed yet. But it does have some passionate believers who are struggling to build one. I met one of them on Saturday mornings at the Wychwood Barns farmers market. Baker Dawn Woodward, her feathered hair ringed by a bandana, her face framed by wire-rimmed glasses, can be found behind a mountain of enticing baked goods, all of them uniformly burnished, earth-toned, rustic. She specializes in heritage whole grain rye, spelt, and other wheat breads, crackers, Gâteau Basques, savory root vegetable turnovers, and her own whole grain versions of Pop Tarts and Twix bars. Sometimes she creates social media agitprop through arrangements of pink icing–lettered tarts arranged to shout slogans. One of them reads BE A GRAIN CHANGER. She credits fellow grain activist Sarah Lemanski of Nova Bakehouse in Leeds, UK, for coming up with the term. Woodward advises her followers, "It's good to ask yourself how your baking reflects your region and who your food dollars are supporting—corporations or rebel farmers?"

Another post is a video of her tossing one of her rustic rye rings into the air like the Mary Tyler Moore of whole grains. It reads, "Free yourselves from the toxic sludge of brainless bakers stuck in the mindless mulch of

NO-purpose flour that is lifeless and inert, designed for uniformity, conformity and crushing creativity; there is a new Dawn. The next revolution will be fresh milled and whole grain. It has already begun."

Woodward is the most committed grain activist I know. Holder of a degree in feminist philosophy, she has corralled her reformist zeal and trained it not just on bringing back local grain economies but bringing down global agribusinesses that have stripped our food of its ability to support the health of our bodies and our communities. "Dawn is a very cool baker because she's so avant-garde," says her friend, miller, and baker Carole Ferrari. "Who puts ten percent more bran in bread and sells it? And just the quality of her cookies . . . she's making fucking Twix bars! It's so beautiful."

Social media, so toxic in many ways, connected bakers like Dawn to a like-minded global community. In bread circles, she's more famous in the UK and at the aforementioned Washington State University Breadlab—hotbeds of regional grainshed activity that are leading the way globally—than she is in Canada, and that's in large part due to social media friendships and mentorships, online workshops, and international bread conferences. Her love for rye, an agronomically resilient grain, has created a special bond with the Estonian-born researcher Laura Valli at the Breadlab.

Both love the fact that rye exists outside the commodity wheat system, so its distinctive taste and nutrient density remain intact. "With no classifications, it's been liberated from existing norms," Valli explains. Rye tolerates low temperatures and arid conditions, is a favored cover crop for its ability to fix nitrogen and enrich soil, is remarkably disease resistant, and requires less water than wheat. A social anthropologist by training, Valli is interested in what rye means to different countries, different cultures, and different bakers, and why, with all its spectacular assets to the environment and human health, it is so underutilized. Their shared goal is to increase both production and consumption of whole grain rye.

It's hard to understand just how radical Woodward is without knowing how rare 100 percent whole grain bread or pastries are. Even those artisanal, naturally leavened loaves you see in the Tartine bread book and in countless artisan bakeries across the country use a mix of white and whole grain flours, where a large percentage of the bran has been removed. The commercial rye bread from your local deli contains more white flour than rye flour. Woodward is a lone renegade voice across many provinces and states who dares to go totally unsifted.

Ontario has always been a grain-growing region and was at one time an important source of soft wheat used for pastry flour. But Woodward has noticed that, recently, more corn and soy are being grown, and less wheat. And most of this corn and soy goes to fuel or animal feed, not to feed people. Five years ago, she lamented the lack of access to consistently high-quality local grain, and the lack of small-scale millers, and believed that consumer demand could bring about these changes in agriculture and infrastructure.

Today access to milling is less of a problem. Toronto has three New American Stone Mills machines, the gold standard milling machines for whole grain bakers looking to maximize flavor and nutrition, and there are more throughout the province. But there are still large gaps in the grainshed: "I would love to see a farmer co-op, where grain farmers can come together to clean, store, sort and mill, and deliver to bakers," she says. Grain is much cleaner now, but a high-tech color sorter—which costs tens of thousands of dollars and can eliminate stones, shells, bugs, and moldy grains with a high degree of precision—would take the local grain system to a whole new level.

Again, she believes that consumer demand will gradually bring these missing elements of a complete local grainshed to Ontario, but it requires creating new local whole grain converts, one at a time. And for that, there is nothing that works better than taste. Few of her regular customers care much about fighting the commodity food system, they just love what Woodward bakes; they have a visceral understanding that freshly milled local grains just taste better. "It's flavor that turns the switch for them," she says.

THE ZEN BUDDHIST MILLER-BAKER

THE OWNER OF ONE OF those two New American Stone Mills is the aforementioned friend of Woodward's, Carole Ferrari, a devout Zen Buddhist and a whole grain baker who has mastered a 100 percent whole wheat croissant, and whose savory pies and tarts and impeccably made *viennoiserie* have built her a strong following. Contrary to what many bakers think, Ferrari says, the added bran in unsifted whole grain flours, combined with the effect that sugar, salt, and butter have on it, can give croissants body and moisture, and act as a tenderizer.

Like a number of people I have met in the course of my travels, Ferrari is not someone made for a nine-to-five job but a restless, questing spirit who wants the world to be better than it is. After studying philosophy in college, embarking on a five-hundred-mile solo bike trek from New Brunswick to James Bay, Nunavut, and after a stint living there picking up work where she could, she moved to Toronto and bought a small bus that was both her home and commercial kitchen, complete with two ovens, four burners, a solar-powered chest refrigerator, and two sinks. It was everything she needed to run a small catering business. Baking became her true calling.

She came to buy her New American Stone Mills machine in 2017 because she was frustrated that she could not find high-quality milled grain. The company had only been in existence for two years, founded in 2015 by Vermont bakers Andrew Heyn and his wife, Blair Marvin, who wanted a steady supply of freshly milled local flour for their bakery, Elmore Mountain Bread. When they couldn't find anything that would grind the grains finely but still preserve its nutritional qualities and unique flavors, Heyn designed his own milling machine, using locally quarried Vermont granite. He discovered that local Vermont Barre Gray Granite had ideal milling qualities: fine grain, even texture, durability, and a large thermal mass, meaning that it does not overheat during the milling process, protecting delicate nutrients stored in the wheat berry from damage.

Unlike industrial roller milling, which removes all of the grain's bran and germ, stone milling preserves them, grinding bran, germ, and starchy inner endosperm into the flour. This saves valuable nutrients and draws out and highlights, rather than obliterates, the flavor and aroma of the grain. Both milling machines to make flour from locally grown grains and the millers to operate them are pivotal to creating a regional grain-shed; without them, flour must be hauled in from miles away, likely from a commodity flour mill with none of the live enzymes present in freshly milled whole grain flour.

As a miller, Ferrari had to develop the skill set needed "to create something we can reliably use to make our breads and pastries according to pre-defined recipes and tastes," which includes knowing the correct speed and temperature of milling, and how to correctly store the flour; too much humidity, for example, can cause the flour to begin to sprout, activating enzymes and altering its gluten content, resulting in terrible bread. Freshly milled flour, she adds, "is very easy to ruin."

But beyond the incredible flavor, aroma, and nutrient density a good stone miller and baker can impart, Ferrari says, "I see civilization in the mill, in the technology and the chain of hands it takes to build a mill—powering the mine, mining the granite, building the mill, developing the grain and farming and harvesting it—and the way it comes together in the milling room for the baker." As she articulated these thoughts, Ferrari was in turmoil, torn between her strongly Zionist family and her horror over Israel's attack on Gaza following the October 2023 Hamas-led attack on Israel, and could not help connecting it to bread. "When you break the chain of hands and deny the means of milling and distributing flour and the baking of it into bread," she notes, "it's simple to see how Israel in this way is destroying Palestinian civilization."

These days she mills for herself and other bakers, and bakes under the name Motherdough Mill and Bakery, from a commercial kitchen in Toronto, selling her goods online and at the weekly Wychwood Barns farmers market. None of her flour is sifted.

Despite the addition of her mill, there is still the problem of scarce and inconsistent Ontario whole grains. So Ferrari is left to find pockets of grain that she can access. One source is the organic Buschbeck Farms in Markdale, Ontario, a pasture-raised lamb farm that grows rye and triticale as feed and as regenerative cover crops. Owner Andreas Buschbeck has also discovered their appeal to whole grain bakers. "His neighbor has a combine, so he has the capacity to clean, store and pack," explains Ferrari. "Every farmer has some sort of grain in their rotation, buckwheat, or beans, why not redistribute that within a commodity structure?"

THE MAINE GRAINSHED BUILDER

THE BORDER CROSSING THAT SEPARATES Saint-Theophile, Quebec, from Jackman, Maine, is said to be heavily trafficked. But each time I drive across it, once to enter the United States and once to return home via Quebec, I am the only one there. Heading south on Route du President-Kennedy, the US border guard seems suspicious that someone might want to drive to Skowhegan, Maine, to research a flour mill. He asks me to open my trunk to inspect its contents.

The sparsely populated landscape in these parts is dominated by a dense blanket of evergreens, its wild beauty a reminder of how national borders are arbitrary lines imposed on an ecosystem. This most heavily forested state of the nation is a continuation of the deep forests of southern Quebec, now more cleared. Parts of Quebec and present-day Maine were home to the Abenaki, Maliseet, Micmac, Passamaquoddy, and Penobscot, collectively known as the Wabanaki.

The central Maine town of Skowhegan was at various times a crossroads for traveling Indigenous traders, a trading post for European and Indigenous people, and a hub for the fur, fishing, and timber industries. In its industrial glory days, it was home to paper, wood, and shoe factories and was considered the breadbasket of the Northeast. Farmers grew oats, rye, wheat, corn, and buckwheat. In 1837, Somerset, for which Skowhegan serves as the county seat, produced 239,000 bushels of wheat, enough to feed more than one hundred thousand people. Over the course of the last century, however, that vitality was drained as the regional economy lost ground to large midwestern commercial operations equipped with the latest in roller milling technology imported from Europe, and the economies of scale they afforded. One hundred and fifty years ago, there were fifteen thousand gristmills dotting the Northeast, sometimes as many as three or more in a single township.[4] Gradually, almost all of them, along with small grain farms, shut down, leaving faded mill and industrial towns rusted shadows of their former selves.

I know that the small but mighty mill I'll be visiting is a merc lean-to in a metaphoric grain landscape dotted by the skyscraping silos of global agribusiness, but I want to meet the people who were audacious enough to think they could do it, and have done so.

Today, four large commodity traders, Archer Daniels Midland, Bunge, Cargill, and Louis Dreyfus (collectively known as the ABCD traders), control the modern global agri-food system, including as much as 90 percent of the world's grain trade.[5] Their long reach and gargantuan economic might do not just control the lion's share of physical commodities like grain, but every link of the food chain from farm feed, chemical inputs, the food itself, fuel to grow or buy, clean, store, and transport those goods, and the manufacturing of value-added food products.

These corporations store agricultural products in their own facilities. They are landowners, and cattle, poultry, and biofuel producers. Their size gives them access to land and water resources and to large stores of capital, so they are also providers of financial services ranging from futures trading to asset management, market analysis, and risk management services, effectively serving as the bankers to their own industries. The increasing "financialization" of the commodities markets—turning commodities futures into popular asset classes for portfolio managers—is profitable, but also prone to boom-and-bust cycles, speculation, and crazy price volatility; we will see more of this in Chapter 7 when we turn to the cacao and coffee markets.

Their actions affect climate change and global food security. They are not just monopolies, they are monopsonies, the very few primary buyers of grain who can dictate prices and conditions for a larger number of farmers. They wield their power in Washington and in the corridors of governments around the world. Yet we consumers know little about these corporations because there is little public information available about them. Their growth has left a shrinking foothold for smallholder farmers around the world, who are at the mercy of global price swings triggered by these agribusiness giants. You can see that the deck is outlandishly stacked against the idea of a thriving regional foodshed or grainshed.

All that is background noise in my head today, though. Rolling into downtown Skowhegan on a sunny, late summer day, it's hard to miss Maine Grains. One side of the red-brick-clad, fourteen-thousand-square-foot former jail is partially obscured by a large gray silo that reads:

> Maine Grains
>
> Organic Flour & Oats
>
> Café & Bar
>
> Farmers Market
>
> Livestock Feed
>
> Dry Goods Store

Around the silo there is a cluster of yellow chutes and grain bins, the exterior trappings of the four-story mill within. So central to the town's identity has Maine Grains become that there is a city road sign posted on Highway 2 telling drivers that they are a mere two-tenths of a mile away from the mill that has become the catalyst to its revived economy.

Today, I am to meet a group of women who form the spokes of this rural food and grain hub. They are assembled on the patio of the mill complex, at The Miller's Table, a farm-to-table café and bakery, where a menu of wood-fired pizzas, sandwiches, pastries, and more showcase Maine Grains flours, farro, groats, and oats.

At the head of the table is Maine Grains cofounder and CEO Amber Lambke, a former speech pathologist who moved from Portland, Maine, to Skowhegan in 2001 after meeting her future husband. She is the third person I will meet in the course of my travels who met her partner at a dance, either square or contra. In Lambke's case it was the latter, contra being a New England tradition and apparently fertile ground for matchmaking (see Chapter 4).

The economic hollowing out of Skowhegan left high rates of unem-

ployment and created a cycle of generational poverty. In 2005, Lambke joined an effort to revive the historic downtown by encouraging the
growth of a fledgling farmers market. The area had become a hotbed
of back-to-the-land settlers in the 1960s and 1970s, and the children of
those first settlers were returning to pick up farming. Over the course of
four years, she helped grow the market from three to twenty-one vendors,
brought in a double dollar program for customers who received USDA
SNAP (Supplemental Nutrition Assistance Program) benefits, and in
partnership with physicians, piloted a fruit-and-vegetables prescription
program.

In 2007, Lambke and her friend, baker Michael Scholz cofounded The
Kneading Conference, which brought together local grain and bread fans,
farmers, bakers, researchers, maltsters, and food entrepreneurs so they
could teach and learn from each other. The conference helped galvanize
a movement, starting conversations between isolated grain farmers, bakers, and other amateurs and professionals: What grains could they revive,
grow, and bake with in Maine? How could they grow their markets? This
forum for discussion made all things seem possible.

Once they had brought together members of their local grainshed, it
was time to build the mill that would serve as its hub. New obstacles
presented themselves. "The number of people in this country who still
understood grain processing and cleaning on a small scale could fit on
one hand," Lambke says. "We became aware that we were fifty to one
hundred years out of the last thriving grain economy in our region, and
that we would lose that knowledge soon if we didn't focus on retaining
it." She and Michael Scholz began drafting a business plan for their mill,
embarking on several years of research and travel to learn the milling
business. The duo raised enough money to buy the former town jail in
2009 and launched Maine Grains there in 2012.

As she was researching her new venture, Lambke came to understand that the problem was one of infrastructure. Farmers were growing grains to be fed as straw to dairy cows, and rye and oats as cover crops for potatoes. Most was tilled into the ground because there was no machinery or system to thresh, clean, de-hull, and mill them for human consumption. She enrolled in a week-long course in milling at Kansas State University but it centered on white flour milling. So, she headed to Germany and Denmark, where she says, "Millers were ten years ahead of where we were in the United States." She reached out to others who were building regional grainsheds, Jennifer Lapidus at Carolina Ground and sourdough bread master Dave Miller in Northern California. No one was making four-foot-diameter milling stones anymore, so she sourced her first (of the three that she would eventually buy) from Austria. Maine Grains now also owns two custom-made mills from New American Stone Mills in Vermont.

Lambke also began working on building a pipeline of farmer grain suppliers. Building local foodsheds is often a process of identifying bottlenecks in the supply chain and eliminating them. "When you have no grains in your farm ecosystem, you don't have straw either," Lambke explains. "And organic dairy farms needed organic straw for their bedding." They were buying straw from out of state at great costs, and those costs were going up.

University of Maine's cooperative extension researchers were trying to solve this problem by helping farmers in the organic dairy belt in northern and central Maine grow grains. Potato farmers were planting oats and rye for cover crops, and either tilling it back into the soil without saving the grain ear or selling oats to the Quaker facility in Canada for pennies on the bushel. For most, it was not worth harvesting the crops at all. Lambke began connecting to these farmers, identifying those who had a tolerance for failure and an appetite for risk, offering between $13 and $16 a bushel for their wheat to supply her nascent flour mill.

She started with a handful of farmers, assessing their risk and establishing a Plan B, in case their first crops did not meet mill standards. Did they have animals to feed? Did they have other people they could sell grain to? "We knew that farmers had been burned in the past by entrepreneurs with good ideas who want to grow things in the hills of Maine only to see the markets fall from underneath them. We wanted farmers to have positive stories to tell about selling into our food supply chain." Growth had to come from word of mouth.

On the demand side, Lambke worked on educating bakers and building up her customer base. "There were some bakers ready for our grain products. Alan Scott and Daniel Wing had written *The Bread Builders*, the Bible for artisan bread bakers that taught you how to bake bread and build masonry ovens; this was fueling a surge in home cottage baking." People wanted delicious bread, but not necessarily local wheat because they didn't understand the interconnected web of relationships and the resurrection of a local economy that Lambke was after. Nor did they understand the vastly superior taste and nutritional qualities local, freshly milled grains would give them. But she explains now, "If I had decided I needed to make sure there was a market like this before getting into the business, I would have missed out on this. We had to build that market through education and connections."

Lambke also worked on expanding the network of local businesses who would purchase her flours and add value by meeting various community needs. On The Miller's Table patio, sitting to Lambke's left is her identical twin sister, Heather Kerner, an occupational therapist who has created a combination pizza dough manufacturing company and workforce development company for people with disabilities. The Good Crust, as it is named, located in the town of Canaan, nine miles to the east, has allowed Kerner to graft her occupational therapy skills to a manufacturing operation that is part of that web-building process. After four years in business, 40 percent of her nineteen-person staff is disabled, and she purchases about two thousand pounds of flour a week from Maine Grains, part of which goes to supplying whole grain pizza dough to kindergarten through twelfth-grade students in Maine.

Also present at The Miller's Table are Kelly LaCasse, who, along with her husband, Mark, owns The Maine Meal, located a block away from the mill. They use Maine Grains products in their frozen prepared meals, their wholesale and retail pasta-making operation, their house-made pizza dough, and in baked goods like corn bread, yeast rolls, and apple crisps for the school lunches they provide to the local charter school. Nichole Weaver, who sits at the end of our table, and her husband, Michael, co-own Bigelow Fields in Langtown, about an hour-and-fifteen-minute drive north of Skowhegan. To diversify their bison farm, she learned to bake sourdough bread. She now sells artfully scored loaves, macarons, and other goods made with Maine Grains products and baked in her triple-deck, Belgian-made stone oven, its steam injection function creating shiny, caramelized crispy crusts.

Polly MacMichael has to excuse herself early to get back to the bucolic western Maine town of Kingfield, where she and her husband, Rob Mac-Michael, run the kind of place I wish I had near me, Rolling Fatties. In a pumpkin-colored clapboard building with a wide porch, they specialize in fat, nontraditional burritos and source as many of their ingredients as possible locally, including Maine Grain beans and oat groats. Another menu item, their nutty, deep yellow corn bread, is made with Main Grains cornmeal.

Back on the terrace at The Miller's Table, the talk turns to the special difficulties that rural business owners face, and how creating a rural food hub means safeguarding its future by taking care of a youthful workforce grappling with familial, societal, and economic woes, and none of the advantages of the highly educated big-city people who summer or vacation in Maine. Lambke ticks off the challenges: "addiction, adverse childhood experiences, generational poverty." She sees signs of all these things, and a pervasive hopelessness among teens, noting, "The fix is community connectedness. It's better connections, providing safe spaces for kids. We are the change makers who can alter the course of their lives and ultimately the course of our communities. We have to focus on that long game."

In August, when half her staff returns to school and sports practice, she and other businesses gear up for the busy fall foliage viewing season when urban visitors, used to a much higher level of service, will be sorely tested. I know exactly what she is referring to. The day before, meeting two friends for lunch at the café, we felt like northern American city dwellers traveling to the syrupy slow and courtly rural Deep South—long riven by deep economic and racial injustices—and expecting Manhattan deli-speed service.

But these problems just come with the territory; for local businesses, what matters is keeping that pipeline of young workers flowing. "They recruit their friends, you provide a safe environment, and they would rather be here than doing nothing or being home," Lambke says. The close-knit community, short supply chains, and high-quality products that Maine Grains has created are impressive, the way I would like the world to operate, not just pockets of the world. But a reality of these systems is that they are not going to generate the kinds of return on investment that Wall Street and most shareholders demand.

"There is a network of financiers and philanthropists, lenders at the community level, who accept investing in farm and food operations at a lower expectation of return, or even no return. Maybe they want their money back someday, or don't need interest, or maybe the farm next door wants to protect their view. For all kinds of reasons, we have been able to find lenders and patient investors," Lambke says. Events like the COVID pandemic and Russia's invasion of Ukraine have opened people's eyes to the value of a local food system. "Land trusts and philanthropies are realizing that if our mission is about meeting basic human needs in the community, chemical-free food is part of that, access to land is part of that. They understand that food is one of the largest social issues of our time," Lambke notes.

Communities and governments are slowly coming around to a new concept of governance that acknowledges the connection between resilient food systems and soil and community health, both spiritual and physical. There are signs that our lumbering agricultural grant, subsidy, and loan system, as it exists now under the Farm Bill, is slowly shifting in this direction.

I see it in programs like California's Department of Food and Agriculture's Office of Farm to Fork and its Farm to School program, which connects local food procurement with food-based education as a way of establishing healthy eating habits in children. The program received more than $100 million in allocations over its first three years starting in 2020. In 2023, it offered $52.8 million in grant funding to 120 farm projects across the state. The USDA, meanwhile, acknowledging the supply chain disruptions of the pandemic, in 2022 established a $200 million Local Food for Schools Cooperative Agreement Program "to help build a fair, competitive, and resilient local food chain, and expand local and regional markets with an emphasis on purchasing from historically underserved producers and processors."

In the nonprofit sector, the Philadelphia-based local food distributor

The Common Market, founded by Tatania Garcia Granados and Haile Johnston, connects more than 250 schools, hospitals, grocers, and workplaces to farms throughout the mid-Atlantic. Programs and hubs like these, which combined provide hundreds of millions of meals each year, are a way to move the alt food system forward in a big way.

The grainshed Lambke built now processes more than two million pounds of grain a year purchased from more than forty-two farm families, most of them located in Maine. It includes two malt houses, two mills, and a number of bakeries that mill in house and purchase from Maine Grains. The mill and café now employ forty people, and its regular mill tours, the café, and shop attract more than a thousand people per month from around the country and world. Echoing on a larger scale the microbial changes that are occurring in the soil and the increasingly biodiverse ecosystems of its member farms, Maine Grains continues to gain in complexity, richness, and connectedness.

Maine Grains has also inspired numerous other start-up businesses that include the local grains as part of their core ingredient, everything from crackers, cookies, ice cream sandwiches, fresh pasta, and tortillas, as well as use of its byproducts in mushroom-growing operations, kitty litter products, potting soil, and more. Lambke was instrumental in bringing cheesemaker Amy Rowbottom to the space next door, where the business has thrived. The Miller's Table takes Rowbottom's whey byproducts and uses them in baked goods and summertime probiotic pops.

Still, it takes fortitude measured out in large daily doses to build such food systems. "All of us are fighting the day-to-day fight," Lambke acknowledges. A local grocery store wants more products from Maine Grains, but at half the cost. Smaller, value-added businesses like Kerner's pizza dough company must fight off incursions into their school-, corporate-, or government-mandated whole grain category. Corporate players are adept at touting "whole grain products" that barely meet the 51 percent whole grain minimum school nutrition standards. They are devoid of any local grain and filled with highly processed ingredients: roller-milled white flour stripped of bran and germ, dough conditioners, preservatives, artificial colors and flavors, all designed to be warmed up in their cellophane packaging. "These are our vendor peers," she says with exasperation.

Too much of Lambke's time is spent pleading with legislators to draft clearer language around the federal local food purchasing program because products like the processed cakes or pizza dough can take away funding right under the noses of smaller operations that are hewing to their local, whole grain principles. Yet she adds, "We have a responsibility to be talking to our elected officials about these issues. We need to invite them to our places more often, plant a seed they can carry with them back to the committees they are on and the decisions they make."

During a recent visit from a member of the Federal Reserve Board and the head of the Federal Reserve Bank of Boston, Lambke described an issue that she is trying to resolve: She wants to purchase an adjacent vacant lot to expand milling space for Maine Grains, as well as to incubate and expand local food enterprises. But she can't get a loan because the building will cost $7 million to erect, yet the finished project will only be appraised at $2.4 million due to lack of comparable construction projects in the area. And that lack of construction, she adds, "Comes from decades of disinvestment in this area. There are huge obstacles to doing what we do in rural areas." Here, too, she has to play the long game, supporting other efforts to revitalize Skowhegan, such as the lone remaining paper mill, the New Balance shoe factory, and Maine Wood Heat wood-burning stove factory. "There is a growing ecosystem of entrepreneurship around here, that is based in inspired risk taking," she says.

THE MIDWESTERN GRAINSHED BUILDER

THOUGH ALYSSA HARTMAN GREW UP in northwest Ohio, surrounded by endless, flat expanses of corn and soy fields, the farmers who tended to them were anonymous and their activities were of little benefit to the local community. Instead, their harvests were destined for distant countries, states, and processing facilities, to be sold as animal feed, made into fuel, or sucked into the global commodity food system, stripped down to their component parts and reassembled into untold numbers of ultra-processed foods.

The first time Hartman encountered a food system that put a face to her local farmer and evinced a deep reverence for grain was in Sicily, where she spent seven months as a twenty-four-year-old working at a cooking school. Farmers were a part of the social fabric of the community, and "there was a real celebration and awareness of wheat and lentil variety names—they didn't feel like a side item, they were at the center of the plate," she recalls.

This was a food system that she felt a kinship with, not too different from the grain-centric one she is helping to shape today as executive director of the Artisan Grain Collaborative (AGC). Launched in Chicago in 2016 by a group of farmers, bakers, and conservationists concerned about the environmental impacts of farming, AGC wanted to revive small grain production, and expand the flavors and varieties available to them.

By the time Hartman arrived to serve as executive director in 2019, the founders had laid the groundwork for a coordinated grainshed connecting farmers, millers, maltsters, brewers, bakers, chefs, distillers, and agricultural researchers. Hartman has helped grow membership from thirty-nine to about two hundred; the same type of painstaking value-chain building that June Russell engaged in in New York state and

Amber Lambke constructed in Maine was happening across the Midwest.

Over the past decade, the region has gone from having no small-scale milling capacity to having fifteen community-based, small-to-midscale flour mills; still there are many, many more acres that could be converted to growing a diversified rotation of small grains, and Hartman knows that there is a "big untapped market for local grains and flour."

But what Lambke at Maine Grains called "chokepoints" in the supply chain have to be fixed first. One is better coordination of supply with demand. "We can't stop people from building a flour mill next to another one, but we can provide resources, information, encouragement, and connections," Hartman says. One member might be having trouble sourcing puffed wheat, or the demand for oats might outstrip supply. AGC is now undertaking a detailed survey of what members are growing and what their needs are to be able to match supply and demand with more precision.

The network's strength has been its willingness to share knowledge, to learn from each other through face-to-face meetings. "It's easy to believe that there's some technology that's going to come along and save us, but I just don't agree. If we could tech ourselves out of our problems, we would have by now. There really needs to be a person-to-person connection, a human touch to this work," says Hartman. Her role is to be the human collagen in this process—connecting, lubricating, and smoothing the way for all the grainshed's parts to synchronize with each other.

The work is hard because this system lacks the streamlined, hypereffi- cient movement across states and nations of the commodity grain system, in which a vertically integrated farm operation will sow and harvest tens of thousands of acres of wheat, store it in towering grain elevators, then either sell it to a mill or have it cleaned and milled on site. From there, it heads to domestic and international distributors, to be delivered to bakers who have placed their orders by catalog.

Yet I don't mean to imply that commodity farmers live financially secure lives. For every dollar consumers spend on food, farmers and ranchers only pocket 14.3 cents.[6] As the University of Michigan's Catherine Badgley (see Introduction) told me, "Anyone who is doing conventional agriculture is very likely doing very large land areas in monoculture, which requires very large equipment. This is expensive, so they're constantly in debt. They're also caught in a system that is very hard to change because to qualify for government payments through the Farm Bill, they have to farm and use the land in certain ways. There are some truly bizarre barriers to doing things differently. What struck me over and over is how much debt these farmers are carrying, and how much that weighs on them. It makes it hard to even consider changing course; it keeps them in that system."

Which is to say that farming is hard, no matter how you practice it. In the small-scale AGC system, each step of the supply chain must be built from scratch. Farmers may have to pay the cost of on-farm storage, and unless they add grain-cleaning machinery they will have to drive it somewhere to get it processed before milling. If it is an ancient grain more prone to spoilage, it may need to be placed in cold storage after hulling. Once the grain is milled, someone, typically the farmer or someone from the mill, delivers it to the baker. "There are a lot of steps in this process that require capital outlays that people now don't have, so it's challenging to see what profitability looks like so early in the development of these regional supply chains," Hartman says. "In ten years some of these costs will be amortized, but right now there's not a lot of fat in this system."

By contrast to the efficiencies of the farmer-to-baker commodity supply chain, here is how one small artery in the Minnesota regional grainshed emerged. When baker Christopher McLeod came back from baking in Germany and wanted to start his own Minneapolis subscription whole grain micro-bakery, he assumed he could tap into a strong regional grain economy. The area was considered part of America's breadbasket, after all. But he had to look hard for a farmer willing to sell him small amounts of winter wheat. Finally he found Mark Askegaard, of Askegaard Organic Farm in Moorhead, Minnesota, who, along with his daughter Beth McConnon, grows a variety organic hard red spring wheat that was developed at the University of Minnesota. Askegaard was the right kind of farmer, too, focused on building soil organic matter and healthy soil through regenerative farming methods.

Even though Askegaard is a small-scale farmer, McLeod's small bakery, Laune Bread, could not buy a whole field's worth of wheat. So he found the one small-scale stone mill—the first to re-enter this midwestern city—Baker's Field Flour & Bread, and head miller and baker Patrick Wylie. Wylie agreed to purchase Askegaard's entire field of Linkert wheat, store it, mill it, and then sell the flour to Laune and others. Laune Bread went from bike-delivered subscription model to storefront bakery in 2019, headed by McLeod and baker Tiffany "Tiff" Singh, a native Korean adopted into a White family in Minnesota.

I meet up with Singh, her hair piled in a bun and surrounded by a wide, apricot-colored headband, at Baker's Field, based in the Food Building in Northeast Minneapolis. She has brought with her a box of Laune's pastries, which are so mind-numbingly delicious it is hard to concentrate on the interview at hand: in addition to a traditional croissant, pain au chocolat, and palmier, there is a savory curry roll and a rustic wedge of "flaxipane"—Laune's regional version of the French almond frangipane swaps in golden flax from Askegaard Organic Farm for almond flour and fills it with Wisconsin William's Pride Apples and Minnesota black currants. "We love the challenge of taking a traditional recipe and modifying it with Minnesota grain, seed, or ingredient," says Singh.

As we tour the mill, which processes sixteen different local grains and seeds, Singh describes Laune's commitment to showcasing the flavors of Minnesota grains, produce, and other ingredients. All its baked goods are naturally leavened and contain at least 65 percent whole grain flour to maximize flavor, nutrition, and the health benefits of long ferments. To support its farmers' efforts to enhance soil biodiversity by growing a variety of cover crops, Laune, too, has diversified the grains and seeds it uses in baking; its ratio of wheat to non-wheat grains and seeds now stands at seventy-five to twenty-five. Half of Laune's budget goes toward Minnesota-sourced ingredients and three-quarters of its spending stays in the greater Midwest; nearly all the flour it sources is grown and milled in Minnesota. The remaining quarter goes toward nonlocal ingredients like lemon, chocolate, and cane sugar.

Singh and McLeod's commitment to community building and accessibility have led them to start a community trade with home gardeners, who can barter fruit and vegetables at $3 bakery credit for every pound of produce. The past summer's take included more than seven hundred pounds of rhubarb, forty pounds of Concord grapes, and nearly ninety pounds of plums, "which we used all the way up to January," Singh reports. Not only does the program offer an alternative way for people to access food, she notes, "it also empowers people to learn more about foods in their own backyards."

Through the individual relationship-building efforts of grain activists like McLeod and Singh and the collective activities of AGC, this region has transformed from one in which it was impossible to source local wheat in 2015 to a local grainshed where consumers can find heritage corn, rye, wheat, spring and winter wheat, buckwheat, spelt, emmer, einkorn, flax, oat, and Kernza (for more on this grain see Chapter 8).

There is still a lot AGC can and wants to do to grow its grainshed:

helping new farmers access land and resources with less risk, adding more infrastructure, connecting with state, federal, and university programs that can help them add capacity, and add more new product channels. But Hartman says, "I feel so confident that all the people we need to fix these problems are in the room together. . . . We've built strong relationships and a two-hundred-plus farm-and-business network that trusts one another and is aligned around common goals."

THE WORLDWIDE REGIONAL GRAIN NETWORK

SPEAKING TO THESE WOMEN WHO are rebuilding their local grainsheds is both inspiring and sobering. They are at different points in erecting the infrastructure of their local movements, a herculean task advanced one hard-fought step at a time. Yet they are still far from the kind of democratization of access that transcends the exclusivity of local food movements.

For this, I look to researchers such as Stephen Jones, Laura Valli at Washington State University's Breadlab, and Bethany Fallon Econopouly at Cornell's Buckler Lab at the Institute for Genomic Diversity. Their focus is on nutrient dense, genetically diverse whole grains that recapture flavor, are widely accessible and affordable, and can withstand the evolving challenges of climate change. It was at the Breadlab, says Toronto baker Dawn Woodward, "that I first saw how non-commodity breeding is essential to a climate-unstable world, as well as breeders who are not beholden to Big Ag, who care about seed sovereignty, farmers, and flavor."

In pursuit of these goals, the research plots at WSU are seeded twice a year with seeds from its own small grains seed bank and other gene banks. The seeds they broadcast, or scatter, include successful crosses using evolutionary breeding—the results of many seasons of seed selection prioritizing yield, climate resilience, and taste.[7] The idea is that if you sow a thousand different varieties of wheat into a one-acre plot, there will be those that thrive and those that do not. Natural selection over time mimics the natural evolution of ecological communities and produces economically viable, affordable crops.

Jones and the Breadlab's Janine Johnson warn against getting stuck on the romance of heritage wheat varieties that were once "modern" but perhaps are not adapted to one's geography and changing climate. They have "a beauty and a value and a place," Jones writes, and "a story unsullied by modern genetics." But they are not the future.

Re-localizing our grain economies, those regional bread baskets eclipsed by Big Grain and Big Ag is just one spoke of the larger alt food system, and shares many of the same attributes that you'll read about in coming chapters: exchanging extractive monocropping for climate-resilient farming methods that reduce the load of chemical fertilizers and pesticides, building healthy soils, and returning ecosystems biodiversity to the land; restoring local economies and offering consumers an alternative to global agri-food monopolies. It is also about connecting with a global network of like-minded advocates.

Dawn Woodward is a member of an international WhatsApp group called "Imagine Biscuits," many members of which are part of the United Kingdom's growing local grain network. Hodmedod's British Whole Foods in Sussex connects local farmers of pulses, grains, and seeds through its line of products, expanding the baker's universe beyond bread and baked goods to meals and snacks. Hodmedod's has also helped spearhead policy changes in the UK and Europe that are ahead of what we have seen in North America so far.

There are many more local grainsheds across North America today than there were back in 2010 when June Russell, Farmer Ground, and the

West Coast early adopters were beginning to bring back locally grown and milled whole grain breads. It is no longer hard to find an alt grain system that will free you from global grain monopolies and the inert supermarket white bread loaf.

As wheat breeders and researchers Jones and Janine Johnson say, the researcher and farmer's job is to develop varieties of grain that carry the DNA of the thousands of lines that got us to this point, and can adapt and flourish.[8] The craft baker's job is to figure out how to make delicious breads with these grains. Our relatively easy and delicious role, as consumers interested in fixing our broken food system and searching for restored taste and nutrition, is to advocate and support these local grain networks and help them flourish.

CHAPTER THREE

FIGHTING BIG FOOD ON THE PRODUCE FRONT: WOMEN WRANGLERS OF THE ALT SUPPLY CHAIN

DURING ONE OF CALIFORNIA'S SEVERE winter rains, I've come west to the Asilomar conference grounds in Monterey, site of the forty-third annual EcoFarm gathering. The conference has provided connection and community to generations of farmers and ranchers who have shaped the organics and the good food systems movements, promoting sustainability, local and regional foodsheds, and the right of all to have access to nutritious and delicious food.

Farmer Dru Rivers, an elder stateswoman and revered icon of the event, has attended the conference for the last forty-two years. With her long, flowing brown hair, beatific smile, and gentle cadences, she exudes an earth mother vibe, opening the conference by speaking of the importance of love for the land and love for all our fellow creatures. Her message captures a core tenet of the alt food system: that humans are not at the center of it, but part of an interlinked whole.

In addition to joining a bus tour of Central Coast farms, I attend sessions by the Coalition of Immokalee Workers on protecting farmworker rights, seed breeding, and agricultural land equity. Writing about this sector and advocating for its growth while living in the dominant industrial food system world can feel lonely at times. Here, we are all like fish who have found our school, and are taking pleasure in synchronous swimming with the thousand other like-minded food system reformers who have gathered this year—a bubble, no doubt, but a growing and comforting one.

At the end of the conference I head north. California is a good place to begin my exploration of the alt food system's produce sector, the women who farm it, haul it from producer to wholesaler and retailer, and those who are fighting for equity in food distribution and access. More than three-quarters of the nation's fruits and nuts and more than a third of its vegetables are grown here. California also leads the country in organic food production, clocking a more than 18 percent growth between 2018 and 2022 for a total of over $11 billion in sales.

My plan is to start here and navigate the streams and tributaries of the shorter and more direct alt produce system, links in the supply chain that are restoring ecosystems and mitigating climate change, strengthening local economies, eliminating environmental racism, and putting flavor, diversity, and nutrients back in local produce. My first stop is Full Belly Farm.

FULL BELLY FARM:
A WOODSTOCK FOR AGRICULTURE ARTS

IN 1982, THE FIRST YEAR she attended EcoFarm, Dru Rivers was a twenty-four-year-old sheep farmer. She square danced with a twenty-eight-year-old organic farmer from Woodland, California, named Paul Muller. "He was super handsome and definitely had farmer hands," was how Rivers would later describe their attraction.

The two married, raised a family, and in 1989 formed the nucleus of an organic farm in the Capay Valley north of San Francisco. They named it Full Belly Farm because Rivers was pregnant with the first of the couple's four children. Today the name also signifies the overflowing organic bounty the farm produces: vegetables, fruits, nuts, herbs, and flowers, as well as chicken, sheep, goats, and cows. It has achieved the rare feat of supplying twelve hundred CSA (community supported agriculture) subscribers with weekly boxes of food—all of it produced on farm—and becoming a player on the bigger stage of regional grocery stores.

The counter-culture-ish farm has, improbably, prospered on its own terms, a diverse alt food system unto itself, separate from the Big Produce hubs of industrial monocropping of the nearby San Joaquin and Central Valleys. The day I was scheduled to visit the farm came with torrential rains that turned the fields to mud. The day before that, I had fallen victim to a routine San Francisco "smash and grab" car break-in, in which I lost all my luggage. Too late, I noticed all parking garages warn people about the city's specialty crime ("It takes less than a minute!"). The delays this incident caused pushed my farm visit forward to what turned out to be the one brilliant day of the week—one of the few silver linings of my misfortune. Since the ground was still muddy, Rivers and I set out on a motorized cart to tour the four-hundred-fifty-acre farm. Low, scudding clouds gave way to brilliant sunshine as she pointed out the twelve acres of original walnut trees, where as many as a thousand visitors—just one portion of the total who attend—camp out for the farm's annual "Hoes Down Festival," a kind of Woodstock that celebrates not music, but the agricultural arts.

More than just a love-in for soil nerds and nature lovers, the event helps drive food system change: Judith Redmond, one of Full Belly's founding owners, has played a key role in managing the festival, helping to attract up to five thousand people, and raise hundreds of thousands of dollars for local and statewide organizations that support sustainable agriculture and rural communities. Her work helping Full Belly navigate state and federal agricultural laws showed her how much work needed to be done to change government's regulatory mindset to one that would truly support diverse regenerative farms, and how deeply calibrated its current laws are to supporting fossil fuel–based industrial agriculture.

One example involved progressive California legislators' attempt to rid farm communities of toxic nitrogen in their groundwater. "There are lots of small communities in the Central and San Joaquin Valleys where residents can't drink their water because there are so many nitrates in it, and that's directly related to runoff from chemical fertilizers," Redmond explains. But the paperwork required to comply with this regulation was geared toward giant chemical fertilizer–dependent farms growing a single crop, or monoculture, not a farm like Full Belly that strives for diversity. It was easy for a mega almond farmer, for example, to plug in one set of numbers, but much harder for Full Belly—with its eighty different crop varieties that harness the power of the sun and complex ecological interactions to build soil carbon—to comply with the regulations.

"For a grower like us, who has diverse crops, lots of vegetables mixed in with some perennials and animals on the farm, those forms are just laughable to even attempt," she says. This is just one example of the kind of systemic barriers in our current agricultural system that keep small- and mid-sized regenerative farms from thriving. I see this diversity for myself as we pass groves of pomegranate and persimmon trees on the left, which double as wind breaks for the fields, and fig trees on the right. Most of the fields we pass are blanketed in about a half dozen varieties of thick green, unruly cover crops, including bell beans, peas, vetch, and oats. By extending their roots into the ground, they minimize disturbance to the soil ecosystem, promote diversity of soil microbes, enrich soil matter, and prevent erosion, balancing out soil nutrient deficits that might have been left by the previous crop. If time allows, a herd of sheep will graze their fill, adding their microbial-rich manure and massaging the land with their hooves. If not, crops will be mowed at the end of the season and left on the ground as mulch.

We hop off our cart to tour the twelve-hundred-square-foot commercial kitchen, used to make the many value-added products Full Belly sells to its retailers, from fruit preserves, pickles, and fermented products, to olive and safflower oil, to nut and grain products. The three-story building is sided with reclaimed redwood and designed and erected by Dru and Paul's son Amon and a family friend; the upstairs houses Amon, his wife Jenna, and their three children. The building, outdoor patio, and fields are also the site of many weddings, and other events, and classes that make up another income stream for the farm; these grounds have provided camp sites for up to four thousand additional visitors to the Hoes Down Festival who can't find a spot in the walnut orchard.

The farm's internship program has taken in roughly three hundred interns over the past forty years, who have gone on to spread its farming methods. Unlike industrial produce farms, where workers may have picked beets for years yet never tasted one, Veritable Vegetable and Full Belly both offer free produce to employees; at Full Belly, eighty to ninety workers are provided with daily staff lunches heavy on the farm's produce. The farm has given loans to staff members to help them purchase housing, and partnered with the organization California FarmLink to help four crew members purchase property. On the day of my visit, a meeting is underway about another project: the purchase of a property that will be used for multiple farmworker housing units in the Capay Valley. "There's a huge dearth of farmworker housing here; we're trying hard to make both food and housing not just available to those who can afford it but also to those who can't," says Rivers.

In addition to this nurturing attitude toward workers, Full Belly has grown along with one of its first customers, Whole Foods. The chain only had a few stores in the Bay Area in the mid-1990s when it began to buy Full Belly tomatoes. Today, even though it is now owned by Amazon, Rivers says, "We're big enough where we have the capacity to keep up with the technology, food safety, and insurance programs that they require," such as the right computer software for labeling, invoicing, and field tracking, and field maps for food and water safety reporting.

Diverse income streams and a diversity of customers is a strong suit of Full Belly's. But Rivers acknowledges that the $80 billion organic food market has grown less transparent as big corporate players have moved in, and adds, "It's important for us to continually reevaluate and reinforce our values. It's easy to get a little lost in the vastness of the culture that's happened around organic."

On both East and West Coasts, the alt food system is the direct descendant of an organic, back-to-the-land movement that has waxed and waned throughout North American history. In 1915, after University of Pennsylvania economist Scott Nearing was dismissed from the faculty for his outspoken anti-corporation attitudes, he and his wife, Helen, took to homesteading in Maine, building their flagstone home by hand, and living according to their pacifist, vegetarian, and socialist values. Their 1954 book *Living the Good Life: How to Live Sanely and Simply in a Troubled World* became the *Walden* of its day. It inspired the next generation of organic, back-to-the-landers like Eliot and Sue Coleman, to whom they sold farmland for a song in 1968.[1]

In 1962, the publication of Rachel Carson's *Silent Spring* alerted complacent consumers to the dangers of DDT (dichloro-diphenyl-trichloroethane, the first industrial chemical pesticide, eventually banned in 1972 for its toxic effects), and the threat that industrialization posed to the natural world and its interconnected ecosystems. On the West Coast, the organic and environmental movements overlapped with 1970s Bay Area political activism. It was a time when the Civil Rights Movement was raising awareness of the harsh injustices of one hundred years of Jim Crow laws. Mounting casualties in the Vietnam war provoked passionate anti-war protests, heightening a sense of social unrest and instability.

My father's beloved Monterey Park food co-op was another tendril of this movement, based on a belief that good food and food education were vehicles for social change, and should be accessible to all. In San Francisco, the People's Park idea helped inspire what was called the People's Food System, a network of grassroots, cooperatively run operations that included the food co-op Other Avenues, Rainbow Grocery, and Veritable Vegetable, all of which, remarkably, still exist today.

WOMEN WHO HAUL PRODUCE

I HAVE PLANNED A VISIT to Veritable Vegetable, a radically different women-owned vegetable distribution business, because I want to find out how it has survived for so many decades in the sharp-elbowed, male-dominated world of food distribution. VV, as its members call it, is located, appropriately enough, amid a strip of warehouses on Cesar Chavez Street in the Dogpatch neighborhood of the city. Bu Nygrens, the company's director of purchasing and a founding member, is on hand to greet me.

The daughter of an American Ballet Theater dancer and a choreographer father, she drifted west dreaming of exactly the kind of back-to-the-land life that was enjoying a renaissance in the Bay Area. She joined VV in 1978, thinking it would be a short-term stint before moving on to a farm. But something about the everyday challenges of figuring out how to move large amounts of produce from farm to co-op, grocery store, or restaurant; coordinating a network of moving parts subject to scheduling and weather changes, vehicle disasters, and staffing problems felt familiar to her—it was a version of putting on a show as she had seen her parents do night after night. She became a core member of what became a solidly woman-led organization.

Amid an assortment of worn baseballs and Giants' figurines in her boss Evans's office—both she and Nygrens are die-hard fans—Nygrens regales me with tales from deep within the produce distribution system, an invisible, unsung, yet crucial component of any thriving local food-shed—the larger counterpart to the regional grainshed, a geographical area in which the food grown and produced is also consumed, and the basic building block of the alt food system.

The network of a regional distributor like VV, compared to a global, long supply chain distribution system, sounds so simple and easy to cobble together. But as I've seen in many instances on my travels through the alt food system, it is inefficiencies and bottlenecks in local distribution systems that keep a foodshed from growing and can foreclose any chances it has for success.

Large distributors, plugged into the vast economies of scale of the industrial food system keep goods flowing through international supply chains. They keep out small and mid-sized grocers, independent retailers, or local co-ops through their high minimum-load sizes or demands for sophisticated software systems. They dictate what ends up on supermarket shelves. To truly change our food system and keep small rural farms and food businesses connected to centers of commerce and individual consumers, VV understood they had to master the same challenges of routing, scheduling, and resource management that global supply chains faced, but on a miniature scale, without the benefit of monopoly-level cash reserves and highly diversified income streams. They needed to cobble together efficient supply chains that started in the fields and threaded through the challenging "last-mile logistics" that take products from warehouse to the customer's doorstep.

VV began in 1974 as one of the collectives that supplied the People's Food System, part of a closed distribution loop that included local farmers and producers, storefronts, co-ops, and buying clubs that shared the motto FOOD FOR PEOPLE, NOT PROFITS. By the time Nygrens arrived, the People's Food System as a functioning structure had collapsed, a result of political infighting and rivalry between two paroled prisoners who were admitted as members of an oppressed minority. Evans and a small group of five or six other VV members, mostly women, decided to try to continue VV as an independent for-profit venture, delivering organic and natural food to health food stores, co-ops, and the remaining People's Food System retail stores. "The term social enterprise was not in use yet, but that is how we identify," Nygrens says. "Profit is not, and never was, the goal."

For its first several decades, Veritable Vegetable's capital came in the form of sweat equity, and it did not take on loans or investors for the first forty-two years of its existence. Then the company acceded to minimal financing for equipment such as trucks, tractors, forklifts, and trailers. More recently, it has taken on a loan to help remodel its warehouse operation for increased effectiveness and efficiency.

VV would remain true to its commitment of supporting independent businesses and growers working to uphold organic values, even though with no national certification process at the time, the definition of "organic" was murky. While private, mostly nonprofit organizations began developing organic certification standards in the early 1970s and many states launched their own programs in the 1980s, it was not until 1990 that federal national organic standards were outlined, and 2002 when the

USDA finally put into effect a rule requiring that organic farmers and processors be certified by a state or private agency.

Just keeping the focus on hauling fruits and vegetables short distances is radical in an age when both the United States and Canada, in terms of value, import most of their fruits and vegetables. In the United States this is driven by growing demand for imports such as mangoes and avocados, lower labor costs in the global south, and the North American Free Trade Agreement (NAFTA)[2] in Canada.[3] Weather challenges and the agriculture sector's dependence on foreign labor pose additional challenges.

VV has won the fierce loyalty of many a farm by ensuring the highest return on its produce, as well as services that include working with farms on crop planning, sharing market information, and educating them on packaging. The company has provided loans for customer start-up costs or to aid in crop failure recovery, offered loaner trucks for cold storage, and below-market freight services.

Another thing VV has been committed to is providing women with executive and leadership roles as well as nontraditional tasks such as loading and driving trucks. Its path was not easy. "Like many small and mid-sized businesses, we carry the heaviest weight of accountability. We pay higher taxes and higher fees to conduct business without the same benefits that huge corporations receive." Nygrens adds, "We had no mentors, no role models, nobody else was interested in providing opportunities for women in an otherwise exclusively male field. One of our guiding principles is that when women control the finances of a community, people do not go hungry, children are fed, and everyone gets a fair shake. It's about cooperation not competition."

Today the company maintains a staff of one hundred, has relationships with more than a thousand growers of high-quality organic produce, and serves five hundred independent grocers, co-ops, restaurants, and food institutions. Nygrens takes pride in its fleet of low-emission tractors and trailers and its thirty-six trucks, which are among the cleanest on the road. Solar panels attached to the roof of the sleeper cabs connect to batteries that power the electric climate control system.

Two of those have been fitted to be all-electric, while the rest of the fleet runs on renewable diesel. Delivery of certified organic produce, dairy, nuts, grains, dried fruit, and beans happens across five states: California, Nevada, Arizona, Colorado, and Hawaii. The company also diverts 90 percent of its waste from landfill. Being energy efficient means never driving with an empty truck, too. "We run our trucks full in every direction," Nygrens tells me. "We outhaul to customers and backhaul (fill the truck for the return trip) from farms and LTL (less than truckload) freight customers."[4]

Though a women-run distribution company may seem like an anomaly, VV is not the only one of its type. Annie Myers learned from her job as the organic produce and meat wrangler for several New York City restaurants that there was a need for a regional distribution system. So in 2013 she scraped together $50,000 in funds from friends, clients, and family to launch Myers Produce, a woman-owned regional trucking company based out of hubs in New York City, western Massachusetts, and northern Vermont. Today her staff of twenty full- and part-time employees connects close to three hundred retail, restaurant, grocery store, and institutions like schools throughout New England. "Though trucking is not exactly known as a woman-dominated industry, there are a lot of women interested in the industry," she tells me. "We're trying to be a really appealing place for nonbinary folks and the LGBTQ population."

Especially exciting is the company's 2023 purchase of a thirty-thousand-square-foot large warehouse in Hatfield, Massachusetts, which allows it to lease shared space to like-minded organizations—such as

Deerfield, Massachusetts–based berry growers Nourse Farms. "The overnight storage thing is huge for trucking companies, knowing that you can drop something off and it'll be held at the right temperature until another company can pick it up," she says. "Most distributors don't want other companies doing that. But the more places our product can be aggregated, the more efficient our systems become." Indeed, in the alt food system universe, this seemingly mundane added service is a big fat slice of logistics heaven.

Back at Veritable Vegetable, Jennifer Doan, director of marketing, gives me a tour of one of two VV warehouses. In the back office, a set of twelve varieties of mandarin oranges are labeled and on display, to help the staff learn their names. A plum and pluot sizing guide is tacked to a cubicle partition wall next to a chart displaying the images of two dozen apples, ranked by tartness. The more informed VV staff members are about the salient characteristics of the products they sell, the better the job they can do representing their farm clients. "We're a conduit of information from farmer to eater," explains Nygrens.

Seeing all these varieties, a nostalgic pang for the riot, the abundance of California produce that I grew up with shoots through me, along with an undercurrent of existential dread. Without more companies like Veritable Vegetable and the regenerative farms they represent, how long will California's lengthy, golden run as the salad and fruit bowl of the nation last? Underneath giant industrial farms, massive overdrafts have led to depleted water tables, and eighty years of chemically treated soil is degrading our land and polluting our waterways. Above ground, a rapidly changing climate and endangered pollinator species cast their long, ominous shadow.

And then there are outlier events like pandemics. Weathering the pandemic was in some ways easier for Veritable Vegetable than long supply chain distribution businesses, which were left with nothing to deliver when the gridlock of oceangoing container ships occurred. Although the widespread adoption of remote work meant that VV's accounts with tech companies like Google and Facebook dried up, the highly diversified nature of its business saved it. "No one customer is more than five to eight percent of our business," Nygrens explains. "For most distributors twenty percent of their client base provides eighty percent of their business. For us it's the other way around. We don't work with large chains like Whole Foods. The biggest chain we work with is four or five stores." The company also offers freighting and independent logistics services, which includes customers in the beverage, flour, grain, and other industries.

The pandemic also boosted public interest in the work that she and her partners have been doing for close to fifty years, and the importance of shorter, more agile, less fragile supply chains that aren't as likely to break down during a crisis; the notion that the businesses you spend your money on makes a difference. "People who want to support a truly green, BIPOC and woman-run business are willing to go the extra mile to do things in the best rather than the cheapest way," she says.

THE HYPERMARKET ALTERNATIVE

FOR EACH CUSTOMER WHO IS willing to go that extra mile and pay more for a more local, equitable, and transparent food system, however, there are scores of others who want or who can only afford to pay as little as possible for food. It is all too easy to go this route, too. Consumers only need to go as far as their nearest "hypermarket" such as Walmart or Costco—which combine grocery store, department store, pharmacy, and appliances—to get access to a warehouse full of cheap produce, both in and out of season. Walmart, Kroger, and Costco account for nearly half of all grocery sales in the United States, with Walmart's market share exceeding the combined total of Kroger and Costco.[5] Consumers' love for low prices and the success of these warehouse stores have put relentless pressure on mid-tier grocery stores, and their distributors to compete on cost, logistics, and ever-evolving technology.

Every superstore purchase is captured by data collection agencies that use artificial intelligence and predictive analytics to pick up on trends and to forecast next year's sales. This allows automated purchasing of the next year's products as well, which are funneled through a shrinking number of distribution channels. "Ninety to ninety-five percent of the products on those shelves were not chosen by the retailer," Alan Lewis, an agricultural policy expert with the Colorado-based Natural Grocers chain, told an audience at an organic food symposium in March 2019, but dictated by this system of data collection and aggregated buying.

That image of embarrassing abundance and variety in North American grocery stores is largely an illusion. Look closely at the thousands of SKUs lining the shelves, including the proliferating category of private label or organic brands (Costco's Kirkland, Whole Foods' 365 label, or Cascadian Farm Organic, for example) and you'll see that they are owned by a small handful of multinational corporations. And because the mega-chains keep an obsessively detailed track of both the global flow of products and their profit margins, when harvests of avocados or bananas slump or prices fall, they can instantly adjust prices or absorb the changes and make up for them in another part of the supply chain.

Not only is it impossible for an alt supply chain to compete with this kind of global logistics clout, a mega-chain like Walmart—leveraging buying power that can grant or deny a food supplier access to 30 percent of American households—can make it impossible for the small to medium-sized retailer to procure even basic items for its shelves. Food suppliers can be pressured into giving mega-chains first dibs on a limited supply product, and sell for less than market cost. Independent grocery store owner Anthony Pena testified before antitrust enforcers in 2002 that it was impossible for him to buy orange juice because the competing big box stores had cornered the market and were selling the product for half the price of what his wholesale cost would be—had there been any product available to him.[6]

Although Veritable Vegetable and its producers operate outside this globalized marketplace, they must still compete with rock bottom retail prices that the dominant supply chain has established. As so many farmers and producers have lamented to me, we are hooked on what the British sheep herder and author James Rebank calls "the cult of cheap food," with little understanding of how harmful to farmers and the environment this is. Americans spend an average of 11.3 percent[7] of their income on food, among the lowest in the developed world, compared to 46 percent in 1901,[8] while the farmer's share of every food dollar spent has shrunk to under 15 percent.[9] Those profiting are the giant corporations who own and control the supply chain, and give little thought to the depletion of soil, the pollution of our waterways, and the exhaustion of our labor force that this system perpetuates.

In the produce sector, this downward pressure on prices paid to farmers comes to roost on the largely migrant laborers harvesting the fields. Climate change–driven record high heat indexes in California and Florida have led to numerous farmworker deaths. There are more than three hundred thousand migrant workers in California alone, who are vulnerable to wage theft, debt bondage, and abuses by labor recruiters.[10] On Mexican mega-farms that supply hypermarkets like Walmart, investigative reports have uncovered abuses ranging from lack of schools in the worker camps, to inadequate food, withholding of medical care, and physical and sexual violence by supervisors.[11] The recent surge in child labor in the United States addresses a labor shortage in part caused by a decline in immigration, a problem that will only worsen under a second Trump administration. These are the natural consequences of the ongoing tide of anti-immigrant sentiment and policies. Labor issues do not even merit inclusion in the $1.5 trillion Farm Bill (the cornerstone of federal food and agriculture policy that overwhelmingly supports industrial and chemical over regenerative and organic agriculture) though they should be right up there with crop subsidies and supplemental nutrition assistance benefits.

Mega-farms and their troubling labor history have all but superseded the small farmer, who could at one time drive his or her pickup loaded with produce to the local grocery store chain, shoot the breeze with the produce manager, and settle on a fair price; that scenario is now rural nostalgia. Big Food relies on efficient delivery of produce by truck, train, or freighter, from the mega-farms of South America, Mexico, or central California. "The problem is, there's no one at the store buying produce, buying anything," says Lewis. "Purchasing takes place in a globalized computerized system, now abetted by artificial intelligence that is missioned to provide nonseasonal, standardized delivery of products and maximize profit."

The result has been a vast consolidation of the grocery industry that has been going on over the past decade as small and mid-tiered markets have been gobbled up by the large chains. Despite rote claims by merging corporations that new synergies will result in cost savings for the consumer and a win for all, things generally do not work out this way. As the headline to one *Los Angeles Times* business column put it, "When companies say a merger will result in lower prices, try laughing in their face."[12] As consolidation in the cable, drug, insurance, and banking industries have demonstrated, when companies merge, prices rise and service declines, yet federal regulators have continually looked the other way.

Until, that is, the Federal Trade Commission (FTC), under the direction of a much more antitrust-inclined chair Lina Kahn, announced a long-awaited decision in February 2024 to file a lawsuit to stop a pending $25 billion Kroger–Albertsons merger, noting that the loss of competition in the market would lead to higher prices for consumers, lowered wages for workers, and lower quality products and services. In December 2024 a superior court judge in Washington State deemed the merger unlawful, putting the kibosh on it. But this hopeful trend could end abruptly with the change in federal administration happening at the time of this book's writing.

If so, the relentless economic pressure that alt food system stalwarts such as Veritable Vegetable—big, but not monopoly-size big—are under could well continue and worsen. "We have to knit inventory from hundreds of farms, keep track of each small order, and the bigger we get, the more expensive that gets," Nygrens explains. "To take care of those small farmers as the cost of fuel goes up, we have to subsidize the costs. And the pressure our retail customers are feeling to survive amid labor, fuel, and climate crises is pretty discouraging; they're feeling so much competitive pressure that it's hard for them to support businesses like ours." Contrast this to Walmart at the height of the pandemic: When a massive shipping supply chain bottleneck left a half billion dollars' worth of food imports floating at sea for lack of port docking space, Walmart opted for the costliest but most expedient solution: It simply bypassed the whole system and hired its own fleet of ships.[13]

WIDENING THE ORGANICS
TENT, MINIMIZING COMPROMISE

THE TRUTH IS THAT GREENWASHING in the industry is ubiquitous. The 2022 implementation of the USDA's national organic standards for production and processing opened the way for rapid growth in the industry. It also ushered in a heavy burden of paperwork, the need for an independent certifying agency, and the hunt for loopholes that large corporations could exploit. Given that accreditors can be negligent, or easily co-opted, and farmers—some of whom were attracted to organics solely for the premium it could bring them—or brokers can simply lie, it also opened the door to fraud. In his 2018 trial, a smooth-talking huckster named Randy Constant admitted to $142 million in grain sales sold to customers as certified organic, which were in fact not organic.

Corporate mergers in American dairy have led to factory-farmed "organic" milk in name only, produced on mega-farms in the western United States (see more on this in Chapter 4). Meanwhile, regulations governing what can be considered "organic" have loosened as organic production has gone super-sized.

In an ongoing debate over whether hydroponics—a method of farming that uses a water-based solution containing essential ingredients instead of soil to nourish plant roots—should be given organic certification, so far hydroponics advocates have prevailed. Unlike in Canada and the EU, the produce of hydroponic vertical farms—which are growing at an estimated rate of nearly 20 percent a year[14]—can be labeled organic in the United States.

This has hurt soil-based organic farmers, who assert that hydroponically grown produce is nutritionally inferior, with none of the ecosystem benefits of soil-based organic farming. They cannot compete with the efficiencies of vertical hydroponic farms—which grow produce on stacked vertical surfaces rather than on one layer of horizontal soil. The 2017 fight over this change by the National Organic Standards Board (NOSB) over what can be labeled organic was so emotional, and the result so devastating to some organic and regenerative farming leaders, that it indirectly led to the 2019 creation of Regenerative Organic Certified (ROC), a certification label covering food, fiber (organic cotton, for example), and health and wellness products. Its founders, an alliance of regenerative farmers and CEOs at Patagonia, Dr. Bronner's, and the Rodale Institute, hammered out a certification label that would prioritize soil health, animal welfare, and social justice.

As we will see, certification labels can be both helpful and confusing, though most in the alt food system acknowledge that they are necessary to help consumers navigate a slew of competing brands. There is even an international nongovernmental organization that drafts standards for products, services, and systems worldwide, the International Standards Organization (ISO).

Elizabeth Whitlow, executive director of the nonprofit Regenerative Organic Alliance, which oversees the ROC certification program, says its standards are based on those of ISO. Brands must open up their books to trained auditors for inspection, show how they source inputs, what they pay farmers, and how they are building capacity. From a pilot program cohort of nineteen farms in 2017, the Regenerative Organic Alliance has certified more than sixty thousand farms and smallholder farmers, 476 different crops, and more than eighteen million acres of farmland.

Yet despite the vocal objections to changes to the NOSB standards, there are many benefits to hydroponics and the broader category of Controlled Environment Agriculture (CEA), a technology-based approach that creates optimal growing conditions in an enclosed environment. These include reduced water use, improved labor conditions, production for many climate zones, increased yields, lower costs to consumers, and reduced challenges from pest damage. Certified organic Wholesum Family Farms, which grows tomatoes, peppers, and other vegetables in indoor farms in Mexico and Arizona, uses a combination of hydroponic and alternative growing mediums, such as coconut husks.

Wholesum Family Farms products are a mainstay in Walmart's organics aisle, leading some purists to cite this as an example of the "Walmarting" of organics, the driving down of prices, which hurts soil-based organic farmers.[15] But there is another side to Walmart's growing share of the organics market. I want organics to be available to all, at a reasonable price. Producers like Wholesum are delivering a healthier, more chemical-free product to consumers who cannot afford farmers market or health food store organic prices.

"Creating system change takes all the different theories of change," says Jonathan Rosenthal, cofounder and former executive director of Equal Exchange, a fair trade worker-owned Massachusetts cooperative. Some farms opt for Integrated Pest Management (IPM)—an environmentally sensitive approach that combines naturally produced pesticides with synthetic chemical version to manage pests as safely and as economically as possible—while others remain purely organic or biodynamic, Rosenthal points out. "I don't think that's a contradiction. In urban areas, where a lot of folks of color live, hydroponics makes a ton of sense. I support all these forms and am glad there's a choice." While it can be difficult to negotiate the slippery slope of where to compromise, the goal of the good food movement should be to spread the greatest amount of nutritious organic produce to the greatest number of people, while resisting the tendency of corporations to lower costs, squeeze laborers, and compromise on quality and environmental standards to maximize profits.

It may be helpful to look at the issue this way: If a handful of agri-businesses did not control the world's vertically integrated food system, perhaps all of us, including the migrant fruit pickers, farmers, ranchers, fishers, and meatpackers whose labor feeds this system would be able to afford fair, pesticide-free, climate-friendly food. But we are all living in a Matrix-like world controlled by Big Food, and all the other bigs:

Big Pharma, Big Tech, and Big Online Retailing (aka Amazon); we're so deeply embedded in it—and the larger capitalist framework that has given birth to these monopolies—that we can't see that there is another, more equitable way to organize our society.

One way to make improvements within the existing system is to search for equitable, pesticide-free, and safe produce grown on large-scale farms and sold in warehouse stores. The Equitable Food Initiative (EFI) Certification[16] is one example. EFI's goal is to integrate the worker's voice, sustainability, and food safety into the large-scale fresh food supply chain, certifying farms that supply retailers such as Costco and Whole Foods. Look for the EFI-certified label or check the "EFI-Certified Farms" page to see if a product you find at one of these big box stores measures up and thank the store manager for supporting EFI-certified farms. Rather than vilify organic products that don't meet the highest regenerative standards, I want to illuminate the differences between the commodity and alt food systems so that consumers can spend their dollars wisely and choose when to pay more for values and growing practices they support.

We make these choices every day. Most of us, though, don't know enough about food and farming to recognize the kind of high-stakes decisions we are making. In Portland, Oregon, New Seasons Market senior manager of sustainability Athena Petty has noticed that many of the store's highly price-sensitive customers "really understand that the externalities of cheap food are costing us . . . they're a little more willing to pay that extra amount for proteins and fresh produce where they understand there's a human health benefit. Some of the most exciting stuff coming out of this regenerative protein space is that it's so much healthier." (See Chapter 2 and Chapter 5 for more on the health benefits of regenerative whole grains and grass-fed beef, to name just a few examples.)

THE REGIONAL FOOD HUB ANSWER

BALANCING TRANSPARENCY, REALISTIC environmental stan-
dards, and the issues of universal access to healthy, nutritious food is one
of the toughest acts of any alt food system. To trace the beginnings of one
that does all of these things well, I reach out to Sue Futrell of Red Tomato, the innovative food hub based in Providence, Rhode Island. Launched
in 1997 as a hub for local growers in the regional food chain, Red Tomato acts as a go-between for farmer and customer, relaying feedback and
requests from one to another. The organization was founded by Michael
Rozyne, along with Jonathan Rosenthal of the fair trade coffee cooperative Equal Exchange. Between 1986 and 1996 New England experienced
a dramatic loss of small and mid-sized farms. Rozyne saw how these
growers were being edged out in an increasingly consolidated, globalized
marketplace. He wanted to do for local farms what he and his partners
had started doing for coffee in 1986: bring transparency and direct trade
to what was becoming an increasingly niche market.

Almost three decades later, Rozyne, along with executive director Angel Mendez, is still involved, along with a cadre of dynamic women who
are maintaining their legacy at Red Tomato. Though the organization
started as a conventional distributor like Veritable Vegetable, with a warehouse and truck, it soon gave up on that model, instead aggregating and
consolidating produce from local growers and using existing infrastructure and supply chains to distribute its produce. Today Red Tomato is a
combination profit and nonprofit organization, and does approximately
$5 million in trade annually.

The organization's relationship with African American farmer advocate and civil rights leader Shirley Sherrod (see Chapter 1) goes back to
the early 2000s, when she worked for the Federation of Southern Coop-

eratives, and the two organizations collaborated on a watermelon marketing project. Since 2019, Red Tomato has served as a marketing agent for New Communities' two-hundred-acre pecan orchard.

Perhaps one of Red Tomato's most significant achievements in nurturing a regional food system is in its work marketing the regenerative fruit orchards of the Northeastern United States. Although this region has grown some of the country's best eating apples since they were introduced by European settlers, the Pacific Northwest has long outstripped it in organic apple sales because its drier, more temperate climate subjects the orchards to far less pest pressure. So, in 2005, Red Tomato launched its EcoCertified program, gathering a team of farmers, scientists, and advisors—many of whom had been involved in an earlier program called Core Values Northeast—to create an orchard ecosystem and certification process focused on best, ecologically sensitive growing practices: promoting soil, tree health, and pollinator habitat while keeping predator insects in check.

In the twenty years since its founding with six members orchards that had been with Core Values, it has certified more than thirty Northeast orchards and began expanding its geographical reach in 2024. The rigorous EcoCertified protocol is a form of IPM (Integrated Pest Management), which Jonathan Rosenthal alluded to when acknowledging that moving our food system forward requires flexibility, using the best practices for a given region and climate. In the Northeast, where humidity, disease, and insect pressure is far more intense than in the Pacific Northwest, organic, chemical-free orchards are virtually impossible, especially if growers are held to the cosmetically perfect standards of the market. Under the Eco-Certified protocol, chemical pesticides and herbicides are not completely eschewed but are highly targeted and kept to a minimum.

To see the EcoCertified program in operation up close, I visit Erin

Robinson, orchard manager at Scott Family Orchard in Dummerston, Vermont. A nearly six-hundred-acre property owned by a land trust but operated as a for-profit business, it is a magical place of gently undulating land covered with 130 varieties of apple and other fruit trees planted at the turn of the century.

Pomologist Ezekiel Goodband managed the orchards between 2001 and 2018, grafting thousands of heirloom varieties onto McIntosh tree trunks. Every fall each of the orchard's approximately six thousand trees are pruned by hand, a labor of love that yields apples beloved by chefs, cideries, and a network of co-op stores and other outlets mostly within a one-hundred-mile radius of the orchard. Robinson grew up down the road, and when she returned home after a stint on the West Coast, started off here, she says, "as Zeke's [Ezekiel's] grunt."

When Goodband left, she served as interim orchard manager while management looked for a qualified orchardist trained in pomology and etymology. Eventually they realized she was already doing the job, and doing it well, and she was offered the official title of orchard manager.

The July day of my visit, Robinson is dressed in jeans and a tank top that show off arms wreathed in mystical-looking tattoos that celebrate the birth of her two sons with their birth flowers and astrological signs. In the orchard, pollinators buzz through the blue skies and sun beats down on the bucolic orchard. A closer look, though, shows how it is struggling after a catastrophic mid-May freeze destroyed more than 90 percent of its crops—just one of the curveballs climate change is throwing these days, along with drought, heavy rainfall, and smoke from Canadian wildfires. As we zip through the fields in a utility cart, Robinson points out row after row of stunted fruit that resulted from the frost, which can be used for cider, but not for retail sale. She ticks off other threats to the fruit: heavy deer pressure, which must be constantly warded off with new fencing, and maggots that will show up as worms in her apples. The noninvasive battle tactic here are bright red decoy apples that dot the orchard. They will attract the maggots, trapping them on their sticky surfaces while keeping the real apples safe.

There are many more threats in this humid northeastern climate, yet Robinson notes that consumers interested in eating fruit as chemical-free as possible don't know the hoops that the ecologically minded Vermont orchardist must jump through to grow as organically as possible. Because the terms "spray" or "spraying" is anathema to these customers, EcoCertification provides much-needed education, transparency, and reassurance that the best practices possible are being followed. "It's a realistic way of orchard growing; you can trap things, use every mode of action available not to spray, but when pressure is high enough, use minimally invasive ways to protect crops," Robinson explains. "I don't use insecticides until after bloom when the pollinators are finished, although I do use fungal, bacterial, and nutritional sprays before bloom. I don't use herbicides [weed killers]; we string trim, meaning whacking the weeds around the trees, cutting grass, and trimming flowers that will attract pollinators after bloom. The soil is richer without using herbicides and soil nutrients, microorganisms, and mycorrhizae all benefit from this practice."

In addition to developing the EcoCertified label, Red Tomato helps spearhead creative marketing ideas like Scott Orchard's seasonal "Discovery Boxes" sold at retail stores from New York City to Boston, packed with three different heirloom varieties. In the fall, for example, Robinson selected the best apples for pie making: Calville Blanc d'Hiver, Belle de Boskoop, and Bramley, one of the most popular cooking apples in England. Through clever marketing, realistic yet sustainable growing practices, and its network of EcoCertified orchards, Red Tomato is expanding its alt produce network throughout the Northeast, making this regional and regenerative system more competitive with Big Orchard products from the Pacific Northwest . Robinson is proud that most of the orchard's fruit stays in the region, supplying a range of customers from top chefs and restaurants to local cooperatives and, at a much lower cost, food banks. "The whole point is to nourish our community," she says.

Yet for all the good Red Tomato and Scott Farm Orchard are doing in expanding the Northeast's alt produce food system, the reality is that too much of America does not have the luxury of making such small distinctions between "certified organic" and "EcoCertified," and in fact, does not even have a local grocery store to make them in. The loss of small and mid-sized stores has left scores of counties across the United States without a grocery store, usually in the poorest and most economically depressed neighborhoods. What we need, and what so many innovative regional food system leaders are doing across North America, is to increase access to whole, nutritious foods and treating them as a basic human right accessible to all.

THE WOMEN ACTIVISTS BRINGING
FOOD EQUITY TO HARTFORD

IN UNDERSERVED NORTH HARTFORD, CONNECTICUT–WHICH comprises three of Hartford's fifteen neighborhoods, and a part of a fourth—the average lifespan is sixteen years shorter than that of much wealthier West Hartford. If any areas should be special targets for expanding a healthier, more inclusive vision of what our food system should look like, it is areas like North Hartford.

Connecticut's state capital carries the bland image of the insurance hub of the country, its sterile downtown a place to pass through on the way from Boston to New York. Mocked by *The Simpsons* as the site of a free trip given to the winner of a gross-out contest, it has gone from extreme wealth of the post–Civil War era to its present status as one of the poorest cities in the nation. Yet it is also home to the innovative Hartford Food System, which Martha Page headed between 2010 and 2022.

She is my first guide to the city's food system history. Over a rivetingly delicious lunch of "Spasta Pesto"—a brightly colored, lovingly constructed cylinder of julienned vegetables, spaghetti squash, pesto, and fresh tomato sauce—Page tells me that her main goal coming into the job was to connect the disparate food system efforts going on in different parts of the state into a seamless whole.

Page's and Red Tomato's paths crossed when she and Michael Rozyne served on the first networking team of Food Solutions New England, a project of the University of New Hampshire's Sustainability Institute that envisions crossing state borders and creating an integrated regional food system over the six New England states. As I've come to realize, it is networking forces of alt food systems across state and country lines that gives it the tensile, aggregated strength it needs to begin to stand up to the conventional food system. These connections are happening at an accelerated pace, says Page, because "the pandemic revealed some serious cracks in the system; there's more awareness of where our food comes from."

In their Food Solutions New England meetings, Page recalls, "We'd have these conversations about how we're talking mainly about people who have the discretionary income to afford to spend ten dollars on a basket of heirloom tomatoes, you know, that kind of stuff. The community I'm working in couldn't afford that."

Lack of access to healthy foods and neighborhood safety in communities like North Hartford exacerbate rates of diabetes, obesity, and other chronic diseases, which are far more prevalent than in the city's wealthier neighborhoods. To solve for this problem of access and affordability,

Red Tomato's Bypass program was born, a supply chain prototype that would leverage Red Tomato and the Hartford Food System's connections to farmers and connect them directly to communities in need, "bypassing" the retailer to reduce costs.

Red Tomato combined federal and private philanthropic funding to launch the program, and Page applied for USDA grant money earmarked for local food purchase assistance. The program's proof of concept phase started in Bridgeport then moved on to Hartford.

Rather than procuring the Bypass program's produce, dairy, and eggs from long-chain commodity dealers, Page was able to connect to local farmers and healthier products. "The premise is that the grant takes the affordability issue off the table. If we can build up enough volume, then eventually the prices these programs will need to pay will go down enough so that we can wean these programs off the subsidy," Page explains. Here, as I will see countless times during the course of my journey, is the creativity and scrappy hard work of organizations like Red Tomato and people like Page who are plugging holes in the alt food system, hoping that one day the systems they are building will be robust and established enough to either stand on their own, or able to tap into the Byzantine system of government subsidies that currently favors only the giant-sized and Big Food dominated.

The Bypass program also helped fund a food-as-medicine program at Hartford Hospital, a way for doctors to prescribe fresh produce for patients who were, say, suffering from diabetes or hypertension, conditions that are highly diet-sensitive. To Page, whose background includes a master's degree in public health, the food-as-medicine concept was an especially welcome addition to her food system work; more than most people, she understood how closely tied a community's health is to its food system and access to fresh, nutrient-dense produce and other local foods. The food-as-medicine movement in turn was driven in large part by a clause in Obama's Affordable Care Act that required public health hospitals to conduct something called a community health needs assessment every three years. Although the clause was widely opposed at first, it made hospitals that had been mostly focused on medical outcomes begin to look at the social determinants of poor health among the communities they served; in Hartford those were mainly poverty and lack of access to fresh, healthy food.

Later that afternoon, I meet with Page again, this time along with three other women who are making their food system more equitable and community based. After touring the new Joan C. Dauber Food Pantry inside Mount Sinai Rehabilitation Hospital, we sit down in the hospital's visitor's room and the group outlines its four-quadrant blitz approach to solving food insecurity and improving community health in North Hartford.

Carolyn Alessi, Trinity Health's regional director of community health and wellbeing, describes Trinity's Food as Medicine program, now in development for underserved residents that will include nutrition education, food prescriptions, a "food pharmacy" to solve short-term food insecurity, and a family intervention and behavior modification program design to promote long-term health. Community health workers will guide a diabetic patient through a six-month program that includes regular monitoring of weight improvements, blood pressure and blood sugar, medication compliance data collection, cooking demonstrations, counseling sessions, and an allied park program for hiking and forest bathing. The latter two strategies reflect a growing body of evidence showing that the more time spent among trees and nature, the better measurable health outcomes like blood pressure, heart rate, and immune function. Upon graduating from the session, patients join a peer support group network to help keep them motivated and maintain their lifestyle changes.

Denise Holter, they all agree, is the linchpin of the team, the valued community representative who has marshalled community support for a sorely needed full-service grocery store in North Hartford. Wealthier neighborhoods can organize against the merger of grocery store giants like Kroger and Albertsons and the power of extractive Big Food monopolies, but in North Hartford, an alt food system victory would mean getting any kind of supermarket, ideally an independent store with plenty of local sourcing from sustainable farms. Here, too, the fight is about eliminating roadblocks, leveraging political and financial power, and most of all, community support.

Like many African Americans of her vintage, Holter, born March 1956, is just one generation removed from the land and the Jim Crow South. Her parents came north from Florida and Georgia after World War II, where her mother and her family were sharecroppers who picked cotton. As a young single mother in North Hartford in the late 1980s, grocery shopping for Holter meant getting on the bus with a stroller and making two transfers. A three-bag haul was the most that would fit on the back of the stroller.

Thirty years later and in a much more comfortable position in life, she agreed to sit on a focus group on the proposed grocery store. By organizing and building up community engagement, she's helped show potential developers that the slowly gentrifying, mostly Black and Brown neighborhood is an attractive, viable option.

While a potential operator of the store has been identified, there are always more roadblocks: community organizers still need to put together a funding package that will make the grocery store project feasible and are newly engaged, Holter says, in the "diplomatic dance" needed to bring the city's newly installed mayor onboard. Generating change from the grassroots level is slow, arduous work; Holter has been working toward the goal of a North Hartford grocery store since 2017 and says, "there won't be a groundbreaking for at least two more years."

Kristen Cooksey Stowers, an assistant professor in health disparities at the University of Connecticut Hartford, says that it wasn't until she examined a map of the country's food deserts as a young economic intern at the USDA that she realized the Southside Chicago neighborhood she grew up in qualified as one. Like Holter, her mother—contrary to stereotypes about inner-city parenting—knew what a healthy diet looked like. "She worked against an environment designed for disease and lugged us four girls and a shopping cart. We blocked the entire day just for bus transfers and so forth." Knowing no other way of life, it wasn't until she went to college that she realized having to take multiple buses to get to the grocery store was not how most Americans lived.

"My lived experience inspired me to build upon food desert research to contribute more data and information about food swamps—data that consider overall balance and equity in food environments. It is not just about the absence of supermarkets but what's there in its place." Cooksey Stowers went on to write her doctoral dissertation in public policy at Duke on food swamps, structural racism, and how food systems and zoning policies can advance health equity. Now, at UConn, she combines her academic work with grass-roots activity in Hartford. Around the country, she has seen urban food equity plans that have worked and others that haven't. Philadelphia's fell short after it added a supermarket in a food desert but failed to solicit community engagement and support, and so lacked a deep understanding of the cultural food needs of the community. Baltimore, on the other hand, has succeeded thanks to a strong food policy council and director, and the participation of local government, research, student volunteers, and data collection conducted by Johns Hopkins University's school of public health.

In addition to the alt food system activism of these four women, there are a number of other efforts to bring food equity and inclusion to Hartford. Forge City Works, a nonprofit that uses food as the conduit for social change, received funding for its Fire x Forge restaurant, bar, and catering service, which provides job training for residents facing high barriers to employment such as past incarceration, homelessness, and poverty. Part of the funding will also go toward ushering in a long-awaited grocery store in North Hartford, which Forge City will manage. Hands-on Hartford, a social services organization, received funds for its pay-what-you-can restaurant, as did Hartford Food System's urban CSA (community-supported agriculture) for underserved community members.

Page's contributions on the policy side—such as her part in the effort to get Hartford bus routes changed so that mothers like Holter don't have to make three transfers to go crosstown to get to a grocery store—helped usher in a change in the balance of power and an escape from charges of "white saviorism," in which all-powerful White people rescue voiceless, impoverished people of color.

Pointing to community activism around the grocery store, Cooksey Stowers says, "The powers that be, the Hartford anchor institutions, they're aware that residents are taking ownership of what happens to their lives and their community." Reeling off the signs of progress, she adds, "The neighborhood revitalization zones, the community action task force, the work that Trinity is doing—"

"Mayoral candidates talking like it's their idea," Page interrupts, finishing Cooksey Stowers sentence, to laughs of recognition. All are proof that the many years of hard work these women activists have invested in their communities are paying off, in sometimes halting, yet real ways. "You're really starting to see that the power that was typically with large institutions, with corporations, is now moving to the community," says Alessi.

From the work of early organic produce pioneers Rivers and Redmond, to Nygrens's and Myers's efforts to construct the distribution link in the alt produce supply chain, to the work of Red Tomato and the Hartford activists to strengthen regional and equitable good food access, the alt produce system is moving forward. These women and their efforts are still the grain of sand in the oyster of Big Agriculture, that small irritant to the status quo that is gaining in size and luster as they add layers of health, biodiversity, and equity. It is work that deserves our tender care and support in order to speed the process of turning that grain of sand into a luminous pearl dangling on a supply chain that will one day no longer need to be qualified as "alt."

CHAPTER FOUR

SCRAPPY GRASS AND COW
FARMERS VS. BIG DAIRY

ON A SUN-DAPPLED EARLY EVENING in late June, Ashlyn Bristle
logs on to the monthly meeting of the Dairy Grazing Discussion Group
(DGDG). This is not its official name but is what I've taken to calling
this group of ten or so young women and queer-identifying pasture-based
dairy farmers who meet regularly on Zoom to share information on cash
flow management, milk tank logistics, herd health, and grant applications—but most of all to offer each other emotional support in an epically
scary time in their corner of the dairy industry.

They are at the extreme alt end of the dairy supply chain I have set out
to investigate, micro producers with none of the efficiencies of scale of the
handful of highly consolidated dairy groups that dominate the market.
The women of the DGDG do not have cows bred to be super-high-yield
commodity milking machines, or plants that process millions of pounds
of milk per day, or hundreds of tankers that transport milk across the
land. In an ideal world, there would be room for a variety of milk producers, from small, diversified, grass-fed, regenerative farmers who raise
other types of livestock and crops, to large-scale conventional producers.
But the entire industry, as I will learn, is broken; I just happen to be starting at the small end, where the pain is acute.

Bristle is checking in from a strawberry patch on Rebop Farm, her
dairy, lamb, beef, and turkey farm in Brattleboro, Vermont. After her

poultry processor abruptly shut down, she and her partner, Abraham Mc-Clurg, were suddenly faced with the task of slaughtering and packaging two thousand birds. "It put us in a really hard place," she says with New England understatement. They brought in off-farm labor for two days, which took care of some of the birds, and processed about a thousand on their own. Added to the recent elimination of their pig farming enterprise, which they decided was causing too much erosion and landscape disruption, the combined loss of income led them to lay off one full-time employee. Another has run into a raging case of poison ivy. "He can't put on his pants or his shoes and he's on a wild amount of steroids," Bristle tells the group. "He can't work in the milk room with open, oozing sores." Their third employee is down with fever and vomiting. So Bristle is here, harvesting strawberries while she chats with the group in a melodious, calm voice that hides the inner turmoil she is feeling.

Some members of the Dairy Grazing Discussion Group—mostly based in Vermont, New York, and Maine—are generational farmers inheriting established family businesses. Others, like Bristle, are driven, first-generation land stewards who have learned an age-old way of life in a few short years. For people like me who want to see complexity, biodiversity, and interlinked, mutually supportive plant and animal systems on one farm, they are role models for their principled practices and the quality of their products. They sell pasteurized and raw milk, yogurt, farmstead cheeses, pasture-raised lamb, veal, beef, turkey, chicken, eggs, and whey-fed pork, either by direct marketing their products through their farm stores or CSAs, at farmers markets, food co-ops, or other retail outlets.

All of them are owner-operators in the first decade or so of their careers in pasture-based dairy practices. While they hold a variety of certifications, including USDA Certified Organic, "Real Organic," Certified

Grassfed, and Animal Welfare Approved, they all follow the practices of regenerative agriculture centered on pasture-raising their animals. Certified Organic dairy farmers are only required to allow their cows to graze for 120 days per year, during which they must consume 30 percent of their dry matter intake per grazing season in foraged grasses, while Certified Grassfed requires 150 days on pasture per year and 60 percent of their dry matter intake per year from foraged grasses.[1] Most of the members of the group exceed those standards, though they can't stretch too far beyond because of the forage limits of their cold climate.

If they use chemical herbicides, pesticides, or synthetic fertilizers at all, they do it in a targeted manner, similar to the protocol of Red Tomato's EcoCertified fruit program. Their goals are to—as much as possible—operate a holistic system in which grazing dairy cows help regenerate soil and the soil returns the favor by producing nutrient-rich grasses. They are equal parts dairy farmer and grass farmer.

As the DGDG Zoom meeting goes on, the news emerges that Sarah Chase, co-owner of Chaseholm Farm in Pine Plain, New York, has decided that when fall comes, she will downsize her herd to about one-third of its current size. A third-generation farmer, she runs the farm with her brother Rory, who heads up the cheesemaking operation, and her partner, Jordan Schmidt. Like Bristle, she is trying to come up with a formula for the farm that will be profitable and sustainable. Both are realizing that the old dairy farmer's adage of "more milk, more profit" is not always true for their small-scale regenerative and organic farms. "We're operators in a different system and the economics are different for us," she says.

Milking once a day (instead of the more typical two times a day) is more profitable in her case.[2] A topic the group talks a lot about is, "Are we using cows to make milk, or to manage land?" They are doing both, but the business goal is to make more money per pound of milk. Milking less saves labor costs, and, by keeping more energy in the herd and in the pasture, benefits the health of both.

All of which, Chase says, "is hard to remember when you're trying to be a good little capitalist." Chase also realizes she has to minister to herself, too, that by not burning out she's apt to stay healthier as well. "It's hard to quantify, but when somebody is not getting sick, that's reducing costs, which is why I'm keeping a diary this summer—how do I put that kind of thing in my spreadsheet?"

The Dairy Grazing Discussion Group was launched in January 2021 by Brattleboro area–based large animal veterinarian Dayna Locitzer. Her interest in pasture-raised dairy connected her to a number of small-scale dairies with women at the helm. It was their shared burden of "having the weight of ownership on their shoulders" that made her want to connect them. "All of them had strong values, work ethics, and were similar in the struggles they were going through: challenges with employees; decision-making fatigue; [cow] mastitis; managing a dairy herd; or thinking about big-picture changes and how to conceptualize their farm within the larger economy. I wanted to bring them together so they could share their experiences. 'Hey, what are you doing for spring grazing, or employee vacation days, or how are you making decisions with your romantic or business partners?'"

After her own experiences and those of close owner-operator friends of sexism in the industry, Locitzer also knew she wanted the group to be all female-identifying so they could be more open than they might be in a mixed-gender group. "And," she adds, "I only knew badass women who were doing this work."

The sexism, however unintended, "is constant," Bristle agrees, recounting a recent farm dinner where a guest wanted to meet the farmer but looked baffled when she extended her hand. "It was such a small thing, but very telling: I'm not the farmer to you. There are lots of examples like that: contractors who circumvent me and then things are built wrong because I'm the one overseeing our strategic planning and the specifics of production, while Abraham is doing a lot more of our bookkeeping and customer fulfillment. There are just a lot of assumptions that are made about who's doing what."

As the Zoom meeting continues, group member Mercy Larson reports that she was laid up for two days after some welding snapped and a piece of tractor equipment dropped on her foot. "It's all kinds of fun colors now," she says. The summer perennials she planted too late in the season because of equipment failure, and because "farm life happened," all died during a dry month with no rain. Two of her cows are off schedule for their milk and she's worrying about filling her milk quota. Sarah Chase consults her list, and tells Larson, "I do have one available in September, a big Holstein. She could be a temporary cow for you."

This kind of sharing of cows, equipment, capabilities, and knowledge (Chaseholm has done some contract beef growing for Rebop as well) is constant among the group. "When I feel really hopeless about the food system, and about my role in it, or my inability to fix what's broken, it seems like the only power that I have is in collective power, in our ability to support each other through marketing each other's products, or through helping each other with technical questions or whatever support we can give to each other," says Bristle.

Between problems with cow ketosis, a metabolic disorder found in lactating cows, the end of her chicken income stream, and the loss of her last full-time employee, Bristle confesses, "I've been having really bad anxiety about it, multiple panic attacks. My body just needs to go through the grief process of the loss of what I thought the future looked like, and how different it's going to be now. I need to get through those feelings before I can see the opportunities and the good stuff. It's healthy and very annoying to have to go through this process."

"Totally," Chase says. "I probably wear it differently, but I'm anxious, too."

Ashlee Kleinhammer, co-owner of North Country Creamery in Keeseville, New York, joins the conversation to say that she, too, is dealing with anxiety, over processing more milk than ever before, the result of a high breeding rate in the spring. She is trying to curb production and debating with her partners whether or not to sell some of their cows. Still, she says, "I got a ton of field work done, which is nothing short of a miracle. "The anxiety is around the fact that it feels like time to scale down, and what a relief that could be for us." Anxiety and relief seem like contradictory emotions, yet they capture the daunting challenge of making a small-pastured dairy pencil out on the accounting books: For Kleinhammer the fear of loss of income from downsizing is mixed with yearning for relief from the difficulty of making income cover costs.

PASTURE-BASED: WHY ALL THE GRAZING?

LIKE OTHER FORMS OF REGENERATIVE agriculture, grass-fed dairy is based on the belief that the last sixty years of high-input, high-yield Green Revolution–style agriculture has not worked. These practices, which taught farmers in developing countries how to dramatically increase yields of staple crops like wheat and rice with heavy applications of chemical fertilizers and pesticides, do serious damage to soil, ecosystems, and human health. Regenerative farming is not only a much better way to lower the climate impacts of food production, but in essence a return to the way agriculture has been conducted sustainably for millennia, enhanced by modern technological insight.

Grass-fed dairy and meat farmers also believe that the ideal feed for cattle is grass, the forage their four-chambered stomachs evolved to handle best. One hundred percent grass-fed farmers feed their cows only fresh and dried grasses and plants, while organic dairy farmers and most certified grass-fed farmers rely on a mix of grass and grain to meet their cow's nutritional needs.

Recalling an earlier generation of grass-fed dairy farmers, Sarah Flack—a Vermont author, teacher, and consultant on grass-based livestock farming systems—says, "Back in the nineties, it was philosophical. Farmers just didn't want to import grain from the Midwest, externalizing those costs and contributing to the decline of soil health.[3] There are others who do it because they feel their cows have better longevity on grass."

Like other regenerative farmers, grass-fed farmers rely on cover crops, which in addition to building soil and ecosystem health, also serve as forage for their animals. Their preferred cover crops are a diverse mix of perennials that do not have to be re-seeded each year like annuals. Perennial legumes such as alfalfa and clover are magical transformers which—aided by the energy of the sun—turn the inert nitrogen abundant in nature into a digestible form that is essential to life, reducing the need for the nitrogen in fossil fuel–based chemical fertilizer.

Cover crops' long roots thread down through the soil, increasing their ability to hold water and safeguarding the land against both flooding and erosion. And—although this is a sometimes-oversold feature—they draw down and sequester atmospheric carbon, one of the primary sources of greenhouse gases. Flowering perennials such as buckwheat, clover, lupines, and cowpeas support and help conserve the pasture's pollinator and beneficial insect community as well.

When there is a healthy diversity of forage in a pasture, competition among the crops builds pasture resilience and makes the animals that feed on them better able to tolerate increasingly occurring weather events like drought or heavy rains. To prevent overgrazing, which can become detrimental to soil, and optimize forage health, pasture-based farmers practice what is known as adaptive grazing, rotating their animals from one paddock to another, aided by shepherd dogs and movable electrified fences. The goal is to keep a diverse ecosystem in exquisite balance in the face of continual climate, weather, and man-made challenges. Regenerative farming helps create a kind of super-resilient biodiversity that is our best way of mitigating climate change, and it saves money spent on inputs, increasingly important as chemical fertilizer costs soared in the wake of the Russia–Ukraine war.

The cow, sheep, or goat's contribution to this ecosystem comes in the form of soil-building manure, while their rotational trampling and grazing exert a stimulating effect on soil and grass. The cows' placid, implacable pulling and munching may seem mindlessly dumb, but it is genius in the way it encourages root growth and the exudation of plant sugars that feed soil microorganisms.[4]

Providing for all of a lactating cow's nutritional and energy needs on grass alone is exceedingly difficult because the dairy cow is called on to provide much more milk than needed to satisfy one calf. In order to meet a herd's energy needs off one farm, the farmer may have to "run" or maintain fewer cows. While many consumers think that grass-fed should be cheaper because there is no need to buy grain feed, Flack says the opposite is true. Commodity cows have been selected to create large quantities of milk on nutrient-dense feed. Add that to the economies of scale of mega-farms and the industrial supply chain and they easily outcompete grass-fed on cost. This is why many organic dairy farmers rely on a mix of grains and grass to meet their herds' energy needs.

The most skilled pasture-based dairy farmers are constantly working to keep the energy output of their forage on a par with the nutritional demand of their herds: they keep an eagle eye on the balance and height of legumes, grasses, and forbs on their fields; how much rainfall they're getting; the rumen fill of her animals (the mix of liquid and dry matter content in a cows' largest stomach compartment) and when to rotate their paddocks.

"There are folks that have these amazing field maps with each cell blocked out, and there are others who can scan the fields with their eyes and do their intensive rotational grazing by adjusting paddocks on the fly," says Reid Miller, farm services director at the Northeast Organic Farming Association of Vermont (NOFA-VT). "Then there are folks that are feeding grain that do a whole additional calculation of 'My forage tests say this, but can I pull back on grain or do I actually need to give them a little bit of energy from the grain?' The more they let their cows harvest their own feed, the more profitable they'll be."

In addition to their benefits to the land, grass-fed dairy products have been shown to have heart-healthy advantages for humans who consume them. We know that omega fatty acids are good for heart health, but less well known is that it is the balance of omega 6 and omega 3 (whose primary fatty acids are, respectively, linoleic acid and conjugated linoleic fatty acid) that is important. Too much omega-6 and too little omega-3 can increase the risk of heart disease. Milk from cows fed a diet of organic grass and legumes have a far superior balance of fatty acids, nearly 1:1 compared to 5:1 for conventional dairy,[5] and tend to be higher in beta carotene as well.

Heather Darby, an agronomic and soils specialist for the University of Vermont, has been working, along with Sarah Flack, on an ongoing study of Vermont organic and grass-fed dairy that is now in its seventh year. One part of the study analyzes the nutritional and organoleptic (sensory) qualities of grass-fed dairy. "Our preliminary data shows that it's really superior [to conventional milk]," she notes. One published study based on this data noted that organic milk in the Northeastern United States contained "a distinct and more healthful FA (fatty acid) profile," including bioactive conjugated linoleic acids."[6]

Yet despite all of these seeming advantages, dairy economics and the existing supply chain structure have made profitability an elusive goal for even the most imaginative and hard-working pasture-based dairy farmers. During my travels through the world of small, regenerative dairy, my overwhelming impression was one of anxiety and burnout in the face of impossible market forces, lightened by examples of the kind of solidarity of the Dairy Grazing Discussion Group.

THE STATE OF THE DAIRY INDUSTRY: FAILING

TO MAKE A GOOD LIVING as a small or mid-sized dairy farmer in the US Northeast today is somewhat akin to trying to throw a successful on-deck soirée during the last hours of the *Titanic*: both cases require trying to make the best of a slowly unfolding disaster. It's helpful to see how the industrial milk business operates so that we can truly understand what Davids these female-identifying farmers are to the Goliaths of their commodity counterparts. The mechanisms are similar to what we've seen in grain and produce except that the monopolies are a few huge domestic cooperatives—which own dairy farms, haul milk, process it, and make value-added products like cheese and yogurt—and a clutch of global food companies.

This system is abetted by the USDA's convoluted management of milk supplies. "There's an old adage in the dairy industry that 'only five people in the world know how milk is priced in the United States—and four of them are dead,'" writes agricultural economist Michael Nepveux, noting that the Federal Milk Marketing Orders (FMMO) "are among the most complicated commodity pricing regimes across all of agriculture." The bottom line is that the government isn't putting a cap on production and helping dairy farmers survive shortfalls in income with subsidies. Instead, it will try to buy surplus or subsidize exports. But these tactics in a market that involves live animals that can't easily change their output to match fluctuations in demand can result in alternating shortages, surpluses, and wild price fluctuations that only benefit speculators.[7] During the COVID-19 pandemic, the closure of large buyers like schools and restaurants and major disruptions in the commodity milk supply chain led to the dumping of an estimated 2.7 to 3.7 million gallons of milk per day.[8]

Rosalie "Rose" Wilson, a Norwich, Vermont–based farm and food business planning consultant who has worked with a number of DGDG members, says it is instructive to compare America's broken dairy system to that of neighboring Canada, where a milk-supply quota is allocated by region and tallied on a monthly basis to keep supply in line with demand. While by no means perfect, the system guarantees farmers a minimum price for their milk, and further protects them via high tariffs on foreign dairy products. In the United States, Big Dairy producers with their monopoly on the market and access to very cheap milk see no need for this system.

"Canada is structured similarly to the European food system in that a much higher percentage of your salary goes toward your food bill," says Wilson. Food in the United States has been subsidized for so long that Americans balk at paying more than Walmart prices. Meanwhile, the real cost of food is being taken out of farmers' pockets. Vermont farmers joke about a family where one brother has his part of the farm on the Canadian side and the other brother's is on the US side. The house on the Canadian side is painted, the wood looks good, there are flowers out front. The house on the Vermont side is falling apart.

"It goes to that 'me, me, me' mentality that's a really bad American trait," says Wilson, who was born and raised in Quebec. "They don't care if they're screwing the environment as long as they personally get the money out of it at that point in time." A persistent oversupply of milk has lowered prices to the point where farmers have been forced to sell at a loss. The small family dairy of sixty cows cannot compete with the mega-dairies of the West with their tens of thousands of cows creating massive amounts of liquid waste that pollute our air and water.

Their choice, to quote the famous line from former USDA secretary Earl Butz in the 1970s, is to "get big or get out." This is what has happened in Vermont. Between 1950 and today, the number of Vermont dairy farms dropped from eleven thousand to roughly five hundred.[9] (This mirrored a nationwide trend: the number of US dairy herds fell by more than half between 2002 and 2019, with a turbocharged rate of decline between 2018 and 2019.) Yet despite a 44 percent decrease in the number of Vermont dairy farms from 2012 to 2022, the amount of milk the state produces remained steady, the result of the rise of dairy farms in the seven-hundred-to-one-thousand cow head range.[10]

Among the monopolies that dominate the dairy industry is Dairy Farmers of America (DFA), a so-called milk hauler that is actually a co-operative of more than ten thousand family dairy farmers. DFA controls the entire supply chain, beginning with on-farm practices, through hauling the milk to its own processing facilities, and ending with final distribution to markets. In 2020, the DFA spent $433 million to purchase the remaining assets of the failing dairy giant Dean Foods—which itself had gobbled up other brands both conventional and organic, including Horizon and AltaDena. Antitrust objections to the increasing consolidation of the industry have so far failed to rouse federal regulators.

In the early 2000s the emerging organic milk market, with its premium attached to organic milk, seemed like the way to turn a profit. And in the early days it was, because the industry was able provide a price point that supported the cost of production. But as large, conventional producers began to realize they could be making even more money with the addition of organic milk to their product list, the market grew until the same problem of oversupply overtook organic milk.

"Shallow organics," in the form of brands like Horizon, which was recently acquired from multinational conglomerate Danone (see Chapter 2) by the investment firm Platinum Equity, had arrived. These farms are "certified organic within the most flexible, generous interpretation of organic rules," says Miller of NOFA-Vermont, usually coming from states where pastureland is sparse, such as Texas and Colorado. Dairies in those states have faced allegations of failing to adhere to organic standards or animal abuse regulations.[11] The entry of Big Dairy—with its looser standards—into the organic sector, combined with lax regulations, has meant that even going organic turned out to be no guarantee of solvency.

While a patchwork of government funds, both state and federal, have been made available to organic and grass-fed dairy farms, Lily Hawkins, policy director of the Organic Farmers Association, says they are shut out of the lion's share of government funds because of their size, while "large corporate agribusinesses have the lobbying power to urge the USDA to set up programs that are beneficial to them and their economies of scale."

Labor abuses associated with other arms of a commodity food supply chain that prioritizes shareholder returns over safe workplaces and fair labor practices can be even more deadly in the dairy industry, where the occupational injury rate is twice that of all other industries.[12] Add to that the extreme economic pressures that all producers are facing, and it's not surprising incidents have been reported even in Vermont, with its tradition of progressive small farm dairy practices. A *New York Times* investigation of illegal migrant child labor[13] found children in Vermont dairies running milking machines, and one case of a fourteen-year-old boy working twelve-hour shifts whose hand was crushed.

Cows too, are being exploited. The pre-industrial family farm might have had one cow—part of a diverse set of farm animals and vegetables and grain crops—that would be inseminated by a bull. Her nine months of pregnancy would be followed by three months of lactating until the calf was weaned, and the farmer would milk the cow for excess milk until she went dry. An industrial dairy farmer's focus is on getting the most milk per cow. Today conventional US dairy farms produce three times more milk than they did in 1960, but with about half the number of cows. The new super cows have been taken from grass- to grain-fed. Since no grazing is necessary, they can be kept indoors in confined quarters and milked three or four times a day instead of the one or two of today's small, pasture-based dairies.

What is not considered as small farms are swallowed whole are the externalized costs of this switch to large-scale production: to the environment, the quality of life of the animals, and the economic well-being of once-thriving farm communities. "When I think about a dairy farm closing, I don't just think about that family losing their lifelong livelihood, I think about the folks hired on the farm, the tractor repair people, the people who service the milking equipment, all the people that are involved on a single-family farm," says Locitzer. "When you consolidate, you just have the pump guy working on milking equipment, and what used to be ten farms is now only one farm. All that economic activity is gone."

Ninety percent of industrial milking cows are Holsteins, favored for their milk productivity. Most commodity cows no longer get to spend quality time with a bull when it's time to conceive. Instead, artificial insemination is planned right as her udders are drying out from her last calving, about three months after giving birth. The one gallon of milk a day she would formerly have been expected to produce to feed a calf, has grown to more than 7.5 gallons a day (Holsteins can produce up to 9 gallons). This heavy burden—along with the much higher acidity in the cow's four-chambered stomach caused by grain feeding—takes a toll; an industrial dairy cow will last about three years before she is culled and sent to the slaughterhouse to be turned into hamburger meat. (Locitzer, the large animal veterinarian, says that the average age of culling in the DGDG is higher than in conventional dairy but with so many variables, it is hard to say by how much.)

This category of cow is also fed as cheaply as possible, on silage, a fermented mix of grasses, alfalfa, or corn mixed in giant silos, as well as dried hay. Her diet is supplemented with a wide variety of by-products, from soybean, vegetable, and fruit pulp; spent brewer's grain; even candy and bakery waste from gummy bears to stale donuts. She'll get hormones to speed her growth and boost milk production, and antibiotics to treat infection.[14]

The huge soy and corn demands of industrial dairy and meat—40 percent of domestic corn and more than 70 percent of US soy produced goes toward feeding livestock[15,16]—are among the key—and most heavily subsidized—drivers of an industrial food system that is the exact opposite of the alt food system I have set out to navigate. These monocultures—the cultivation of a single crop on a piece of land over time, with no crop rotation—are vulnerable to pest infestations, bioterrorism attacks, and the increasing incidence of extreme weather events, all of which diminish national food security. Their widespread cultivation results in soil erosion, polluted water supplies, pest and weed resistance, and destruction of insect and pollinator habitat.

Most of these feed crops are genetically modified, meaning they are bred to withstand copious applications of the herbicide glyphosate. Monsanto (acquired by pharmaceutical giant Bayer in 2018 for upwards of $63 billion in cash[17]) has settled over one hundred thousand lawsuits involving the alleged carcinogenic properties of its patented version of the herbicide Roundup, paying out well over $11 billion in damages, with tens of thousands of suits still pending.[18]

The commoditization of the dairy industry has led to a race to the lowest possible prices, and lowest possible pay for farmers and every link in the supply chain: a devaluation of agricultural work that has made the lone holdouts, the small, pasture-based dairies, economically untenable. And in the dairy industry, you are seeing the effects of this all over, from farmer burnout to farmer suicide: In 2001, an overworked and in despair Copake, New York, dairy farmer named Dean Pierson shot each of his fifty-one milking cows in the head before turning the gun on himself.[19]

THE GRANT-GIVING FALLACY

THERE IS AID AVAILABLE TO small and mid-sized farmers, through a patchwork of funding that the regulatory, federal, and state systems offer. A federal risk-management program called the Margin Protection Program can be helpful in certain situations as well. But the slew of COVID-era funds that became available to dairy farms is as much a crutch as an aid.

"They have allowed farms to cash flow (times of the year during which incoming cash is higher than expenses) for a number of years and get by, but there's a difference between cash flow and profitability," Flack points out. The Dairy Grazing Discussion Group applied for and got a $57,000 grant from the Northeast Dairy Business Innovation Center to trial different pasture techniques that provides them with automatic gate openers and different seed varieties. The whole small grant-giving process, says Locitzer, means "jumping through enormous numbers of hoops to support basic things on the farm." She adds, "There is a lot of money right now 'available' to farms" in the form of grants from government programs and private funding. But the money is distributed through various nonprofit organizations, which have become the de facto arbiters of who deserves funding.

Wilson, the farm planning consultant, recalls hearing an agronomics advisor tell farmers in a webinar they had to include grant income in their business planning. "That's a horrible message to be sending, but at the moment, that's the position we're in and the problem," she says. "Grants are competitive, not everyone is going to get the pots of money," and the sums available are negligible compared to the need that exists. The grant-giving process disadvantages farmers "who may be the most amazing farmers in the world," but are not computer savvy, or not polished writers, Miller adds.

As these supplementary funds—mere Band-Aids on a critically ill patient—dwindle, Sarah Flack says, "Smart young farmers are looking at how hard they're working, and at what is going to happen with the finances on their farm. They're stressed, they're depressed, they're overwhelmed, and they are selling their herds. In just the last eight years, the number of organic dairy farms in Vermont has dropped from over 200 to 118.[20]

VISIT TO REBOP FARM

NOT LONG AFTER MY LAST drop-in Zoom visit with the Dairy Grazing Discussion Group, I head to Vermont to meet a few group members in person. Heading east from Albany, New York, the lush and gentle slopes of the Green Mountains sparkle in the sunlight. I pass the former Dutch settlement and industrial steel and transport town of Troy, New York, then draw closer to the old spa resort town of Brattleboro, Vermont. Beneath the fresh roadkill and moose crossing signs lie the remains of colonial farmsteads, and even more deeply buried, the invisible, sacred sites and settlements of the Abenaki and Mohicans. Battles have been fought over this land, and foragers, hunters, and farmers have withstood the elements to eke out a living.

Since I was in my mid-twenties and developed an intolerance for lactose, my own relationship with dairy has been estranged, though not entirely absent. As a child, while my father gravitated toward his food co-op, my health nut mother became a devotee of Adelle Davis, the Indiana farm–bred nutritionist who advocated for eating whole, unprocessed foods, and criticized the standard American diet and food system before it was fashionable to do so, decrying its overreliance on preservatives, additives, and pesticides. My sister and brother and I were the weirdos with the whole wheat sandwiches in our school lunch sacks, filled with green pepper- and walnut-studded cream cheese or some other healthy variant. I search for grass-fed yogurt, butter, and local cheeses—which I still eat—and, for use in cooked dishes and baking, similarly sourced milk and cream.

The section of southern Vermont I am voyaging through is home to a mix of small conventional dairies housed in one-hundred-to-three-hundred-year-old barns, and young farmers like Bristle producing niche market products like raw milk and pastured veal, the kind of products my mother would have loved. To get to the farm requires driving partway up a steep mountain, to which Rebop improbably clings.

Bristle first encountered milking and dairying through friends in North Carolina who were starting a raw milk farm. Infatuation turned into true love when she became a counselor, then farm crew member at the Farm and Wilderness camp in Vermont. The work was creative, meaningful, and she knew it was her life's calling.

She and McClurg began farming on leased land in Vermont in 2014, living in a cabin with no running water. They moved onto their current eighty-acre property in 2016, transforming it from an invasives species–covered no-man's land, into a diversified collection of stacked enterprises shoehorned onto thirty open acres, including a pastureland roamed by sheep and cows. As a first-generation farmer, the work was "like learning a second language," says Bristle; to become more fluent, she completed a second bachelor's degree in sustainable food and farming from the University of Massachusetts Amherst in 2021.

Locitzer, Bristle, and Locitzer's Corgi mix dog, Annie, are on hand to greet me. We climb up to the farmhouse deck, where we sip on mint-infused lime water and gaze east toward a spectacular scene: the township of Brattleboro nestled in the valley ahead, and beyond that New Hampshire's Wantastiquet State Forest, Mount Monadnock, and Pisgah State Park, which present as rolling, variegated blankets of green capped by blue skies and flat-bottomed, cottony clouds. I can see what Reid Miller meant when they said, "The simplest argument for pasture-based dairy is that Vermont is really good at growing grass."

Bristle describes her role in her partnership with McClurg as "the gas," and his as "the brakes." She is in charge of production and decides to do "a wild number of things" on the farm. He is supportive and is the job finisher to her role as the job starter. A decade into their farm business, they've whittled down their enterprises to a manageable load by getting rid of their pastured pork and poultry operations, but still, Bristle says she is in a state of "perpetual burnout." She has seen it in plenty of other young farmers like her. Some reach a breaking point, where they have to step back, or scale back; sometimes it happens with the arrival of children, she tells me, a year before she gives birth to the couple's first child. Access to land is a huge barrier; they are lucky in getting some financial support from McClurg's parents.

Their mostly direct-to-consumer business includes a retail store they built on their property, a CSA for milk and meat with one hundred family subscribers, and traffic from travelers from New York City heading north to Massachusetts. Whereas diversified farming pioneer Joel Salatin used to advise farmers like him that if they could grow it, they could sell it, Bristle says that's no longer true. As pasture-grazed meats and local produce have gained more and more adherents, the number of farmers producing these products has also grown. Despite stiff competition, equity of access is important to Bristle: her milk CSA operates on a sliding-fee scale, with higher-income people subsidizing lower-income customers. "It's a pretty bell curve, and so beautiful that people care," she says. "It's one of the reasons I love living here." If SNAP (the Farm Bill's Supplemental Nutrition Assistance Program, which helps lower-income consumers purchase her products) benefits were to be cut, she would lose a good share of her clientele.

Accompanied by Hamoud, Bristle's Great Pyrenees guard dog, and Annie, we head off on a tour of the farm, past the compost bins and the now-defunct mobile chicken coops, wading through grasses to reach the herd of Katahdin sheep, who peaceably share the field with a small number of Jersey and Jersey-Holstein mix cows. (Jerseys are a smaller breed than Holsteins and produce less milk but are favored for their high butter-fat content.) Bristle introduces me to some of her favorites, Flavia and Malaprop. It's plain to see they have a better quality of life than a Holstein in a ten-thousand-cow milk mill. A little removed from the pack, a cream-colored eleven-year-old ewe rests on the grass while her twin lambs—her sixteenth or seventeenth offspring, according to Bristle, birthed earlier in the day, hover next to her on uncertain legs.

We pass an orchard of plums, peaches, and apple trees, then visit the cows housed in the barn, which stare at us with their beautiful brown liquid eyes. Those bearing blue stickers are in heat; one will be bred tonight. "She's a difficult breeder," Bristle explains, she gets one natural shot at it, and then if that doesn't work, I'll work with Dayna to get her inseminated."

That evening, over dinner at a restaurant called A Vermont Table, I learn just what a tight-knit foodshed I am in. My server, restaurant owner Coridon "Cory" Bratton, speaks highly of Rebop Farm and provides me with some sourdough bread to go with the block of pastured butter Bristle gave to me as a parting gift. He regularly buys bushels of apples or quince from Scott Farm Orchard (see Chapter 2), which I visited the day before, and will often cater weddings or events for the orchard. In a later conversation, Bratton tells me he has just purchased eighty pounds of culled heifer ground beef from local organic dairy Lilac Ridge Farm. Even the local pizza place features Rebop farm meatballs on its menu. Yet for all this mutual support, I continue to hear stories of dairy farms in distress.

CHALLENGING TIMES AT THE CORSE FARM DAIRY, WHITINGHAM, VERMONT

MY NEXT VISIT IS WITH Dairy Grazing group member Abbie Corse, sixth-generation farmer at Corse Farm Dairy in Whitingham, southern Vermont, just north of the Massachusetts border. Corse shows me into the house, where her parents, Leon and Linda, and herd manager MacKenzie Wallace have gathered to greet me. Although Abbie is warm and cheerful, the rest of the group's welcome is guarded, perhaps because this is a painfully beleaguered point in the dairy's one-hundred-and-fifty-five-year history, a fact that will become even clearer as we talk.

I've been drawn here in part to learn about the history of cooperative dairy farming in New England, knowing that the Corses have been co-op members for three generations now. Even before that, Leon's grandfather Merrol was president of the local creamery—the first butter-making plant in Vermont—back when every family dairy's income came from less perishable cream, not milk, and you could find a creamery in nearly every town in Vermont. A generation later, when Leon's father Lewis was running the farm, market consolidation had begun; he witnessed creameries around him fold, one by one. "I'm sure he had concerns about the ongoing market as it got farther and farther away from his farm," says Leon. To help protect his farm from becoming the next casualty, in the early 1960s, Leon's father sought strength in numbers and joined the New England Milk Producers cooperative, which later became the Agri-Mark cooperative, which then merged with another cooperative, Cabot Creamery.

Although Leon's father had practiced adaptive, or rotational, grazing before it was known by that term, when Leon graduated from the University of Vermont's College of Agriculture with a degree in plant and soil science in 1976, the message to students was all about growth, yield, plowing, and "telling the soil what it needs to grow instead of listening to it," Leon recalls. A ten-year "unlearning curve" followed. Going 100 percent organic was, he admits, initially a market-driven decision, but it is now a way of farming he is deeply committed to. It just took the kind of close observation of the land that he learned from his own father—a man with a seventh-grade education yet "one of those really observant people who was always taking in whatever he was exposed to"—to learn to listen to what his land and animals had to tell him about what they needed to thrive.

Today Corse Farm Dairy is a member of the Organic Valley cooperative, which includes more than sixteen hundred small organic family farms across the country, including two hundred who specialize in produce, pork, eggs, and a feed pool of hay and grains to supply member farms. The cooperative offers small family dairies—the average herd size is only about seventy-five to eighty head—the protection of a large organization. Its services include on-staff veterinarians, agronomists, producer payroll and accounting services, and more than eighty different milk processing centers across the United States. For the Corses, Organic Valley membership solves critical bottlenecks facing many organic dairy producers in the Northeast: the scarcity of affordable organic grain and feed, and of small-scale organic milk processing facilities, logistics, and distribution.

Organic Valley also offers the kind of valuable advice and support that most independent small dairies would not have access to otherwise, including consulting on animal genetics, soil fertility, forage quality, and grazing. When the Corses wanted to install a solar system on the barn roof, the cooperative's sustainability department vetted the three proposals they solicited, advised them on what questions to ask and wrote the REAP (Rural Energy for America Program) grant proposal that procured funding that covered 30 percent of the total cost. Another valuable benefit of co-op membership, adds Linda Corse, is the peer network it provides. "The most powerful learning is farmer to farmer, especially as there are so few of us; we're two percent of the population in the United States."

Unlike the underregulated commodity milk market, Organic Valley also keeps careful tabs on supply and demand, allotting each farmer a monthly milk production base. If the farmer wants to produce more, she must file an appeal, and if she gets her appeal approved and goes over base, she is subject to a deduction in pay. This system keeps the cooperative from having to sell excess supply at a discounted price; the closer it comes to matching supply with demand, the more profitable it will be.

While the protection of a national cooperative like Organic Valley offers some reassurances, it is "still at the mercy of the systemic realities of the food system in which we exist," says Abbie. For one thing, there is competition from "shallow organics" brands. In August 2021, Danone North America, then parent company to Horizon, announced it was ending all of its contracts with family farms in Maine, New Hampshire, Vermont, and New York. It was simply much cheaper to source its milk from mega-farms in the western portion of the United States.

Yet Danone (now a minority owner) is still flooding the New England market with nonlocal Horizon milk. In the supermarket, Leon Corse says, "There's no way a consumer can easily identify where a dairy product comes from. But what I can tell you is you can be quite certain that if you buy an Organic Valley product, it comes from a smaller local farm."

Toward the end of our conversation, Abbie says slowly, "I do have to say at some point that we are not being paid—"

"Enough," Leon interjects.

"—to cover the cost of our production," she finishes. I understand now the palpable grimness at the start of our visit. One reason for the shortfall, Leon offers, is that where once Organic Valley was able to rely solely on existing processors to handle its milk, it has grown big enough that it now must look at owning its own processing facilities, which Leon says, "is a hugely expensive way to go."

But a much bigger problem, says farm business consultant Wilson, is that Organic Valley locks its dairy farmers into a set pay price for its milk, unlike conventional dairies, where prices rise and fall with the aforementioned, byzantine Federal Milk Marketing Orders. This was not a problem when organic milk was highly profitable, but when prices fell following the entry of shallow organics into the market, farmer payout from the cooperative fell and Organic Valley dairy farmers began to feel the pinch.

Organic Valley dairy farmers are also, by contract, not allowed to divert any of their milk to other customers. Even though Leon Corse has won enough dairy awards to fill two barns, he cannot sell any of his product to local artisan cheese makers or anyone else willing to pay a higher price; it all goes to Organic Valley, even when milk prices drop below the cost of production.

Conventional dairy farmers had fought hard against the big milk hauler cooperatives they were part of, such as the DFA, to be able to divert some of their supply to make value-added products like butter, yogurt, and farmstead cheeses. As milk prices plummeted, this helped keep them afloat—for a while. Then, Wilson says, the added cost of making, marketing, and distributing these value-added products began to mount, and too many dairies were trying to go the artisanal, value-added route, flooding the market. By 2015, "people were calling me and saying, 'Hey, Rose, we need an exit plan.' And that's when I started to realize, whoa, this is not a panacea. Burnout is a big problem. The on-farm premium required by value-added products is just gonna suck you further down the dark hole that you're already in."

Now "the farms that are totally tied to the milk truck [meaning contracted to a milk hauler], which is all of the Organic Valley farmers," are finding themselves in that same dark hole, without even the option of making the mistake of starting an on-farm creamery. "The cost of organic inputs has soared, but the organic pay price never went up," Wilson adds. "So the organic farms are the ones that right now cannot cash flow at all. They're just really under water."

Another factor at play is the decline in consumer demand for cow's milk in favor of plant-based beverages. Fluid milk consumption has been in decline for the last seven decades, from .96 cups per person a day in 1970 to .49 cups per capita in 2019. Plant-based beverages have increased in popularity but according to USDA research, "are not likely to be a primary driver of those trends. Instead, studies have shown the generational drop in milk consumption has more to do with the wide variety of alternative beverage options beyond plant-based drinks, and the high consumption of sugar-sweetened soft drinks and juices."[21,22]

Wilson adds, "I went through this really, really sad period where I was helping people go through bankruptcies." She learned so much about bankruptcy proceedings that she is now in the process of putting together a workbook to teach other business planners how to help companies that need to exit their farm business. "What I came to realize is we can't change the food system, and our business planning is telling us that these businesses are unsustainable. And that's really depressing," Wilson says.

Abbie Corse might, under different circumstances, have taken over as sixth-generation owner operator now that her father is in his mid-seventies. But she is unsure that it is possible for her to take on that role; she has her hands full being a wife, mom, and coping with the depression and anxiety that she has discussed publicly. After becoming a mother, she wrote, "It is only now that I am cognizant of the dual labor that both my parents took on. To entertain the curiosity of a young child without crushing it while carrying out the myriad farm chores is no small task.

"For me, the result of this mother-farmer collision is massive guilt, anxiety, and panic and middle-of-the-night worries; a near-constant sense that if just one thing shifts, the entire house of cards—on the farm and at home—will flutter down. Despite my privilege and love for my work, I dwell in uncertainty." In her most recent email to me, Abbie told me she is at last being properly treated; it turns out ADHD, not anxiety, is her principal diagnosis. The future is uncertain, but she has the full support of her family, and a more positive outlook on what is possible.

Yet during our interview, she tells me, "People do not seem to understand that farming is an everyday gamble. They think of farming as tough and we're at the mercy of the weather and all these things. But it's not just weather. It's animal health, not knowing when the next cow is going to have a health issue. It's human health. Farmers are people, and there are so few of us that it's much harder to make the bottom line work. If you're trying to farm regeneratively, sustainably, organically—whatever you want to call it—in this day and age with the food policies and food pricing that we have, you have to extract from humans, because you're no longer extracting from your soil, your land base, or your animals."

ORGANIC VALLEY IN THE
AGE OF TOO MUCH ORGANIC MILK

HAVING SEEN HOW HARD IT is for small dairy farms like Rebop, Chaseholm, and North Country Creamery to compete with Big Milk, I thought that the Corse family, by being a member of the highly regarded Organic Valley cooperative, would be having a much easier time of things. Now, the shine is slightly off the business I have long admired, though I still want to believe in the power of the cooperative model. To find out more about Organic Valley, I reach out to Elizabeth McMullen, a cooperative spokesperson who works out of its Cashton, Wisconsin, headquarters.

The cooperative's origin story has taken on the aura of myth: In 1988, a group of seven farmers in Coulee, Wisconsin, fed up with an industrial agricultural system that told them to get big or get out, and that chemical inputs were the only way to go, decided to fight back. They were concerned about their own health, that of their animals, and of the environment. A farmer named George Siemon put up posters calling for a community meeting at the county courthouse in Viroqua. Once they decided to form a cooperative, he visited farmers one by one to talk up the appeal of organics. Within a year, they began selling their organic dairy products, expanding across the Midwest and then the country.

To address some of the most pressing problems facing the industry—including farmers retiring with no one in the family to take over, or prohibitively high land costs that are barriers to young farmers who want to break into the business—in 2005 Organic Valley launched the Generation Organics, or "Gen O," a group of young farmers that meet several times a year. Regional meetings for all farmers happen twice a year, and there are monthly call-ins that keep farmers connected. Forty percent of members are from Plain Communities: Amish, Mennonite, or Anabaptist, she adds, a tight-knit community within a community. In 2011, Organic Valley became the first national brand to launch a 100 percent grass-fed milk label nationwide, with the trademark "Grass-milk."

All this sounds wonderful, but I've heard too much to think all is well in Organic Valley-land. Through McMullen, Shawna Nelson, executive vice president of membership at Organic Valley, issued a statement pointing to "a six-month collaborative process with farmer-owners" that was instituted, which aims to "balance supply with demand and ensure stable member pay." When I ask McMullen about the current plight of Organic Valley dairy farmer members who have been struggling for months without turning a profit on their milk, she says, "I hate to see my farmers suffer, so it's been hard, I'm not going to sugarcoat it." Echoing what the Corses told me, she says, "It comes down to education: explaining why it's good to buy local, and why our products are priced at a premium."

SEARCHING FOR SOLUTIONS
TO A DESPERATELY BROKEN DAIRY SYSTEM

FEELING AN ALMOST OVERWHELMING, HEAVY sense of sadness for so many deeply skilled dairy farmers, who are passionate about their land and animals but are being ground down by an almost comically (if it weren't so tragic) broken food system, I remember something Sarah Flack, the dairy consultant, told me: that fixing our broken dairy system does not mean championing the alt food system over all others. It is about knitting together an ecosystem of production styles—grass-fed, organic, and conventional farms using the latest clean energy technology—that are all focused on improving practices and arcing toward sustainability in pasture, animal, and human management.

"We need all of these farmers, not just grass-fed, or grain-fed organic," Flack says. "It's good to have that diversity of different ways to produce milk on these farms, because we need to have enough thriving dairy farms in the community to be able to support the veterinarians, the feed dealers, the wonderful man who does house calls and will fix your tractor in your barn. We need enough farms here that are able to keep him in business. In most communities here in the Northeast, our fire departments are entirely volunteer run. Most of those volunteers are farmers; if we lose our dairy farmers, we will lose all of the volunteers that make our towns function."

But just having a diversity of dairy farm styles is not going to keep the DGDG farmers afloat. Structural change will come through active lobbying and legislative changes, and the kind of grass-roots activism in which consumers can play a role.

On the legislative front, in addition to a few new organic certification rules that have been passed, the big victory for the organic dairy movement has been the introduction of what is called the "O Dairy Act," Lily Hawkins of the Organic Farmers Association tells me. It calls for a robust organic dairy data collection system that will enable the USDA to create a safety net program for organic dairy programs similar to its conventionally oriented dairy margin coverage program, which provides financial aid when the price of milk falls too far below the cost of feed. Introduced by Vermont Senator Peter Welch and cosponsored by Senators Bernie Sanders, Tammy Baldwin, and Kirsten Gillibrand in October 2023, its passage would be an important step in making system change to advance organic dairy across the United States.

Meanwhile, the Dairy Grazing Discussion Group will continue meeting, and continue supporting each other. They are the survivors. Recently, Bristle pulled out the business plan that she wrote a decade ago to rewrite it for her new, retooled format. She noticed that every farm she had mentioned in the "local competition" section was gone, no longer in business. Yet she's determined to keep some cows to milk. "We're always thinking about how we'll subsidize the dairy because we'll let go of everything before we let go of that. Because that's the great love. For everybody in the group, it's a calling before anything else," she says.

On the return trip from Vermont to Toronto, I stop to visit friends in the Berkshires. Along with a dinner of grilled pastured chicken, roasted mushrooms, and marinated zucchini salad, we cracked opened a bottle of Scott Farm Orchard's Chèz Memé French-style hard cider and dug into a creamy and extraordinarily flavorful disk of Chaseholm Camembert cheese. The entire meal evoked the season, the place, and my visits with these two producers. The gratitude I felt for this rich bounty and the love I felt for my friends was complicated by all that I knew about the Dairy Grazing Discussion Group's struggle to stay afloat, and my recollection of Sarah Chase sharing her existential anxieties.

During my travels through the alt food system, I often queried my sources, "What is your biggest ask of the consumer?" Many advised consumers to speak up: to their local grocery store manager, educational institution, hospital, and other large institutions whose buying power can favor local alt producers over long-chain commodity products. Elizabeth Whitlow, executive director of the Regenerative Organic Alliance (see Chapter 3) advises consumers to "buy local, find a farm you can visit, learn about their farming practices. Have some skepticism, ask questions about their practices, the nutritional density of their products."

Sarah Flack gave me perhaps the most urgent and important response for this chapter: "There's a lot of attention being paid to soil health and regenerative ag, animal welfare, and carbon sequestration. But with rising land prices, it's more important than ever to make sure that the next generation of young farmers—who want to practice good land stewardship and thoughtful animal husbandry—are able to make it financially. Consumers need to be asking their farmers, "Are you getting paid a fair price? Can you afford to put money in a 401(k)? Do you have health care? Do you ever get a vacation? We need economic justice for farmers, and if consumers started to pay attention to that, it might help pull together a fuller picture of how their food choices are supporting the wellbeing of farmers and their families."

CHAPTER FIVE

MEAT AND POULTRY
THAT TASTES GOOD *AND* IS GOOD
FOR THE ENVIRONMENT

GROWING UP ON TRADITIONAL JAPANESE and American fare, with liberal allowances for the Mexican food that was woven into our Southern California landscape, meat and poultry were present but not dominant in our diet. I did love my grandmother's epic sukiyaki feasts and her comforting *oyako donburi* (chicken-and-egg rice bowls). Steak was an occasional treat that my meat-loving mother relished. I, though, could not understand its appeal. Arriving in our home on white Styrofoam trays wrapped in plastic, these flat slabs of meat were grain-finished feedlot beef purchased at our local supermarket, and to me they were tough, only moderately flavorful, and unappealing. It was not until we moved to Japan and I tasted my first wagyu beef that I understood how tender and appetizing a steak could be.

Cow flesh was not consumed in Japan until the Meiji Restoration (1868–1912), when foreign imports, including all manner of foods, were introduced to a country that had been firmly closed to trade for more than two hundred fifty years. In 1872, the Meiji Emperor himself broke the taboo against eating beef, shocking and angering temple monks. A small group of them attempted to break into the Imperial Palace to express their outrage and belief that this new trend would "destroy the soul of the Japanese people"; half of them died in the ensuing fracas with guards.[1] More people, however, wanted to eat beef. Newly arrived Brown Swiss, Shorthorn, and Devon cows, among others, were crossed with smaller Japanese farm cows, and the highly marbled Japanese wagyu was born.

Wagyu (literally "Japanese beef" or "Japanese cattle") was so prized that beginning in 1968 trade unions began monitoring genetic lines, overseen by the Japanese Meat Grading Association. A 2003 traceability act created a system under which each animal is provided a ten-digit ID number and barcode so that its genetic lineage and movement through the entire supply chain from birth to retailer can be traced.[2]

Stories of wagyu calves guzzling bottles of beer that their owners hand-fed them, being massaged like elite sumo wrestlers, or having their coats brushed with saké only enhanced the meat's mystique. Today, however, I realize that wagyu is so tender in large part because the animals are confined and encouraged to put on fat instead of being allowed to run free and develop their muscles.

The North American meat and poultry alt food systems that I will be exploring on this leg of my journey are highly transparent and traceable, but in most other ways the opposite of Japanese wagyu. They are based on the proposition that the healthiest and happiest animals are those that are allowed to roam on chemical-free pasture, according to a way of ranching and farming that not only yields the most flavor, but also happens to be good for the soil, climate resilience, and the planet—including humans who consume grass-fed protein.

Before going further, I probably should, in the words of lawyer and grass-fed beef advocate Nicolette Hahn Niman, "defend beef" as a positive food choice for any ethical and climate-conscious eater. She writes, "It's time to focus on improving how we raise cattle and turn them into food. Only then can we tap into the full ecological and nourishment potential these remarkable creatures provide."[3] Factory-farmed livestock production accounts for somewhere between 11 and 17 percent of global greenhouse gas emissions,[4] yet despite admonishments from climate experts to stop eating meat, this is extremely hard for humans to do. According to one large-scale study, 84 percent of vegetarians and vegans abandon their diets.[5] Only about 2 percent of Americans are vegetarian, and an even smaller percentage are vegan.

Plant-based meats are one alternative, but there are many choices and complex issues at play. One study found that for frequent meat eaters, switching to at least one type of plant-based diet lowered risk of cardiovascular disease as well as LDL or "bad" cholesterol levels.[6] Another found that plant-based and grass-fed meat each contain very distinct and different valuable metabolites (nutrients produced during metabolism). The authors noted the dangers inherent in trying to mimic only a fraction of the nutrients found in whole foods and voiced reservations about the ultra-processed nature of some plant-based foods.[7] While only thirteen nutritional components are tracked on nutritional labels, they represent a mere fraction of the twenty-six thousand metabolites in the "human foodome," a term coined to encompass our food system in all its complexity, as mapped with the aid of artificial intelligence.

I believe that a better, more realistic alternative to giving up meat is to source pasture-based alternatives that regenerate soil, increase biodiversity, support local ranchers, and prioritize animal and human welfare. And by all means, reduce consumption of meat, too! Since 1950 meat consumption has doubled among the world's richest 20 percent of people, and not at all among the world's poorest three percent.[8] Wealthy nations are also the primary producers of greenhouse gas emissions, yet their effects disproportionately harm poor nations by exacerbating climate change. Reducing factory-farmed meat consumption is one of the most effective means of reducing your dietary environmental footprint. More practically, it is one way to make room in your budget for more expensive pasture-raised meat.

A VISIT TO CARMAN RANCH

IT IS MID-OCTOBER, AND MY day's journey has taken me due east from Portland, Oregon. The steep inclines and vivid greens and blues of the Columbia Valley Gorge give way to the gentle, orchard-strewn Hood River Valley. A few miles later, I cross the sparkling river via the towering steel Bridge of Gods to Cascade Locks, once the gathering spot for the Nez Perce, Umatilla, Warm Springs, and Yakama tribes. I pass the old trading post town of Pendleton, where thousands of Chinese transcontinental railroad workers once lived. Gradually, the drab scrub of the Umatilla Plateau gives way to lush greens as I wend my way through the Ponderosa pine- covered Blue Mountains, then descend into the high desert grasslands of the Wallowa Valley.

I'm here to meet Cory Carman, the fourth-generation rancher who turned the eight thousand acres that she leases and owns in Wallowa into a 100 percent grass-fed beef ranch. Carman's expressive brown eyes and gentle demeanor camouflage a highly efficient multitasker, ranch owner, and single mom who keeps close track of her brood. During the course of our visit, she is in contact with her son, who is playing a rugby game at his college in Vermont; her mother and sister, who are there to visit him; and her twins, who are attending a volleyball game in nearby Enterprise.

Ranching is bred in the bone for Carman. Growing up on the ranch, every Saturday she would squeeze into the feed pickup truck with her grandpa, her uncle Kent, and her dad, Garth, and drive off to feed the cows. Her grandparents lived next door and kept horses for Cory and her sister to ride. She loved the rural life (Wallowa's population is less than eight hundred) and these rolling grasslands, where the imagination roams free. Her father held a doctorate in agricultural economics, and they shared an intellectual curiosity and a love of the land and their animals. When he was killed in an on-ranch accident when she was fourteen, her life lost its moorings.

Though she grew up in the 1980s and '90s during the peak of the wars between conservationists on one side and ranchers and timber harvesters on the other, she saw how hard her family worked to care for their animals and land, and the many sacrifices they made. It wasn't until she was on scholarship at Stanford that she gained a more nuanced perspective of the world she had grown up in, learning from her advisor, Wally Falcon, an expert in global food security and agricultural economics. She also began to understand the harmful effects of one hundred years of intensive cattle grazing, which eroded meadows and polluted rivers and streams, and the rapaciousness of Oregon's timber industry.

Carman was interested in a regenerative way to raise livestock. When she returned to the family ranch in 2003, her role model was Connie Hatfield, a charismatic Oregonian who founded a grass-fed beef cooperative in 1986 with her husband, called Country Natural Beef. Since then, it has grown to encompass more than ninety family ranches across the West. Country Natural Beef raises its cattle on grass and sends them to conventional feed lots to standardize the animals and finish them on grain. Carman wanted to take her cattle operation one step further.

She and her then-husband, Dave Flynn, were committed to holistic range management that was being popularized by South African biologist and ecologist Allan Savory. This practice keeps animals on grass from start to finish, rotationally grazing them on land and balancing fresh forage and the right level of trampling and manure leavings to build soil microbial matter and renew grasslands, which in turn nourishes the animals. As we have seen in our foray into grass-fed dairy, fields that are rotationally grazed are better able to retain water, resist drought, and store atmospheric carbon than continually grazed land, making them more climate resilient. And although ranchers may have to pay for supplemental hay during the winter, they do not pay for chemical fertilizers or other inputs. One hundred percent grass-fed beef is less fatty and marbled than grain-fed, but it offers deeper flavor and, as studies have shown, significantly higher levels of nutrients such as omega-3 fatty acids, antioxidant vitamins such as vitamin E, minerals, and omega-6.

While the main component of Carman's business is growing and selling grass-fed beef, like the grass-fed dairy farmers we met in Chapter 4, she also wants to restore the land to a state of robust, nutrition-rich health that will support the local ecosystem and grazing cattle, and sequester carbon.

But doing this on the rangeland of the arid West is a very different proposition than grazing cattle on the lush green pastures of Vermont, where lack of water is generally not a problem and forage is plentiful. The four hundred fifty to five hundred acres of irrigated land Carman manages in the Wallowa Valley, just a fraction of the land she has access to, can produce as much as ten times more forage as her non-irrigated land. On those rangelands, each animal requires a hefty fifteen to twenty acres of forage per growing season. Carman's cattle will often graze on dry, leased rangeland just once a season, which still requires the erection of fencing and creation of paddocks for perhaps eight days of rotational grazing. While critics of regenerative rotational grazing note that it requires two-and-a-half times more land than factory-farmed beef, it is in areas like Carman's corner of northeastern Oregon—extremely dry, rocky, uneven, tree covered, and not arable for crops except for extractive dryland farming—where the full value of regenerative ranching can be realized. Unsuited to other forms of food production such as machine-tilled row crops, this land's fertility and the health of the entire ecosystem will be greatly improved by conscientious grazing practices.

As with the grass-fed dairy farmers, balancing land restoration with the creation of enough energy to meet beef cattle's forage needs requires fine-tuned rotational grazing: "You want a cow to take one bite, because when it takes two, you're stressing the plant," Carman explains.

The work is twofold: on the one hand, spending time, money, and energy experimenting with new techniques solely in service of the land, with the goal of leaving more forage behind that will protect the soil and create habitat for wildlife. On the other is the money-making imperative: operating costs have to be covered before any profits can be made. The challenge for the rancher is balancing what Carman calls the "cool, fun work" of doing right by the land with the commercial realities of the farm. And there is always a trade-off.

Carman's neighbors, rancher Dan Probert of Lightning Creek Ranch and his wife, Suzy, are getting help for their land restoration work. They have teamed up with the Nature Conservancy (TNC) and The Climate Trust, negotiating a conservation easement that protects the working ranch from tilling or development while allowing Probert to pursue a grazing management plan that restores the grasslands and riparian areas on 12,225 acres. The easement covers part of the Zumwalt Prairie, the largest known remnant of a once-extensive Pacific Northwest bunchgrass prairie, rich in hawks, eagles, grassland songbirds, and other wildlife; it allows TNC to influence the restoration of land and share the task of fighting invasive plant species through managed grazing without the expense of purchasing it.

The arrangement is an example of how the old rancher vs. conservationist dynamic that Carman grew up with has been flipped. Rather than the extractive ranching practices of the past—when heavy equipment reshaped the land, and ruminants were left too long on pasture—regenerative practices have made their alliance possible. Both ranchers and conservationists want to preserve and enrich the land and restore native ecosystems.

To get a close-up look at Carman's land, we hop on her John Deere side-by-side ATV. Her border collie, Fritz, no longer a spry pup, struggles to jump on the vehicle to join us for a bumpy ride over the prairie grasses. Carman has made substantial progress in fighting back the invasive medusahead rye, fiddleneck, ventenata, and cheat grass, which outcompete the native plants that provide important habitat for wildlife.

We visit a group of cows who have just been "pregged," or pregnancy tested, and some yearlings. Wild quail scatter across the ground as we carefully approach a skittish new mother and her calf. In another part of the ranch we see Carman's small pig operation, four sows that produce from forty to sixty piglets a year, but whose main use is for land rehabilitation. Their propensity for tearing up the land was a liability on Rebop Farm in Vermont, but an asset on dry, depleted soil rife with invasives; they offer a natural, herbicide-free and large-equipment-free method of ripping them out and provide an income stream as well. Our tour of the ranch gives me a sense of its arc toward a more complex biodiversity, but also how far it still has to go to recover from a hundred years of industrial agriculture—including large populations of sheep prior to World War II, which Carman says "eat everything"—and extractive dryland wheat farming.

When I ask if meat from different pastures and ranches are each unique expressions of terroir, Carman's quick yes is without hesitation. For one producer event she held, she solicited a rib roast from each rancher, to be prepared and served to a group of chefs in a blind tasting. Each could detect significant differences in flavor and level of gaminess or grassiness. Carman noticed another indicator of terroir when she harvested (meaning slaughtered) her first set of lambs last year. Despite clear differences between the taste of lamb and beef, there was a strikingly familiar undercurrent of flavor: an earthiness, minerality, and clean finish; it could only be Carman Ranch terroir. This complexity of flavor is one of the hallmarks and many benefits of grass-fed beef, which you'll hear more about later in this chapter.

A COMMODITY BEEF INTERLUDE

ON CARMAN'S RANCH, AND ON other ranches I pass throughout the Wallowa Valley, the wide-open rangelands dotted with munching cattle are a bucolic scene from the vanishing past. Many ranches do a very good job of using cattle as a tool to manage the land, as she does. But few, says Carman, are "doing the crazy thing" she is: direct marketing. Instead, they put their animals into the commodity system.

Grass-fed, regenerative ranching constitutes less than 5 percent of all beef production in the United States and is in stark contrast to the global commodity beef system. Single-minded on-farm efficiency—which prioritizes productivity and yield over animal welfare—rules a precision-engineered supply chain, where value is added at every step to meet target market specifications. Breeders sell their seedstock, or genetic material, including bulls, heifers, calves, and semen to cow-calf producers. Those producers' weaned calves, or feeder cattle, are sent to a concentrated animal feeding operation (CAFO). Though they may spend their first year on grass, after that most are fattened on a mix of corn, barley, silage, and whatever low-cost feed is readily available until they reach from 1,150 to 1,500 pounds. Then they are sold to a packer for slaughter and boxing.

The industrialized, commodity livestock model that has taken over much of the world's meat production accounts for 1.7 billion animals (including cattle, pork, and chickens) in the United States alone, a figure that has increased by nearly 50 percent over the past twenty years.[9] In CAFOs, cattle are densely packed in indoor or outdoor pens, where their concentrated, untreated waste is stored in deep clay or concrete pits, lagoons, or holding ponds before being spread or sprayed on farmland, often overloading fields with nitrogen, phosphorus, pathogens, pharmaceuticals, and heavy metals.[10] These unwanted substances filter into nearby streams and waterways, causing algae blooms, in which the rapid cycle of algae and aquatic plant growth, proliferation then death depletes oxygen stores, kills fish, and reduces biodiversity. Livestock standing in their own manure can lead to respiratory illness and infectious foot rot.

The difference between an agricultural commodity like cattle or grain and non-commodity agricultural products is that the former are grown in large, uniform quantities that can be traded as financial assets such as futures and options. This allows corporations to offset the risk inherent in growing livestock (although it does not make it immune to boom-and-bust cycles), create another income stream, and set global prices. The world's four biggest meat conglomerates—Cargill, Tyson Foods, JBS, and Marfig (represented in the United States by National Beef Packing)—control from 55 to 85 percent of the hog, cattle, and chicken markets. To understand just how much power Big Meat holds, witness its price gouging during a crisis: The big four's net income surged more than 500 percent during the COVID-19 pandemic,[11] becoming the major driver of inflation at our grocery stores.

Big Meat has not been shy about greenwashing its practices either. In 2024, the New York Attorney General's office sued JBS USA for misleading claims that it will achieve net zero greenhouse gas emissions by 2040, when its documented plans indicated it would actually *increase* its carbon footprint.

As if competing against monopolies like this was not enough, post-pandemic climate change and global events have ushered in an even more fraught time for alt meat producers like Carman. Many years of drought, the pandemic, and then the massive instability that rippled out from wars in Ukraine and the Middle East have created a situation of low cattle inventory. Prices for commodity cattle have spiked sky high, yet the global giants are cushioned by their many-tentacled enormity; their alternate sources of income, for example, from the different forms of proteins that they grow and sell, offset losses in the meat sector, allowing them to keep meat prices stable at the retail level. "Companies like ours that live outside the mainstream beef world who didn't gouge customers during COVID don't have all these retained earnings," Carman explains, "so we're seeing various branded meat companies, and smaller processing plants shutter."

The government, recognizing the problem of a lack of regional meat processing capability, invested heavily in grants and financing programs to rebuild them.[12] But just as they were coming online, small and medium cattle ranchers were experiencing record low inventory. With no cattle to process, many of those new regional processors opened and closed in short order, Carman says. Fixing a broken system is hard, especially when it is done piecemeal and not holistically, or, as Carman puts it, "not solving for the whole picture."

HOW TO BUILD A BETTER, SHORTER SUPPLY CHAIN

AS WE HAVE SEEN IN other alt food systems, it is the small- and medium-sized processors that are driven out of business by the consolidation of the corporate monopolies that control the parallel commodity system. To build a local food chain from the ground up, it usually has to happen link by link. Carman's vision is of a regional alt meat system based on shared values and practices, similar to what Veritable Vegetable created with its five-state network.

When they first set out to create a more direct, transparent, and ethical meat supply chain, Carman and Flynn launched a direct-to-consumer cow share program, selling quarter cows that have been carved into various steaks, roasts, ribs, and brisket, and even "mini-shares" of one-eighth of a cow. Ranchers like Carman love this type of program because it maximizes "carcass utilization" in an extremely low-margin business where every scrap of the animal has to turn a profit.

Between sixty to eighty head of Carman Ranch cattle are brought to maturity and harvested each year for the cow share program. They are slaughtered on-farm by the same man who has been doing this on the ranch since Carman was twelve, Dale Baker. In town, the same butcher, Kevin Silveira, with whom she has been working for twenty years, does the cutting and wrapping before the cuts are trucked to Portland or Seattle. Although she worries that the program is dependent on two men in their sixties and seventies, Carman says, "It's super cool that we're a part of their lives and we get to feed them."

To widen her reach—and aided by a patient investor more interested in the success of a pastured-meat model than in harvesting large and immediate profits—Carman created a separate, wholesale entity under the Carman Provisions label, which is supplied by her ranch and a group of seven other family ranches in three states who share the goal of rebuilding soil, prioritizing animal health, and creating a local and regional food economy. The producers' group also enables efficiencies in the grass-feeding phase of production. If one of her producers runs short of forage for the season, Carman can take some of the herd on for its last weeks of finishing on her land before they are harvested. She will also take cows from other member farms for her breeding program.

One of these family producers is Dan and Mary Flitner of 4 Lazy F Ranch. The day of my visit with them is overcast, with gray clouds slung low, dry scrub covering the mountains, and lush green cover crops spread across the field where the finishing cattle are grazing. Eighteen months old now, two months from attaining their finished weight, they are a mix of beautiful red-brown and black angus cattle.

The herd looks sleek, robust, and bright-eyed to me, but Flitner tells us they have gone through the toughest winter he has had on the ranch and gained little weight. Still, he has been pleased at their rate of growth since the fall, which he attributes to the strong nutrient mix he has created in the grasses. He points out a mix of about ten different cover crop varieties: three or four types of clover, along with millet, brassica, bird's-foot trefoil, sorghum, and sudan grass. "The more sugar the better—there's a lot of energy in this clover. But where we get into trouble is in the heat of July and August, when the energy of the grasses just tanks," he explains. It's a race against the clock to get the cattle to their finished weight of 1,100 or 1,200 pounds during the twenty months they have on grass. This is one reason he has prioritized small-framed cows instead of larger commodity animals that will reach 1,300 to 1,500 pounds.

While grain-based diets promote the growth of *E. coli* in cattle, grass-fed cows are far less likely to contract the bacterial infection. Furthermore, *E. coli* that grass-fed cows do have in their stomach are less likely to survive the human gut microbiome defense because they have not become acid-resistant, as have the *E. coli* in the grain-fed cow gut.[13]

Nearly all of Carman Provisions products are sold through its wholesale distributor Corfini Gourmet, which has plants in Seattle and Portland, among other West Coast cities. The remaining 2 percent or so of products, mainly hot dogs and jerky, are sold direct to customer via a small Portland warehouse. Instead of the typical producer-distributor relationship, in which the distributor buys only what it needs to satisfy customer demand, Corfini will take Carman Provisions' entire weekly inventory, delivering to wholesale customers including hospitals, schools, corporate dining halls, retail stores, and co-ops throughout the Pacific Northwest.

It is a big give on the part of the distributor, who could easily get cuts on demand from a commodity supplier. But the catch is that Carman has to guarantee sales for the entire shipment, including what exceeds customer demand. This means time spent on identifying or generating customers to send to Corfini, or sometimes even taking orders.

Each Tuesday of the year save two (during the holidays), a rotating member among Carman Provisions growers will send a shipment of cattle by truck to the group's Animal Welfare Approved processing plant in Brownsville, Oregon. (This, remember, is part of the wholesale Carman Provisions group, not the smaller cow share program that Carman Ranch alone supplies.) The cattle are harvested the next day, processed on Thursday and Friday, the cuts boxed and palleted according to restaurant and retail specifications. The trim is ground and shaped into patties for the Burgerville chain, Carman's longtime staunch ally in the fast-casual restaurant sector, then distributed by Corfini Gourmet.

CERTIFICATIONS:
SO MANY, BUT WHAT DO THEY DO?

TO HELP MARKET HER BRAND, Carman teamed up with her biggest retail partner, the Portland-based eco-conscious grocery chain New Seasons Market, to get her entire producers' group certified under the "Regenified" label. Because most consumers are unfamiliar with the principles of regenerative agriculture—or if they are, want proof that it is fulfilling its promises—at least six different certification programs have been launched in the last five years or so. The Big Meat version of these would be the USDA grade shield sticker you see on packaged beef, which is divided into a half dozen different classes, ranging from highly marbled "prime" to less marbled "choice," to "standard," and "commercial."

Although a surfeit of organic and regenerative labels can confuse consumers, Athena Petty, senior manager for sustainability for New Season Market in Portland, says, "Third-party certifications help companies rise above the greenwashing that is so rampant in food." In working with Carman to select a program, New Seasons looked for certifications based on verifiable environmental outcomes, not just having ranchers swear to uphold certain practices. They decided Regenified—which was launched by regenerative farming and grazing pioneers Gabe Brown, Allen Williams, and soil scientist Doug Peterson—was the most rigorous program, calling for yearly improvements, measuring soil health with in-field tests, stressing what the organization calls "adaptive stewardship," and ecosystems processes such as the cycling of water, minerals, and energy through the land. Adaptive stewardship is based on the belief that ranch practices, whether good or bad, have a compounding effect on the soil and environment; the goal is always to intensify biodiversity. New Seasons invested $100,000 toward baseline data collection and monitoring of nine Carman

Ranch sites. As we will see in Chapter 7, certifications can turn into further opportunities to greenwash or labor wash. Here, as in all aspects of the alt supply chain, it behooves the consumer to know their certification programs as well as they know their farmers.

THE IMPORTANCE OF
CHEF AND RESTAURANT ALLIES

ALONG WITH RETAIL PARTNERS LIKE New Seasons, every producer in the alt food supply chain relies on chefs and restaurants to help spread the word about their good work. Ultimately it is the superior taste of Carman's products that creates new converts. One of her strongest chef allies is Portland chef Greg Higgins, who, before it became a meaningless cliché, launched Higgins restaurant, the state's first farm-to-table restaurant in 1994. To this day, Higgins restaurant remains a steadfast champion of Pacific Northwest farmers, presenting guests with a copy of its original manifesto in support of local, organic, and regeneratively grown food. It begins with the Wendell Berry quotation: "A significant part of the pleasure of eating is in one's accurate consciousness of the lives and the world from which the food comes."

The day I drop into Higgins in downtown Portland for lunch, the air is soft and the temperature mild. Sunlight streams through large plate-glass windows into the warm, wood-paneled dining room. As I wait for my food to arrive, Higgins himself stops by, wearing a gray baseball cap and black T-shirt that complement his long, tapered salt-and-pepper beard, neatly gathered midway down in a carved silver clasp studded with an amber-colored bead. Like so many of the first generation of new American chefs, he was profoundly influenced by the food culture of France.

"This was in the seventies, and I saw how closely tied really fine food was to agriculture," he recalls. There was a very different system in play there, where a lot of producers would come directly to the restaurant." He took these lessons with him across America and when he found himself in Portland in 1984, figured he would support his art career by cooking. His easy access to top-quality food led him to seek the same type of close relationships with producers he had seen in France; he was on his way to becoming a Portland institution.

As with every one of his producers, he has visited Carman Ranch and says, "I appreciate Cory's care of the delicate landscape, which requires stewardship above and beyond what most would consider 'responsible livestock management.' She's doing a really good job cutting down on invasives and restoring grassland, and you can see the results from one side of the valley to the other."

Higgins acknowledges that grass-fed beef, even the most impeccably raised, butchered, and aged, entails some consumer education. "People are so used to CAFO meat, they want that fall-apart tenderness and greasiness. When an animal is raised well, the flavor is astounding: richer, more herbaceous and complex. Because the animals are working out more, not standing in a pen, there's not a lot of intramuscular fat, but you can really taste the different environment."

In order to give me the full-spectrum Carman Ranch experience, he has asked the kitchen to prepare a special sampler of Carman Ranch beef three ways. A square of braised short rib comes with a thin cap of fat, bathed in a two-day reduction of red wine, its own roasted-bone beef stock, and a mirepoix of thyme, garlic, and shallots. A cube of tenderloin brochette is topped with a caramelized chanterelle mushroom and miniature garlic flower. Both fill my mouth with a deep, meaty savoriness, richer than any beef flavor I've ever encountered before. By contrast, the cured brisket has been transformed into a silky, rose-colored pastrami, its delicate seasoning drawing out the natural umami of the meat. There's a sidecar dish, too, a juicy, pink-in-the-center mini burger, which comes on a grilled brioche bun slathered with aioli and some sliced dill pickle, the perfect bit of fatty accompaniment. Although I did not try it, Higgins also makes a koji-cured eye-of-round, which he says creates a beautiful, fascinating, and yeasty bresaola-style cured meat.

In between Carman Ranch and the Higgins dining room, there has been just one or two links in the supply chain, one of them being Revel Meat Co., run by two chefs turned meat cutters, Jimmy Serlin and Ben Meyer. The duo can trace each cut it processes to the farm where it was raised, and with the animals Higgins buys from Carman Ranch, they will dry age them for more than three weeks before breaking them down.

FIGURING OUT A FIX

AS WE HAVE SEEN IN every other food supply chain, producers committed to repairing the land, treating animals well, and maximizing climate benefits find it exceedingly hard to integrate those priorities into a business model that is competitive in a marketplace dominated by cheap commodity food. "You can only sell food for so much money, and you can only ask people to pay for so many things at the same time," says Carman. "Customers are paying for the work on the land, they're paying for the transparency, and they're paying for my smaller-scale processing plant. And they're also paying for my inefficiencies, because I'm not scaled—it's a big ask."

And it's not just cheap commodity beef that is hard to compete with; it is also other purportedly grass-fed and organic beef producers. They, and shifting market trends, are threatening the wholesale arm of Carman Provisions that she has worked so hard to build. Restaurants are struggling as fewer people are eating out. Two competitors in the organic and certified grass-fed beef space, she believes, "are straight-up lying" about being 100 percent grass-fed and/or organic. There is so little enforcement that less scrupulous producers are cutting corners in order to create products affordable to a wider swath of the market. "The market is incentivizing them," Carman explains.

Meanwhile, even retail partner New Seasons, under pressure from the South Korean company it was purchased by in 2019, is cutting grass-fed SKUs, products such as Country Natural Beef's "grab-and-go" program (prepackaged ground beef, for example) and replacing it with packages of commodity beef.

Assuming consumers can see past the greenwashing (a tall order in itself), opting to buy from a producer like Carman Provisions is the right choice for all of us—but can we afford it? There's the short-term fix and the long-term fix, both of which preoccupy Carman's thoughts. For the short-term, she's trying to make her direct-to-consumer products more relevant and appealing to life as we live it today. "It's about meeting customers where they're at and being able to honor our animals more completely and continuing to evolve. This means going through every cut of the cow and figuring out how to offer it to customers in a form that's both easy to prepare and eat and delicious." So, alongside the fifty-pound boxes that go to grocery stores and restaurants, she is replacing the intimidating $25 rib eye steak or the big roast with smaller portion sizes and quicker cooking methods. For some, it may still be a stretch for the weekly grocery budget, but ease and convenience could make the difference for someone who has decided to leave the commodity Big Meat fold and make meat a smaller but more delicious part of their dinner plate.

The solution to the bigger-picture dilemma—how to transform the alt food system into one that can go head-to-head with the commodity system—involves solving the big question of how to pay for all of the externalities, those hidden costs that the commodity food system lets consumers, governments, and health systems pick up. They include the cost of cleaning up environments polluted by toxic pesticide, fertilizers, and CAFO runoff; the costs of the epidemic of obesity and malnutrition that have been tied to the Big Food–enabled Standard American Diet (SAD); and the costs to laborer health and wellbeing.

"Land and ecosystem restoration won't take forever, but it needs upfront money now," Carman says. "Beef can only pay for so much, and the support mechanisms that are available to us are massively overshadowed by direct subsidies that the commodity industry benefits from." The patchwork nature of government funding available to grass-fed producers like her reminds me of the arduous and unpredictable task of securing funding that alt dairy farms face.

Regenerative grass-fed farmers can access programs through the USDA's Farm Services Agency, including direct subsidies and its crop insurance program. Then there's the federal National Resources Conservation Services (NRCS), whose Environmental Quality Incentives Program (EQIP) provides both technical assistance and funds to farmers for improving water and air quality, soil health, and climate resilience. There are Conservation Stewardship Program (CSP) enhancements, bundles, and supplemental payments designed to allow farmers "to take their conservation efforts to the next level," as its informational brochure promises. The problem is that these programs are evolving all the time and are competitive grants, with no guarantee of securing funds. They are also tied to specific practices that the farmer may or may not be able to implement, and more importantly, subject to shifting political winds at the federal level. Landing funds takes a long time, and if you don't have a good NCRS person in your local office willing to alert you to available funds and help you through the application process (and this is assuming you can find a contractor to help you execute said practices, whether it's incorporating "wildlife-friendly fencing" or reducing surface water nutrient loss by utilizing precision agricultural technologies), your odds are diminished.

One example of how removed these programs can be from rewarding actual farming practices is the set of USDA federal allotment programs designed to protect farm revenue. There are livestock price protection programs, crop insurance programs, and drought insurance programs. Administered by private insurers, the premiums are subsidized by the federal government. Drought insurance is structured so that it pays by the acre, according to changes in average rainfall over the past seventy or so years. In recent years, climate change has created some big winners among those located in parts of the country where there has been a significant change in rainfall patterns. It has helped some ranches stay in business, and created something of a gold rush for speculators who realize that on a forty-thousand-acre ranch eligible for $300,000 in drought insurance in a year, for example, the ranch could be paid off in a handful of years. "It's created some massive disasters, too," says Carman. "All of a sudden, the reality of managing forty thousand acres hits. You have to buy the cattle. There are wolves out there, weather challenges. You can't just hire some cowboy to go out there and tackle this.

"We spent fifty to seventy years making that system unbelievably efficient and productive," Carman says of the industrialized commodity food system. "There's no reason why, if we put the same or even a fraction of those resources toward reintegrating livestock on crop grounds, that we couldn't achieve a similar level of productivity without all the externalities."

The choice Carman sees is between working inside the entrenched system or "standing on the outside and trying to paint a picture of an altogether different way of doing things." Country Natural Beef, the Oregon-based meat collaborative, is doing the former, putting together $10 million in USDA Climate Smart Commodities funding and $500,000 in private money to create a climate-smart, regenerative ranching program that spans six-and-a-half million acres across the western United States. Based on the carbon that it draws down and sequesters, the program will sell carbon credits to industries that create greenhouse gas emissions.

What Carman and her good friend, Mimi Casteel—ecologist, botanist, and owner of the biodiverse Oregon winery Hope Well—are doing, by contrast, is weaving a holistic vision of a food web that begins with the goal of restoration of entire ecosystems. Using Carman Ranch's grass-feed beef operation and its semi-arid climate as its testing ground, Casteel, supported by a grant from the Portland-based Salmon Nation Trust—which helps fund people working on regenerating natural ecosystems and local culture—has outlined a plan utopian in scope but grounded in concrete first steps. It is founded on the idea that any sustainable agricultural system must be regional. Instead of prioritizing extracting profits, it puts healing the land and people's relationship to it first and trusting that abundance will flow from lands that are managed for lasting sustainability. It requires patience and a long view.

Casteel believes that inviting people onto the land to connect with it in a visceral way, through hiking, music, or speakers, will help locals remember their ancient connection to it. Part of restoring those ties involves bringing First Nations members back on the land to forage for traditional foods. To solve for the parched terrain that has resulted from generations of extractive use, Casteel envisions first restoring forest health through a redistribution of biomass and carbon via biochar production (which turns organic matter into a charcoal-like substance that stores carbon while producing clean energy) and then controlled burns. To bring water and vegetation back to sere grasslands, her plan calls for methods ranging from simulating beaver dams on rivers to, bit by bit, creating biodiverse gardens, multi-animal grazing relationships, and reintroducing wildlife populations onto the region's vast ranch lands.

While she acknowledges that her utopian vision of a regional food web is not 100 percent achievable, Casteel says, even "seventy to eighty percent food autonomy will balance these ecosystems."

Visionaries like Casteel are necessary: They urge us to think big, broadly, and holistically about what is possible, and aim for that. But just as Vermont dairy farmer Ashlyn Bristle described her role as the gas and her husband's as the brakes, we also need people who, in the near-term, can turn that vision into reality. Again, finding the time and money needed for land and ecosystem restoration is one of the biggest hurdles to large-scale adoption of more regenerative, eco-friendly, and equitable food systems. The metaphysical divide between pre-restoration and post-restoration, when profits are not coming in and capital may run short, is known as the "Valley of Death." To see how one farm venture is bridging this gap, I head to Northfield, Minnesota.

TREE-RANGE FARMS: BRINGING LESSONS FROM THE CENTRAL AMERICAN JUNGLE TO MINNESOTA

THE MOST CONSUMED LIVESTOCK IN America today is chicken, the culmination of a century's worth of industrialization. It began with Arthur Perdue's idea of contracting with local farmers and building grain receiving and storage facilities, which created a vertically integrated supply chain that includes feed-growing farm, breeding farm, hatchery, battery cages and barns for housing the chickens, processing and rendering plants, and a distribution system.

Chicken production accelerated with the FDA's approval of antibiotics in the industry in 1951, leading to the ever-growing factory farm, which mushroomed from one-hundred-thousand-chicken capacity forty years ago to the half-million-plus poultry factory complexes of today.[14] The phenomenon has been called the "chickenization" of the American food system by the USDA and author Ellen K. Silbergeld.[15] Among the many environmental costs associated with factory farming are the polluting of groundwater (water found underneath the soil), waterways, and air. But there is another one that deserves attention: the hidden toll on underground aquifers (below-ground rock or sediment that holds groundwater in usable quantities) that are being overdrawn to grow the soy and corn that feed these animals, as well as to process the poultry. Consider that in 2023 the average American ate one hundred pounds of chicken per year, more than double the amount forty years ago, and that each grocery store rotisserie chicken requires hundreds of gallons of water to produce,[16] and you can see that we need a better way to farm chicken.

Inspired by traditional Indigenous farming methods of the Latin American jungle, Tree-Range was co-founded in 2022 by Guatemalan-born farmer Reginaldo Haslett-Marroquin. Tree-Range is made up of a network of smallholder chicken farmers who create one-and-a-half acre multi-storied paddocks on which native hazelnut and elderberry trees provide the protective overstory for fifteen hundred chickens that forage not on commodity corn and soy, but on a combination of plants, organic sprouted grain, and insects, and fertilize the land with their droppings.

It is a system reverse-engineered to maximize the symbiotic relationship between chickens and hazelnut trees and build soil biodiversity and climate resilience. Each hazelnut will grow roots twelve feet deep and spread about ten-and-a-half feet across. Above ground, they will grow to about twelve feet in height and are planted in rows twelve feet apart so their branches will form a canopy to keep the chickens cool in the searing summer heat and protect them from aerial predators. Their overlapping roots create a microbiota-rich mass communication network between trees and increase water retention. The chicken's organic feed is grown in Wisconsin and southern Minnesota. Jennifer Zepeda, Tree-Range's head of operations and marketing, notes, "very little of the crops are irrigated and rely on rainwater only."

Research at the University of Minnesota has shown that an acre of hazelnuts can absorb and store up to three hundred pounds of nitrogen—a crucial component for the creation of proteins, vitamins, and hormones—per acre. So Haslett-Marroquin planned a flock size whose manure will provide each paddock with two hundred fifty pounds of nitrogen per acre and add twenty-six different nutrients to the soil, which will help the trees develop immune systems strong enough to fight off invasive pests without any chemical fertilizers or pesticides. The goal is for each level of the Tree-Range multi-storied system to generate income while regenerating the land.

The day I visit Haslett-Marroquin and Zepeda at his sixty-three-acre Salvatierra Farms in Northfield, Minnesota, it is windy, the sun alternatingly emerging and hiding behind fluffy clouds. His is the largest of the Tree-Range's network of eight farms, five in Minnesota and three in Wisconsin, and it operates three chicken houses, each containing fifteen hundred coops. Meant to be replicable and scalable, this system reminds me of the modular nature of GreenWave's regenerative ocean-farming paddocks, which you will learn about in the next chapter. And like GreenWave founder Bren Smith, Haslett-Marroquin sees the low bar to entry as a powerful way to build the alt food system, one unit at a time, accessible to immigrants, farmers of color, and people who lack the means to get into Big Ag.

Haslett-Marroquin points out the six hundred hazelnut trees he has planted so far, and the Guatemalan heritage corn he's been experimenting with, which will be intercropped along with mammoth sunflowers among the rows of hazelnuts. Their added foliage will provide more protection for the chickens below and another layer of biodiversity to the soil while the hazelnut canopy grows to full maturity.

For member farmers, the Valley of Death will last for six to eight years. The first two years are devoted to planting and tending to the perennial hazelnuts and elderberries. Poultry are added in year one as well, as soon as coop, fencing, water lines, and feeders are installed. The canopy spreads and matures between years three to five, and in year six, hazelnut harvests reach economic viability. By year eight, the majority of the ecosystem has reached a sustainable level.

The job of taking Tree-Range farmers from year one to eight and helping them make it through the Valley of Death alive falls to Diane Christofore, executive director of the Regenerative Agriculture Alliance (RAA), the nonprofit arm of the Tree-Range ecosystem. Her indispensable skill is unlocking corporate and government research grants and loans and connecting those assets to farmers, processors, distributors, retailers, and chefs to weave together a regional and resilient business ecosystem. RAA is a major sub-awardee of a $5 million USDA Climate-Smart Commodities Grant, $3 million of which will be available to the organization over a period of five years. One use of those funds will provide rebates to climate-smart poultry producers for purchasing poultry feed to supplement the plants and insects the chickens forage in the developing fields.

These funds will enable Tree-Range to add another layer of complexity to its regional alt poultry system by connecting to the local grainshed that AGC (see Artisan Grain Collaborative, Chapter 2) executive director Alyssa Hartman is spearheading, and to explore an experimental sprouted grain feed system. Sprouting grain feed before it is offered as feed breaks down its starches to make nutrients easier for the chicken to digest and absorb. So far thirty regional grain producers have enrolled under the Climate-Smart grant, and Christofore expects the relationships connecting RAA and AGC to be mutually beneficial and long-lasting.

"The grant sounds like so much money but its goal is to transition seven thousand, five hundred acres over the next five years, and also measure, monitor, and track the grain," says Christofore, a drop in the bucket compared to the scale of the commodity grain system. It is the connecting of two different strands of the alt local food system, grain and regenerative poultry, that for me is most exciting to see.

FROM FARROW TO FINISH TO FENNEL SALUMI: KINDERHOOK FARM AND LA SALUMINA

THE LAST STOP ON MY pastured meat tour will be to trace a short supply chain that starts at Kinderhook Farm in Valatie, New York, a former conventional dairy that in 2004 was converted into a farm for 100 percent grass-fed and pasture-raised beef, lamb, pork, chicken, and eggs. Rotational grazing and a diversified mix of animals have restored the depleted lands, drawn down carbon, and helped the farm become a valued piece of the Hudson Valley foodshed.

The first animal I meet during my visit is Okra, a beautiful red-coated pig with a small wattle hanging off her neck. She's come to the fence of her pen to give her caretaker, Grace Cannan, a nuzzle. The daughter of Olive, a Red Tamworth sow, and Banjo, a Red Wattle boar, Okra, along with her sisters, Onion and Omelet, is one of three quality "replacement gilts," or female offspring who have not yet mated or given birth to piglets.

"Their mother Olive was a really beloved sow of mine, and she's given us these beautiful daughters," says Cannan—a tall tweedy-looking farmer dressed in a gray cable-knit sweater and muddy rubber work boots—who christens each of the dozens of piglets born at the farm every year and is the only one who can tell them apart.

As with farmers who have embraced heirloom wheat, rice, or vegetable varieties, pig growers seeking taste have returned to older breeds that have gone out of style because they are not well-suited to the intensive production of factory farming. They're willing to engage in a slower form of farming, allowing a small number of pigs to forage on open pasture rather than being raised in pig CAFOs. Heritage breeds can be factory farmed as well, however, so you can't assume that every cut of Berkshire pork lived as idyllic a life as those at Kinderhook. To Cannan, it is the combination of the inherently superior taste of these older breeds and the nurturing environment they were brought up in that make Kinderhook Farm's pork so delicious.

Kinderhook aims to be a farrow-to-finish operation, meaning that the animals spend their entire lives on the farm, where Cannan is the one human constant, kind of like their on-premises governess. Keeping a closed system of pigs that are born and live on one farm their entire life builds resiliency in an era when, Cannan believes, it is only a matter of time before swine flu becomes an issue in North America. It has already swept through South America, and in the United States the rampant feral hog population and its propensity to be a reservoir of transboundary disease leads Cannan to predict, "It's going to happen."

The low-stress conditions of the farm, including the pigs foraging together on pasture, the pregnant sows with their nests in close community with each other, and Cannan's emotional bond with them create the best possible birth outcomes: robust and contented piglets who will eventually be transformed—at the other end of the short supply chain—into savory cured meat by Eleanor Friedman of La Salumina in Hurleyville, New York.

On every livestock farm I have visited, I have seen the palpable love each farmer feels for her animals, and how accepting—if not sorrow-free—each is of the fate that awaits their animals. The message here is not the "Christmas is Carnage" cry of the 1995 film, *Babe*, which created many a vegetarian, and led actor James Cromwell to move from his longtime vegetarianism to veganism. Cannan and Friedman, I discover, are respectively a former vegan and a former vegetarian, something that is surprisingly common in the pastured meat world. I have met countless butchers, livestock farmers, and chefs who shed vegetarianism or veganism when they encounter pasture-raised, whole animal butchery. By becoming part of the circle of humane birth, caregiving, death, and renewal on the plate, they feel they can honor their animals in life as well as in death. "Meat is amazing and delicious, and it helps connect people," Cannan says simply.

Yet she adds, "It's hard. There's this perennial grief that I have to deal with." That grief is specific to the sows that she has helped give birth, and bonded with, and less so for their piglets. She recalls an incident in 2019, her first year on the farm, with a sow named PJ, who gave birth to thirteen still-born piglets. As a sow's pregnancy advances, she will make a nest of hay, roots, and dried leaves. (I was fascinated and delighted to learn that each piglet, by the end of its first day of life, will have selected its own teat, which it will return to for each feeding, like assigned seating in an elementary school classroom.) One day, PJ didn't come to her own feeding trough. Although it was premature, she had started and then stopped making her nest. Cannan had seen that her mammary glands were not yet swollen with milk, which is typical for mothers about to give birth. She knew something was wrong, so she sat quietly by PJ as she fretted. After PJ produced thirteen stillborn piglets that looked like little bowling pins, Cannan could tell the sow was grief-stricken, recalling, "I just sat there and cried with her."

On this day, she is grieving the loss of Olive (Okra, Onion, and Omelet's mom), who has just been culled this week at age four—the typical age to cull at Kinderhook—and sent off to be butchered and then processed by Friedman. "I can send off six- to eight-month-old market pigs and feel nothing but pride in how they turned out," she notes. But the sows are a different story. These nuanced, maternal caregiving impulses reminds me of a comment made by Abbie Corse of Corse Farm Dairy: how it is odd that dairy farming has traditionally been so male dominated when it is about caring for lactating animals. "I hated cows most of my life, then became a mom and thought, "Oh, my god, I understand you!'" she said. Cannan agrees. "Being female helps me do my job well, in a lot of different ways. A big part of that is that I'm a little more eager to talk about the emotions around farming with other female farmers," she says.

Just like Carman's cows, Cannan's pigs are raised outdoors and moved from pen to pen to forage grasses. In a factory-farm setting, pregnant sows will be confined to individual gestation crates on hard floors that allow little movement and no socializing. Industrially raised piglets will be weaned after five or six weeks rather than the average eight weeks they have at Kinderhook Farm. Yet Cannan is not completely critical of this system, which has been outlawed in some states. Industrial iron farrowing crates are structured so that when a sow lays down to give birth, she can't stand up, eliminating the risk of her stepping or sitting on a piglet and crushing it. "Part of me understands this because there's an ongoing theme of freedom versus safety when it comes to farming, especially farming pigs."

When it is harvesting time, Kinderhook Farm pigs are sent by truck to Eagle Bridge Custom Meat and Smokehouse an hour north toward the Vermont border. The facility, run by siblings Stephen and Debbie Farrara, is a key link in the local niche meat supply chain, prized for its humane and meticulous treatment of animals. "It's clean, respectful, and what they do is as humane as killing can be," says La Salumina's founder Eleanor Friedman. From cutting, to cooling, to not overbooking so that there is adequate air circulation, the Farraras keep a close watch over the entire process. If Friedman's vendors will not allow her to have their animals processed at Eagle Bridge—for some it can be too far from their farm, or difficult to book because the company will turn down clients if they lack the space to do the work—she will not accept their animals.

All the care taken in raising livestock can evaporate in an instant on the killing floor if an animal is not treated properly at the slaughterhouse. In cows, the adrenaline rush and depleted glycogen stores that result in an animal that is highly stressed at the time of slaughter will result in meat with much higher pH levels and lower levels of lactic acid than a calm, non-stressed animal. This leads to what is known as Dark, Firm and Dry (DFD) beef of an abnormally dark purplish color. In pigs, the result is PSE, or Pale, Soft Exudative meat, and in both cases, the resulting meat is inferior in both taste and texture and will spoil more quickly. Humane killing, on the other hand, involves stunning the animal and then killing it in a short span of time to reduce suffering.

When her four-pig, one thousand-to-thirteen-hundred-pound bi-weekly order from Kinderhook Farm arrives at her facility in Hurleyville, Friedman, sometimes aided by her Italian-born chef husband Gianpiero Pepe, will break them down, grinding the whole animal trim for *salsiccia* (sausages) and *finochietta* (petite fennel sausage), taking care that the fat to lean ratio is correct. She uses the whole head plus skin, other bones, and feet for Tuscan-style *coppa di testa* (head cheese), and trim and liver for her pâté. They will also grind muscle for any additional meat needed for their salumi.

As a young teen, Friedman took up vegetarianism as a protest against factory farming and stayed with it for over a decade. But through her work in both the front of house and in the kitchen at Blue Hill restaurant in New York City, she saw there was a way to reintegrate meat that was conscientiously raised into her diet. And that, much like Cannan's farrow-to-finish-to-slaughter impulses, led her to visit an eleven-hundred-acre organic farm in Tuscany called Tenuta di Spannocchia, to work with livestock and try her hand at making salumi. She liked it enough to return for a formal one-year apprenticeship.

"It was very old-school, like you make coffee and you only cut off feet for six months before you're able to do something else. And you're happy to do it for ninety hours a week and room and board, because you're absorbing so much. I was the foot-and-head girl, that was my thing," Friedman recalls. She went on to deboning shoulders, putting muscles in casings, massaging the prosciutto, and finally, breaking down a whole side of a pig. Being a woman, and on the small side, however, she was frustrated to see larger men come in and be allowed to take on bigger tasks sooner than she was. Her tenure in the slaughter room, hands deep in pig guts, rinsing out duodena, was short, too. Her boss forbade her to return, because the comments the male staff made about her were too unbearable, to him more than to her.

Yet by the time she departed, she had proven herself; it took three hires to replace her and the work she was doing, she tells me proudly. Today, Friedman trains her own employees the same way (minus the sexism), because making salumi "is a very long haul and you need to see it over time."

Although running her own salumeria was never her dream, her jobs back in New York—working as a butcher at Marlow and Daughters and the restaurant Del Posto and running the whole animal program at the Wythe Hotel—left her missing salumi making and wanting to push the no-waste and ethical boundaries of whole-animal butchery even further. She wanted to fill that hole in the local supply chain between small producer and consumer, and to be "a little bit of an educator, but not in a preachy way"—to offer consumers an alternative to overprocessed charcuterie, which, even when the label looks like that of a small independent brand, is often co-packed by a large industrial company and not transparently sourced. So she and Pepe opened their salumeria in April 2020.

Unable to benefit from the economies of scale of industrial production, one goal of whole animal, "nose-to-tail" butchery is to sync supply and demand perfectly, so that no part of the animal is wasted, and even less desirable animals are used to best advantage. Cannan, for example, loves that Friedman will take older, less valuable carcasses that other customers won't touch, like the cull sow Olive over whom Cannan[17] was grieving, and make delicious products out of them. Most customers will not want these because as larger, older animals, their muscles won't be as tender; they may have also just come off weaning their piglet, which also changes their bodies. Friedman will also not balk at taking undersized younger gilts (ranging from two hundred to four hundred pounds) with fertility failures or other issues that make them less desirable to keep on the farm.

Yet no matter how seamlessly producer and artisan salumist work together, there is no getting around the higher price she, like Carman and every other genuinely ethical producer, must charge. This does not mean that consumers have to go over budget and in debt to stay within the alt food system. As Hartman of the AGC learned in Italy, she didn't need a big chop or other hunk of meat at the center of her daily plate; a delicious serving of Friedman's *coppa* or *proscuittello* (sirloin cured and aged like prosciutto) can play a supporting role to grains and vegetables and leave the family grocery budget intact.

Each of the alt meat ranches and farms I have visited have shown me how, when ecosystem restoration and animal welfare are elevated to the same level of importance as feeding people, the economics of the resulting model are exponentially more challenging than those of the streamlined supply chains of global Big Meat, the modern, multinational, "protein-focused" global giants such as JBS and Tyson Foods. Theirs is the system that the USDA, and the profit-chasing commodity markets and supermarket monopolies prop up, and which we buy from.

Challenging the status quo requires a lot of things: legislative change, creative financing, and for us consumers, a shift in consciousness that involves searching for our local alt meat producers and decentering meat on our plates so that we support them and the vision of a balanced ecosystem that they represent. Challenging the status quo is hard, yet as Friedman says, "If we want to show that this work with small farms is doable, we have to survive—this is a work in progress."

CHAPTER SIX

WOMEN WHO HARVEST THE SEA

DURING MY ADOLESCENT AND TEEN years, a minor character known to me and my family as "the fish man" would regularly drive his van up our suburban cul-de-sac, a 100 percent Japanese American enclave of settlers who had relocated west after their World War II imprisonment. It was a narrow shop you could enter from the back and come away with fresh tofu and newspaper-wrapped fillets of freshly caught tuna, mackerel, and sardines that were best eaten raw, as sashimi, with grated daikon, soy sauce, and steamed white rice.

The fish was most likely caught by Japanese and Japanese American fishermen out of Terminal Island in Los Angeles Harbor. From the turn of the century until the outbreak of war, this was home to a vital community of nearly three thousand Japanese, many of them from the coastal fishing villages of Wakayama Prefecture. They lived cheek-by-jowl on the island's Fish Harbor, lined with canneries, barrack-like worker housing, and small fishing boats packed tightly together. Japanese fishermen were prized cannery recruits because of their mastery of harvesting albacore with bamboo sticks and barbless hooks.[1] Young second-generation *Nisei* could play hooky from school to pick up a few bucks working in the cannery, or diving for abalone. Fittingly, they called their village *furusato*, or "hometown."

Later, after the outbreak of World War II when every Terminal Island fishing license holder and resident was rounded up and imprisoned, members of this close-knit community—with its hard work and hard play ways, its community samurai movie nights, and fierce kendo, judo, and baseball rivalries—would remember this interval in history as an enchanted age of community, despite their material poverty and the reality that no other work was open to them as a shunned minority.[2]

Today, remnants of that spirit of community remain in my mother's neighborhood; her Japanese-born neighbor Nao will occasionally stop by to give her neat, vacuum-sealed fillets of bluefin tuna, caught on one of his deep-sea fishing excursions in Mexican waters. The taste of the fish, slightly metallic and fine grained, brings back memories of my grandmother, and I think how delighted she would have been with such a prized dinner. On my tongue, the marriage of cold, silky fish, salty soy sauce, and hot, glistening grains of steaming rice holds echoes of both the joys and the hardships of those early immigrant years.

This present-day Japanese alt food system is connected to its prewar predecessor on Terminal Island, and similar enclaves of immigrant Japanese fishermen up and down the West Coast, from Mexico to Washington State. In British Columbia (BC), they settled in the fishing village of Steveston near the mouth of the Fraser River. As in Los Angeles, most were from Wakayama Prefecture, and as a highly skilled, concentrated minority they were also among the first to feel the sting of resentment and discrimination by a majority Anglo fishery. One family that stood out in the community was a fishing family of six brothers named Kimoto that had begun arriving from Wakayama in 1890.

In 1921, when the government began limiting licenses issued to Japanese to protect the White fishermen, the Kimotos were denied access to sockeye salmon runs on the Fraser River. "There were three boats and twenty-seven people, and they were all turned away from Tofino with weapons," third-generation Japanese Canadian Ellen Kimoto, the daughter of one of those brothers, told me. This was several years ago, when I met Kimoto on a reporting trip to Tofino, the untamed, remote surfing outpost on the westernmost point of Vancouver Island. She was then eighty-one years old, recalling a story that was handed down to her by her father and her uncles. During that lean year of 1921, her father, Masaru Masanobu (nicknamed Bob) and his five brothers—denied a livelihood on the waters by White settlers—were taken in by the local First Nations Tla-o-qui-aht tribe.

Decades later, she and her family faced another form of discrimination when they were incarcerated as enemy aliens during World War II. In 1949, as soon as the ban on Japanese Canadians re-entering the protected zone along the BC coast was lifted, Bob and two of his brothers returned to Tofino to reclaim their livelihood, no easy task in the racially fraught climate of the time. "They knew how to handle it, they were very stoic, never confronted anybody, except for my uncle Tom," Kimoto recalled. "He was my hero. He would take on whoever got in his way. He walked into the local bar and faced a lot of heat. He was only about five-foot-six, but he was tough as nails and he could rage. People just backed off and left him alone."

It was Kimoto's uncle Tom who, every New Year's after his return, visited his Tla-o-qui-aht friends. "He would fill his fishing boat with goodies, snacks, booze, toys for the kids. Only the men went. They would take food, stay for three days, eat, and get drunk," recalled Kimoto. It was not only their way of celebrating their lifelong bond of friendship and fishing. It was also a miniature alt food system of its own, based on mutual aid and forged under the shared burden of discrimination.

INDIGENOUS SALMON
PRACTICES OF THE PACIFIC NORTHWEST

THOSE INDIGENOUS FISHERS WERE HEIRS to Pacific Northwest indigenous salmon fishing practices that stretch back millennia and once comprised a vast, interconnected network of fisheries that they sustainably managed. Tribal fishers set up fish weirs (wooden fences built across salmon-bearing streams and rivers), traps, wheels, reef, and dip nets.[3] They assessed the health of the run, leaving spawning salmon alone, returned unwanted species to the river, and maintained generations of sustainable fisheries. Their large catches were designated for the tribe's own use, but also for their extensive trade networks. Salmon was not just a form of sustenance, it was a symbol of regeneration, something to be revered and cared for, part of an ecosystem that included the grizzly bear, the deer, the wolf, and the eagle.

In both Canada and the United States, starting in the mid-nineteenth century, indigenous resource management systems were disrupted and replaced by a colonial approach to fish management focused on extraction and export. By the 1830s, indigenous fisher people were trading salmon at Fort Langley, the Hudson's Bay Company fur-trading outpost on the Fraser River. When canneries began lining the shores in the 1860s, canning technology and the remoteness of coastal areas made West Coast fisheries a much more concentrated, large-scale industry compared to East Coast fisheries. And, as in every other area of post-contact (with European colonialists) expansion, this industry was built on a system of caste labor, with jobs strictly segregated according to race. Indigenous and Asian men and women fished, unloaded and cleaned the fish. European women and men filled the cans and served as managers, engineers, and machinists.[4] Their products were so in demand globally that in 1942, British Columbia's entire canned salmon pack went to feed British civilians and Allied forces.

Today, one of the principles of agroecology (a food and farming system based on ecological, economic, and social sustainability) is respecting a diversity of knowledge. One knowledge base being increasingly recognized for its ability to return balance to the earth is the rich body of global indigenous traditions. And yet, though much lip service is being paid to respecting those traditions and learning from them, the reality on the waters of British Columbia is different.

A VISIT WITH SKIPPER OTTO AND THE TSESHAHT FIRST NATION FISHERS OF VANCOUVER ISLAND

IN JULY 2023, TSESHAHT FIRST Nations fisher Melanie Fred sent out an email to potential customers informing them that the sockeye salmon were returning to Vancouver Island's Somass River and she was looking for buyers. "I wrote that I was looking for someone who would work in partnership and purchase these beautiful sockeyes that we were going to be catching and working so hard for yet were being paid two dollars and fifty cents a pound for—not even, it had dropped down to a buck-twenty-five," Fred recalls. Seeing the price drop like a rock gave her "this terrible sick feeling inside. Not only because of the hard work you've put in, but also because it costs me twelve hundred dollars just to put my boat in the water."

She made an agreement with a Vancouver contact who offered five dollars and fifty cents a pound if she gilled and gutted the fish rather than leaving them "in the round."

Post-pandemic, sockeye prices—already lower for members like her of an Indigenous Economic Opportunity fishery—kept falling, in part, according to the buyers who underpaid them, because of record catches in Bristol Bay that year, which drew business away from Vancouver Island fishers. Yet because of the opaque, long supply chain they were at the supplier end of, the Tseshaht fishers never knew the exact truth of what was holding prices down; it was all unverified hearsay to them.

Fred and her twin sister, Melissa, spent from 4:30 a.m. to 9:30 p.m. on the water, hauling in the netted fish by hand in two "sets" or circle formations, then transferring them to the boat, cleaning, and packing them. By the time she had processed and packed the fish in slush-ice, the salt-water slurry that is the best way to keep fish fresh, and filled her totes, it was 3 a.m. Fred contacted the buyer to say she needed to catch a few hours of sleep before making the six-hour round trip by road and ferry to Vancouver to deliver her catch. She would catch the 9 a.m. rather than the 6 a.m. ferry. His response was to drop her like a hot potato. She ended up freezing some of her catch and giving some to relatives, spending two days sitting on the roadside with Melissa to sell the remaining ice-packed fish to passersby.

I am sitting on the patio of Pescadores Bistro on Johnston Road in Port Alberni, Vancouver Island, as I listen to Fred's story. This burg shares the feel of other western Canadian frontier resource towns: low-slung diners, hotels, and gas stations, wide streets and wide-open skies fringed by mountains. I have made the three-hour trip here from Vancouver by highway and ferry with Sonia Strobel, cofounder and CEO of Skipper Otto, the community-supported fishery (CSF) she founded in 2008 to create a more direct, transparent, and fair supply chain from small fisher to consumer. One reason was so that fishing families like Fred's don't have to bear the brunt of the risk and responsibility for their catch, as they usually do when dealing with corporate or private buyers.

In 2020, when a conflict between Indigenous and non-Indigenous lobster fishermen on the east coast of Canada broke out into violence, Strobel realized that with Skipper Otto's deep ties to the British Columbia small and medium-sized fishing industry, she was in a unique position to begin a dialogue and build bridges to local Indigenous tribes. She immersed herself in readings from the Fisheries Act and court rulings on First Nations rights, then embarked on a series of conversations with Indigenous and non-Indigenous fishers, government officials, environmentalists, and academics.

She learned from Indigenous fishers firsthand how their rights had been gradually stripped from them. Skipper Otto was by then doing enough volume to allow her to prioritize adding Indigenous fishers to its roster, especially women. She began the long process of building a relationship with the Tseshaht and Hupacasath First Nations fishing communities on Vancouver Island, first with a strong and articulate Tseshaht fisher named Jocelyn Dick. Over the course of nearly a year, they had meandering telephone conversations about family, kids, and the legacy of trauma experienced under colonialism in the Tseshaht community of thirteen hundred members.

In 2021, Dick and eleven other members of the two tribes joined Skipper Otto. Our visit today is a chance to visit with the CSF's Port Alberni fishers Dick and another veteran fisher, Les Sam, as well as Dick's ten-year-old daughter, Parris. Strobel has also invited Fred, a hardworking and reliable fisher who is not yet part of the Skipper Otto family but who she has been hoping to recruit for the past three years. Skipper Otto's membership has grown large enough to allow the addition of one more fisher, and Strobel hopes that it will be Fred, whom she is meeting in person for the first time.

Up until the late 1980s, Indigenous communities in Canada were only allowed to fish for their own "food, social, and ceremonial" purposes, and not sell their catch. Exceptions were those few who could afford costly licenses and gear to fish commercially. It was a remnant of colonialist exclusion on waters where, as Sam points out, "we once controlled one hundred percent of the fishery."

The federal government eventually gave in to Indigenous demands and in 2022 invested $11.8 million to support Indigenous fishing enterprises. The Economic Opportunity fishery established for the Tseshaht and Hupacasath First Nations opened up a new income stream for small-scale fishers of chinook and sockeye salmon—as long as they did not used modern equipment such as hydraulics and retained the tradition of hand-hauling nets onto their small aluminum skiffs.

Yet even after the ruling, in a provincial fishery increasingly dominated by corporate and hedge fund investors, fewer buyers were interested in these small-scale catches. Indigenous fishers have been consistently paid approximately a third of the market rate, says Strobel, kept at the mercy of sometimes unscrupulous buyers. Fred's story of being left high and dry with a boatload of fish she thought she had sold was all too common.

Today, as our lunch orders begin to arrive at our table, Strobel has exciting news to tell the group: She has secured a provincial grant for close to a quarter of a million dollars, that will allow Skipper Otto to outfit a flatbed deck truck with a winch—a hydraulically operated spool wound with a cable that can lift, pivot, and offload fish direct from boat to dock—to create a mobile offload station. Offloading fish has been one of the choke points in their short supply chain. Where before, buyers would try to keep Skipper Otto fishers off the wharf by monopolizing the single winch available and making them wait, the new grant and their own winch will allow Dick and Sam to offload their boats whenever they need to.

As it is, the fishers' days are long enough: Dick starts at 6 a.m. and fishes until 1 or 2 a.m. the next morning, then has to offload the boat. Sam has been kind enough to do the early morning round-trip, drive-and-ferry trek to Vancouver to deliver members' catch to the Skipper Otto processing facility in Richmond.

After lunch, Strobel, Dick, and I drive to "the dam," on the grounds of the Tsehshat First Nations north of Port Alberni. The name refers to a former paper mill and dam that once stood here, but it does not do justice to the idyllic beauty of this stretch of tree-lined, blue-green Somass river, a swimming hole for the Tseshaht community, where eagles can be seen wheeling overhead. "If there's a place that is a church for Tseshaht, that would be it," Sam had remarked at lunch. "Many of our people go up there for prayer, just to ground themselves."

This is the site of many a fishing exploit as well, both difficult and jubilant: Fred's ill-fated 2023 sockeye catch, and a glorious June 2016 catch of 958 fish made by Dick. Although two nets were destroyed, the latter one will be forever enshrined in Tseshaht legend. Making a "set" is a modern form of Indigenous fishing that Dick says is best suited to the quiet dam setting. The fisher anchors one end of the net and then drags the other end through the water by boat to make a circle formation, pulling in all the fish as she closes the circle. On that fateful June morning, Dick and her crew of four family members were out on their two aluminum boats, nineteen and twenty-five feet long, respectively. The first set yielded zero fish. For the second, she had tied one end of the net around a green piling, when out of nowhere, a swarm of sockeye salmon rose up like an aquatic mirage. Then the arduous work of closing the circle began.

To avoid getting beached as the tide receded, Dick and her crew pulled the bursting net into the boat and began to make their way to the marina dock as quickly as possible. It was filled to the brim and teetering, so laden with glistening sockeye that the ten-minute trip took hours. Several hours more went by as they transferred the fish by hand from boat to dock. Speed was of the essence because Dick's Vancouver buyer was waiting on the dock, and the fish needed to be processed as soon as possible. After seven straight hours of hauling fish in and scooping them from net to shore, Dick remembers walking around the marina like a zombie, covered in slime, green algae, and scales. "To this day, people can remember driving by, jaws to the floor," she says. Even though the price of salmon had dropped, she walked away with $25,000 in cash. When the buyer offered to send her off with a bodyguard, he was only half joking. Aside from birthing her children, she says, "it was one of the best days of my life."

MARRYING A FISHERMAN, DISRUPTING THE INDUSTRY: SONIA STROBEL

THOUGH STROBEL GREW UP IN Vancouver in the 1970s, surrounded by ocean and some of the world's prime fishing grounds, seafood was not a regular part of her family's diet. Then she married into a fishing family. "Suddenly I was having the best seafood of my life. I couldn't believe that my whole life I hadn't been able to access this," she says. Growing up, her family ate fish from the supermarket. "There was no way of knowing exactly what it was, how old it was, where it came from, or how it was caught." Since 90 percent of the local British Columbia catch is exported while 80 percent of what is available locally is imported, she now knows that it could have imported fish that "sat in an auction until it was almost rotting, then thrown into a slow-freezing freezer and stored there for years before being slacked off (defrosted) and sold at the fish counter with 'previously frozen' in fine print. It was fishy and made me gag."

Strobel was also horrified to learn how difficult it is for fishing families to make a living, the risks that they take, the uncertainty around what they will catch, who they will sell to, and how much they will be paid. She saw the huge disconnect between the local fishermen and what should be their local market.

She launched Skipper Otto in 2008 as her schoolteacher maternity leave project. The idea was to put together the equivalent of a community-supported agriculture box, designed to support fishing families and find a more efficient way to get her father-in-law Otto Strobel's catch to friends and family. Solving one problem at a time, Strobel built a movement. With only word of mouth promotion, Skipper Otto grew from forty CSF members to two hundred CSF members the following year. Otto's catch alone was not enough, so he enlisted some of his buddies.

Today, Skipper Otto includes about forty fishing families in British Columbia and the Canadian territory of Nunavut, ten full-time staff, another ten who work part time, and an online marketing presence. It provides fish shares to eight thousand members across Canada, with about one hundred pick-up hubs from Victoria to Montreal, and southern BC to southern Quebec.

Just as Maine Grains' Amber Lambke does with grain farmers, Skipper Otto sits down with fishers to talk through their costs, their expenses, and what they need to bring in to support their families. "We work as the best and most ethical buyer," Strobel explains, "and a lot of it is business mentorship. Often, people haven't thought through issues; they're spending money on ice but they're not even factoring that into cost recovery. We try to come up with the right price, knowing that if we pay more, we might sell less fish because the cost to the member will be higher. What's the competitive market paying? What is the sweet spot? We're making sure we come up with a price that's not astronomically higher than you would pay somewhere else, but the dollars are going to the fishing family."

Because Skipper Otto members are paying for their share before the season starts, the organization also has the capital to help its fishing families out with, say, $10,000 culled from member pre-payments so a fishing family can lease a fishing quota, or buy camera equipment to monitor and verify the catch, as is mandated in certain fisheries—both big financial burdens for small-scale fishers. During its fifteen years in business, other than membership fees, Skipper Otto has taken on no investment money or debt. Its members invest in both the fishing families and the coming fishing season—the exact opposite of how fishing for a large corporation works, where the fisherman comes last and has no idea how much he or she will be paid until long after the catch is delivered.

To make this short supply chain work, it must be as tightly constructed as possible, with full transparency and open communication with members. A Skipper Otto fisher will call in from the fishing grounds to report, for example, a five-thousand-pound catch of sockeye and two thousand pounds of Chinook in its hold, and that it is heading toward land. Strobel's team will figure out how many fillets the catch will supply, then print labels for each. Processing is done at Skipper Otto's plant in Richmond, BC, instead of being sent to China for processing and then shipped back to Canada, as happens to so much of the local catch sold to other fish companies. "We have a very tight chain of custody of the fish. It comes from the fishing family directly to us, and not through anybody else," Strobel says. "It's really about community. There has to be a personal connection, not just a QR code to a website."

Skipper Otto started with fresh fish only, then, realizing its reach was limited by how long the fish would stay fresh, found a processor that would cut and freeze the catch for them. Although access to a good small processing plant is often a bottleneck for local, short-supply-chain food systems, Strobel was able to identify one that would fit Skipper Otto's fish in around its other work. Then the COVID-19 pandemic hit. The processor lost all its export clients overnight, while Skipper Otto, the more resilient local supply chain, grew 300 percent. "It was a beautiful synergy and partnership because they've always been willing to think a little differently and do things a little differently," says Strobel of the processor. "And they've come to see that domestic markets are important—that we're so vulnerable when it's all export and industrial scale."

To ensure equity of access, Skipper Otto keeps the minimum price for a share to $100, with no membership fee for the first year, and a small one after that. The average share price is $400. On offer at various times of the season are five species of Pacific salmon, halibut, tuna, ling cod, rockfish, and hake; shellfish including oysters, mussels, and spot prawns; a variety of canned seafood products, and a range of dried kelp products.

For consumers used to deciding what type of fish they want that evening and going to the supermarket to buy it, Skipper Otto "flips that around and looks at what the ecosystem is providing in abundance any given year," Strobel explains. This year, for example, there was no hake to be found. Skipper Otto alerted customers in a blog post and let them know what to expect instead. "The proposition to members is that you're going to eat with the ecosystem," Strobel explains.

A GRIM TALE: THE INDUSTRIALIZED
SEAFOOD SUPPLY CHAIN

THE SAME FORCES THAT COME into play when comparing the alt land-based food systems with its commodity, or globalized counterpart, exist in ocean-based food systems—everything is just on a vaster scale. Supply chains, which can start in the remotest waters off West Africa or North Korea, are especially opaque and especially long. As we've seen, salmon caught in Alaska is often shipped to China for processing before re-entering the global supply chain for worldwide distribution. This is confusing for the buyer because salmon caught in Alaska but processed in China will be labeled "Product of China" or something similar.

As with other areas of the food system, the free-market ideal of putting the care of the commons—the cultural and natural resources available to all people—into the hands of corporations was based on the neo-liberal belief (at least on the part of nobler minds) that the profit motive would incentivize them to care for the oceans, the farms, and the ranches that they owned. But things didn't work out that way. Instead of the hoped-for sustainable fishing practices, profit became the prime objective, which meant figuring out how to extract maximum gains for the least amount of money. Implicit in such operating practices is the idea that nature is a bottomless well to draw from, an ever-renewing resource that asks for nothing in return. When the whole globe is at your feet for you to harvest, you can deplete one reserve and simply move on to the next great untapped fishing ground, mine, ranchland, or planet.

The industrialization of our oceans has happened over the past one hundred years, aided by favorable government policies and rapidly modernizing technology. As the most popular fish stocks collapsed, technology allowed trawlers and other large fishing boats to travel farther and faster offshore, and fish deeper and deeper into the ocean, detecting fish with the aid of sonar, more efficient engines, the ability to corral vast harvests with more durable, petroleum-based fishing lines and nets, and preserve their catch with mobile freezing technology.[5] As with chemical fertilizer, many of these innovations were products of World War II–era research that found a home in our domesticated lives.

It is also easy to overlook the grave human rights and environmental abuses that have been well documented in global seafood supply chains—both at sea and on land in processing plants—because they are happening at such a far remove from our busy daily lives. The Washington, DC–based nonprofit The Outlaw Ocean project has reported the widespread abuses on hundreds of boats in the Chinese distant-water fishing fleet. With over six thousand boats, it is by far the largest seafood supplier in the world, and within it, Outlaw Ocean reporters have documented forced labor by

Uyghurs and North Koreans, debt bondage, beatings, passport confiscation, and death by violence. Seafood from this supply chain as well as the overseas processing of North American caught fish—everything from pollock to salmon to haddock—ends up in North American and European supermarkets, restaurants, food service companies, and in the purchases of the biggest buyer of all, the US federal government, which supplies these products to the military and public schools.

Around the world over the last century, the traditional low-yield methods of small, independent fishers—hook-and-line, longline, and gillnetting—have given way to trawlers and other deep sea fishing vessels that do not target just a single species of fish. Trawling is like opening a giant suitcase and dragging it through the middle or across the bottom of the ocean, trapping target fish as well as enormous quantities of bycatch. And there has been the same consolidation, the same global setting of prices, and the same marginalization of the smallholder producers that we've seen in other sectors of the industrial food system.

As the industrialization of the world's fisheries made raiding oceans of their edible bounty increasingly efficient, the realization dawned that wild stocks would not be enough to meet global demand. In 2007 the Food and Agriculture Organization (FAO) reported that globally, 77 percent of wild fish stocks were either fished to capacity or overexploited. In the Pacific Northwest, fish farmers began Atlantic salmon cultivation in the 1950s, and by the 1970s net pen aquaculture, using large underwater net pens, or cages, was established. By 2016, farmed Atlantic salmon was British Columbia's top exported agrifood.

Industrial salmon farming accounts for 70 percent of today's global aquaculture and has become a twenty-billion-dollar-a-year industry. Between 1980 and 2000, farmed salmon overtook wild to account for most of the salmon consumed globally. But the way salmon aquaculture has been practiced—on an industrial scale, focused on yield, under poorly regulated conditions, and close to shore—has had a devastating effect on ocean life, ocean habitat, wild fisheries, and the economic well-being of local fishing communities. To see what this globalized system looks like from the local, British Columbia level, I spoke to Sonia Strobel's husband, Shaun Strobel.

GROWING UP IN THE FISHERY: SHAUN STROBEL

STARTING AT ABOUT AGE SEVEN, from the day school let out for the summer to the day he returned, Shaun Strobel lived on the water with his father, Otto. They would head out from Steveston Harbour south of Vancouver in Otto's thirty-foot gillnetter, a wall of netting that hangs in the water, catching the fishes' heads and gills. Surrounded by a small cadre of other gillnetter friends, they scooted up the coast through the Georgia Strait, pulling fourteen-hour days until setting up their fish camp, often at a place called Rivers Inlet south of Haida Gwaii, once home to the thriving Wadhams Cannery.

This was in the 1970s, when, despite owning a license, it was already hard for a small fisherman like Otto to make it on his own, and large companies ran the game. Strobel likens the fishermen's role to that of coal miners in a company town. His father sold to British Columbia Packers, the largest of them all, a conglomerate that had consolidated many smaller packers, and whose reach once extended to the United States, Mexico, and Southeast Asia. After fishing all night and landing maybe one hundred or, on a hot night, two hundred salmon, the water would look like a city, so lit up was it with the red and white lights of hundreds of small fishing boats, Strobel recalls.

"You'd sell your fish to the fish company, and they'd keep a ledger of what you sold, and give you scrip money, basically coupons to spend at the company store." Fishermen bought their fuel from the company and, on Sundays, could go to the radio house to make calls home before the fishing run. "It didn't matter if you owned your own boat, or if you fished a company boat," Strobel explains, "you were still dependent on them, because where we were was so remote." It was a hardscrabble life but if you were born and raised on the sea, it was one you were loath to give up. For fishermen, "the company" was the equivalent of the dairy farmers of Chapter 4 who were tied to and dependent on the milk truck, their supply chain connection to the market.

Starting in the 1960s, and ramping up in the 1980s and 1990s, the federal government began to limit the number of licenses issued to combat the boom-and-bust nature of fisheries and control overexpansion and overharvesting. Individual Transferable Quotas (ITQ) that could be bought, sold, or leased gained popularity in the 1980s. This system was based on the theory that reducing the number of fishermen on the sea, setting limits on fishery catches, and letting the free market regulate the outcome would create the most rational market.

Without rules in place to prevent consolidation of ITQs by wealthy fishers or seafood processors, the system has opened the way to increased corporatization of the seas and foreign ownership, further squeezing out small owner-operator fishermen. Large, vertically integrated companies bought out small fishermen's licenses and quotas, combined them, and built seiners triple the size of the small fisherman's boat, which could bring in far more than triple the small boat's catch. ITQs became so expensive and ownership so difficult to trace that eventually there were virtually no generational boats, licenses, or quotas to be passed down. Halibut fishing, once a reliable way for a small fisher to make a living, was no longer within reach. "The small boat fleet all but disappeared over a twenty-year span," says Sonia Strobel. Enforcement has been difficult, as well, allowing large ITQ holders to overfish, dump bycatch, and under-report their hauls. The system helped make Canada the world's biggest exporter of fish in the mid-1980s.[6]

The most famous failure of the quota system came in 1992, after decades of overfishing led to the closing of the nearly five-hundred-year-old cod fishery in Newfoundland and Labrador. The government-imposed mor-atorium led to the single largest layoff in Canadian history, putting forty thousand mostly fishers and plant workers in the Atlantic provinces and Quebec out of work.[7] The collapse led to a restructuring of entire marine ecosystems in Atlantic Canada; over time, the cascading consequences of the cod's disappearance began to emerge.[8] The decline of top predator cod led to surges in snow crab and shrimp across the waters of Nova Scotia. Yet at the same time, the die-off and slow recovery of the primary forage fish that cod rely on, including capelin, has significantly slowed the recovery of the cod stock in Newfoundland and Labrador. Although it might seem that without its prime predator, the population of these forage fish would explode, the complex movement of energy and nutrients along intertwined food chains has resulted in the opposite outcome. Long-term exploitation of a single species in the ocean is akin to the single-minded monocropping of industrial agriculture: both result in ecosystem imbalances that the alt food system tries to restore and preserve.

Above water, in another complex web, the role of the vanishing cod is played by the small and medium-sized owner-operator. Even those lucky enough to own ITQs, or Individual Transferable Quotas—often through inheritance—rarely own enough to be independent. Instead, they have to lease more, or lease quota for bycatch they might accidentally net, such as rockfish. And the price and terms of those quotas, as well as the fish they catch, are determined by the large export-oriented fishers/processors who control the system and global market realities. Small harvesters are still caught in what Sonia Strobel calls "a modern feudal system."

Although a small, short supply chain CSF such as Skipper Otto, she adds, "must work incredibly hard" to cover huge quota costs, remain competitive with global industrial supply chains, and pay harvesters a living wage, their alt supply chain does provide more stability and consistency for both harvesters and consumers. To see another example of a successful alt seafood supply chain at work, I head east, to New York.

SUPER SUSTAINABLE AND WELL MANAGED: BRISTOL BAY'S ILIAMNA FISH CO.

ON A SUNNY, NOT-TOO-CHILLY DECEMBER morning in Manhattan, I take the subway uptown to meet Emily and Christopher Nicolson in front of the Hargrave Senior Center at West 71st Street and Columbus Avenue. It is the first members' pick-up day of the salmon season for Iliamna Fish Company, a family-owned fishing cooperative with roots in the Indigenous culture that has managed the Bristol Bay salmon run—the largest and most sustainable in the world—since time immemorial.

The couple unloads and stacks a neat pile of large black insulated bags used to transport today's stock—nine hundred pounds of frozen salmon and cod and forty-five pounds of canned salmon—and wait for shareholders to arrive to pick up their portions. The first arrival, a woman in a brown parka, gives Christopher a big hug and offers to get him a coffee. Another arrives by bicycle and stuffs Iliamna's twelve-pound boxes in large panniers; still others arrive in cars with coolers at the ready to pack, or on foot with large IKEA totes. "One member buys at least ten shares of everything; he owns a farm and entertains a lot," says Emily. Others drive in from as far as Maine to pick up their shares.

The Nicolsons are one offshoot of "a big, messy, hippie, bohemian enclave" of a family, with roots on Iliamna Lake, the terminal spawning grounds fed by the Kvichak River, one of six that feed Bristol Bay, to which native salmon populations return every summer. Christopher's mother is a member of the Iliamna Village Council, an offshoot of the larger Athabaskan group and the Dena'ina tribe, one of thirty-one tribes in the Bristol Bay region. He and his cousins grew up spending summers on Bristol Bay, catching salmon by hand with fifty-fathom nets on a twenty-foot aluminum skiff fitted with an outboard motor, and working various jobs around the country in the offseason.

When farmed fish was at its ascendancy in the 1990s and beginning to compete with wild-caught salmon, wholesale buyers at the dock saw their profits plummet. The loss was reflected in the price fishers would receive from the buyers for their hard-won catch. There was no way the Nicolson's family of fishers could continue to fish for larger companies and make a profit on the rock-bottom prices then being offered. So about twenty-five members of the family started their direct-to-consumer CSF.

Their ten CSF members grew to thirty-five and kept growing. Christopher's cousin Reid Ten Kley set up the cooperative structure for the CSF, and soon they were selling in Portland, Seattle, and other satellite cities. Today their network stretches up and down the East Coast from Boston to Philadelphia, Maryland, and Texas, serving between five and six thousand customers, about fifteen hundred of whom live in New York City.

So fecund is the Bristol Bay salmon run that during the June and July sockeye run, Iliamna fishers stay close to shore to net their catch, running it to shore every hour, where it is loaded onto a truck and driven straight to the small processing facility they work with that Nicolson says "would fit in a two-car garage." In 2023, fifty-four million wild salmon crowded

Bristol Bay's waters to make their way upstream. (Like farmed salmon did to wild-caught salmon in the 1990s, the Bristol Bay fishery has—at least according to the BC Indigenous Tseshaht fishers' buyers—lowered demand for their catch.) Master cutter Amanda Wlaysewski deftly carves the fish into fillets, which are packed, flash frozen, and sent by barge to Bellingham, Washington. There, they will be boxed and trucked to member cities in continuous cold storage.

Although Sonia Strobel could find no other organizations like hers in 2008, today there are about two hundred community-supported fisheries like Skipper Otto and Iliamna Fish Co. in the United States and a few in Canada (many fishers sell directly to local customers through farmers markets). As with the other branches of the alt food system I have explored, these individual supply chains are connecting with each other to form a vital network of like-minded organizations that share knowledge, tactics, and resources. The Local Catch Network, founded in 2011 by Joshua Stoll, an associate professor of marine policy at the University of Maine, supports local fisheries and the communities that depend on them through technical assistance programs, help in applying for grants, and knowledge sharing on how to build a decentralized local supply chain.

Strobel founded the Canadian branch of Local Catch in 2023, a group that is primarily focused on building Indigenous food sovereignty, ensuring that fishers have access to fair markets, and community members have access to their traditional foods. The network is working with a Nunavut community to build an equitable route for "country foods," or traditionally harvested meat and seafood that will replace the commodity, junk, and highly processed food that is routinely shipped north, and which many Indigenous communities are forced to survive upon.

SMALL INDEPENDENT FISHERS' PROBLEMS ARE GLOBAL: SUPAPORN ANUCHIRACHEEVA'S THAI STORY

THE DIRECT-TO-CONSUMER INNOVATIONS HAPPENING IN Bristol Bay and along the British Columbia coast are not unique to North America but can be linked to a movement of smallholder fisher people around the world who are working to wrest ownership and profit from middlemen, and to manage stocks to ensure the livelihoods of many generations to come. This lesson came home to me on a trip to Thailand I made in June 2023, when my friend Dharath "Tot" Hoomchamlong took me to meet Supaporn "Nuch" Anuchiracheeva at the organic fish market she founded, Pla Organic, one of several global alt food systems that I will be looking at in my travels.

The direct-to-consumer venture was just one arm of a large project that Nuch, an academic whose background is in coastal zone management, has spearheaded for the past ten years. When she learned about the plight of small fisherwomen she was studying, she pivoted to promoting their work to big city consumers. The fishers were directed by middlemen to douse their catch with formaldehyde to preserve it—an illegal but commonly used preservative in some countries, and a human carcinogen[9]—and were paid a mere 15 percent of the market price of their fish. For the Bangkok consumer, despite their country's more than sixteen hundred miles of coastline, it was impossible to buy fresh, locally caught fish; those supply chains had all but disappeared with the industrialization of the oceans.

In 2013, Nuch was able to land a 750,000-euro, five-year grant from the European Union to develop a small-scale organic fisheries project, which targeted seven areas in seven different provinces. The Pla Organic retail shop is located in a part of Bangkok that Tot described as the

Bangkok outer-borough equivalent of the Bronx, on land donated by a supporter. It is a sunny, wood-and-glass construction that resembles a fishing boat, stocked full of local catch and organic vegetables and consumer packaged goods—a COVID-era addition that saw it become a fully rounded food hub. "Our focus is environmental rehabilitation, the fisher people's quality of life, and a fair price for the consumer," Nuch tells me. Pla also returns 60 to 70 percent of market price to each fishing village, with the rest covering marketing and staffing. Even so, the organization manages to sell its products for less than top gourmet supermarket prices, and its catch is represented in some of the top restaurants and hotels in the country.

GREENWAVE CULTIVATING SEA VEGETABLES: BREN SMITH AND EMILY STENGEL

FOR AN EVEN MORE RADICALLY regenerative way to harvest the sea, I turn to GreenWave, the Connecticut-based nonprofit founded in 2013 by former commercial fishermen Bren Smith and Emily Stengel. Smith's life took him from the small-scale fisheries of his youth in Newfoundland to harvesting the Bering Sea in giant trawlers at the height of the industrialization of the oceans. Eventually, his body broken and conscience battered by the massive carnage and waste he witnessed at sea daily, he came up with a way to stay on the ocean, but on his own pacifist, regenerative terms.

His first foray into ocean farming began by cultivating eco-friendly shellfish at his Thimble Island Oyster Company on Long Island Sound. Unlike open-net pen-farmed salmon that pollute the ocean, adult oysters, mussels, and other shellfish can filter up to fifty gallons of water a day, removing excess algae or nitrogen from fertilizer and industrial or animal waste runoff. GreenWave was born when he created his concept of "three-dimensional ocean farming," in which modular farms of twenty acres each are outfitted with a rope scaffolding for four vertical layers of crops ranging from sea kelp, to oysters, to clams, mussels, and scallops. The ropes can be raised or lowered to avoid storm surges or to find nutrient sweet spots. These crops need no fertilizer, grow quickly, and can act as artificial reef and storm surge protectors, shielding coastline communities.

In recent years kelp has transformed from a fringe edible in the West to a nutritional and ecosystems superhero. Not only is it good for your body, kelp is also able to absorb ten times more carbon—a contributor to ocean acidification—than land-based trees or plants[10] and remove the excess nitrogen and phosphorous that can cause toxic algal blooms. Kelp forests are biodiversity hotspots, ecosystems that nurture and protect thousands of species of fish, algae, and other forms of marine life. Kelp can serve as a replacement for toxic, fossil fuel–based fertilizers or mono-cropped corn-based ethanol; as additives to pet and animal feed; binders in anything from salad dressings to shampoos; or for bioplastics.

While Smith supplies the vision, his cofounder, Emily Stengel, is the one who makes it all happen. When Stengel, fresh out of graduate school, met Smith in 2015, he had endured the low point in his career, the loss of all of his gear in back-to-back hurricanes Irene and Sandy in 2011 and 2012. The twin disasters left his shellfish farm in shambles and him $100,000 in debt. That forced him to return to the drawing board and come up with his radical plan to make sea kelp an integral part of his dense, biodiverse, and completely input-free ocean farms.[11] His plan was so simple, yet innovative and compelling. Stengel managed the fundraising and put together a women-led, nearly twenty-member-strong team scattered across the country.

As a graduate student at the University of Vermont focusing on agricultural economics, Stengel had, with the help of a USDA grant, visited two hundred farmers across the country to find out what the barriers to growth were. She learned that small to medium-sized farm families often could not afford childcare or health insurance. The economics of Big Agriculture, compounded by the challenges of a changing climate, meant these families could no longer afford to just farm; they needed to diversify, whether through different crops, value-added products, or agrotourism, or by taking off-farm jobs to supplement their income.

At GreenWave, she found that the problems of East Coast fishers mirrored those of land-based farmers. The sea and its warming waters was no longer able to provide them with the predictable livelihood it once did. Farming the ocean regeneratively, it turned out, offered benefits similar to that of land-based regenerative farming. Among the programs she oversees is the Kelp Climate Fund, which has provided more than sixty kelp farmers with funds for climate mitigation practices in exchange for collecting data on everything from growth rate and yield to carbon and nitrogen removal. GreenWave also offers online and in-person training, tools, and networking opportunities—efforts to connect farmers to emerging agriculture, ingredients, and biomaterials markets.

The combo of kelp and shellfish farming attracts both seasoned fishers who have seen too much of the rapaciousness of commercial fisheries, like Smith, and newcomers to the field. To meet some GreenWave ocean farmers I head north along the Eastern Seaboard.

Suzie Flores, owner and operator of Stonington Kelp Company, moved from New Jersey to Connecticut in 2016, when she and her husband, veteran Jay Douglass, bought a marina in Pawcatuck with plans to rehabilitate it from the studs up and rent out slips and kayaks. GreenWave helped them set up the front end of their ten-acre commercial sugar kelp farm, guiding them through the permitting and leasing process for state waters.

At first, Flores kept her job in market development for a publishing company, but the lure of the kelp farm convinced her to move it from hobby to more of a full-time job in 2017. "It's more satisfying in *so* many different ways, and it brings a unique sort of joy you can only get when you're growing something to feed people," she says.

In the fall, she buys sugar kelp seed stock from GreenWave and the nearby Indigenous Shinecock Kelp Farmers, cultivating her kelp beds in Fishers Island Sound. Regular harvests two to three times weekly between March and May require hauling up ropes laden with one hundred to two hundred pounds—and up to five hundred pounds at the end of the season—of long, ruffly edged ribbons of kelp from up to six feet under the ocean, something she's had to develop the muscles for. Between the farm, helping Douglass run the marina and its bait and tackle shop, and parental duties, she is busy.

While Flores has made sugar kelp cultivation her sole occupation, Azure Cyglar of Rhody Wild Sea Gardens, located off Portsmouth, Rhode Island, juggles her job as a fisheries and aquaculture specialist at the University of Rhode Island with farming her five acres of oyster and kelp beds. Where Flores can command top dollar, anywhere from twelve to twenty dollars per pound for fresh kelp sold directly to local chefs, Cyglar sells mostly to bioplastic firms for a lower price. Achieving a price of sixty cents per pound, the research shows, is the point at which a kelp farm can become profitable.

Cyglar grew up in San Diego exploring tidepools, snorkeling, and surfing. She worked as a research diver while at UC Santa Cruz studying fisheries management and marine biology. She served as a crew member on a small fishing boat in Australia, then worked in commercial fishing in Australia, American Samoa, and Alaska. As part of her job working for a

Cape Cod nonprofit fighting the new wave of Individual Fishing Quotas (IFQs), she interviewed small fishermen who jigged for cod and fished for tuna; one family was the last squid and scup (porgy) fishing group to use traditional Native American weir nets, a rare experience that she treasures. "You build friendships, do a lot of drinking, eat a lot of chowder," she recalls of those days.

What she learned during her time embedded among fishing families informs her view of fishing today. Of the many commercial fishers and their wives or former wives that she interviewed, she says, "Not one of them said, 'This was a great life, I would do it again.' Instead, it was, 'This is really hard, and for what? We're not making the planet better.'"

Having seen up close how badly the fishing food system is broken, she says, "I've flipped from devoting my life to saving small fishermen to feeling like the oceans should be a reserve: anything we get out we cultivate with not only zero input but positive net gain." The kind of regenerative aquaculture she is doing allows her to "repair people's lives a little and repair the earth—that's a better way to do business," she says. "Call it a career chiropractic."

THE SUPER-AGENT TO THE SUPPLY CHAIN

FOR GREENWAVE, THE CHALLENGE IS to scale up in the face of the growing presence of Big Kelp. A kelp rush is underway, with stakeholders ranging from corporate, government, nonprofits, and Silicon Valley venture capital funds pouring more than $300 million into what they hope is the future of everything from plastics to animal feed.[12] Both the huge commercial potential of kelp and the need to safeguard the future of wild kelp forests have become increasingly evident. The US edible seaweed industry alone is estimated to be worth $1.87 billion,[13] while potential growth of the global seaweed market, according to the World Bank, is up to $11.8 billion by 2030.[14] But will scaling up a harvest that seems to offer so many nutritional, climate, and sustainability benefits simply become another extractive monoculture?

If GreenWave is the regenerative alternative to the gathering tidal wave of Big Kelp, then Sam Garwin is the number-crunching super-agent to this branch of the alt food system supply chain, which, as we have seen, often struggles to connect its links. "No one can make supply chains sound as scintillating as Sam," says Lindsay Olsen, GreenWave's director of training and support. "She brings them to life."

Garwin's background in business analytics software was an asset when she helped Uncommon Cacao (see Chapter 7) source direct trade, organic cocoa beans. Her tenure as the former CEO of the now defunct Fleishers Craft Butchery served as her trial-by-fire apprenticeship in growing supply chains in real time, connecting farmers and processors with transportation, logistics, and cold storage. She learned how to rebuild local supply chains that had been destroyed by the industrialization of our food system from the ground up. The job also transformed her, like pig farmer Grace Cannan and salumi maker Eleanor Friedman, from a vegetarian to meat-loving, hands-on butcher.

Garwin met Bren Smith at a "friendsgiving" dinner in New Haven in about 2016. He was figuring out what the GreenWave model would look like and how to teach new farmers his regenerative ocean farming model but had no idea how to get GreenWave's product to market. For Garwin, solving this problem "was the chance to make a world-class food system from the ground up, learning from the mistakes that land-based agricultural supply chains have made." In addition to collecting data from both farmers and buyers that will help her better match supply with demand, she has developed a seaweed app called Seaweed Source that Stengel calls "a dating app," that connects kelp farmers to buyers. Not only is it important to make sure demand keeps up with supply, Garwin has learned from experience that if everyone in the entire value chain does not make money, the system will fail.

Olsen's job, like Garwin's, is devoted to growing the GreenWave network, but through an open-source regenerative ocean-farming hub catering to more than six thousand registered users who can take an introductory "seed-to-sale" training program on how to start a kelp farm or follow a path that will help them become kelp processors, buyers, or hatchery operators. There is also a community bulletin board that Stengel says is building a network or "hive mind that allows farmers a way to share methods and maximize their production and make them competitive with much bigger farms but using less labor and much lower costs." As Olsen says, "We need to grow the entire network supply chain."

CRACKING THE EDIBLE KELP MARKET CODE: COURTNEY BOYD MEYERS

FOR THE FORESEEABLE FUTURE THE edible kelp market will remain a niche one, what Smith calls "Brooklyn beekeeper food," though I take umbrage at that as a non-beekeeping Japanese American who knows how central seaweed can be to a nation's diet. There are, in fact, a few companies that have cracked the code of making delicious kelp-based products. One of them is Akua, cofounded by Courtney Boyd Meyers, who drew on her marketing, tech start-up, and journalism background, her desire to be a climate activist, and her teenage passion for plant-based eating. The first to make a kelp-based meat substitute, she sells kelp patties, bulk kelp "crumbles," a hamburger alternative, and a vegan crabcake.

The inspiration for a kelp burger came after she met Bren Smith and toured Thimble Island Ocean Farm. She and cofounder Matthew Lebo landed a total of $5.4 million in seed money[15] to get the company off the ground, and launched their first test product, a kelp jerky in 2019. "It didn't go very well, it was way too kelp-y," says Boyd Myers, who goes by the much snappier three-initial moniker "CBM."

To continue the company's work during the COVID-19 pandemic, she built an online kelp burger club of one thousand members and sent out free samples. "It felt really cool. People were looking for ways to connect, and as they gave their feedback, we iterated." Akua can sound like any number of other plant-based tech start-up companies in its unbridled "we're saving-the-planet" messaging, but CBM's commitment to working with GreenWave—she sources from about five farms in the organization's network—keeps the patties more sustainable than highly processed plant-based meat alternatives.

Akua purchases freshly harvested kelp from Maine and Massachusetts farms. It is blanched, blended, the water pressed out, packed in large drums, and frozen at their Portland processor. Since they've outgrown that facility's capacity for assembling the patties, the company ships the drums to its sister facility in Atlanta, where the kelp is combined with olive oil, cremini mushrooms, pea protein, black beans, and nutritional yeast, among other ingredients. A bonus cache of publicity came when the cable television network Nickelodeon reached out and asked to partner with Akua for a healthy option for kids. The result was Akua's Sponge Bob kelp patty line.

As the example of GreenWave competing with Big Kelp illustrates, the alt-food-versus-technology-driven-Big-Food story continues to evolve. The challenge will continue to be how do we keep to our regenerative, equitable, and affordable ideals, while scaling up in a way that makes a difference? All of the tools that Food Tech has at its disposal (from artificial intelligence and big data to robotics and nanotechnology) can be deployed in service of alt food, and will have to be as climate change advances and more of the world becomes unfarmable and uninhabitable. The language we adopt does not have to be that of war and battle, however, but of continuing to strive for a meeting in the middle: change that benefits the most people, for a democratic rather than oligarchic food system.

WHERE DO WE GO FROM HERE? RATANA CHUENPAGDEE SHOWS THE WAY

EARLIER IN THIS CHAPTER, I noted the growing recognition of the value of traditional indigenous ways of ecosystem management in the face of encroaching climate change and an industrial food system that accepts habitat destruction as the cost of doing business. Indigenous people manage only about a quarter of the world's land, yet that land supports about 80 percent of global diversity[16]; they have been stewarding the land responsibly for millennia. They are holders of deep, practical wisdom and expertise.

Yet calls to listen to those voices constantly bump up against the opposing forces of extractive, business-as-usual practices: not just in the realms of agriculture and large-scale ocean harvesting, but in oil and gas extraction, mining, logging, and the harvesting of other natural resources.

In the Pacific Northwest, we need to listen to the highly specific, place-based information safeguarded in tribal lore, and begin to think about salmon not as a commodity, but as a way to enter into a relationship of mutuality, helping each other survive in a way that benefits fish, ocean ecosystem, and humans.

One person who has thought a lot about the power of indigenous knowledge and the ecosystem of global small-scale fishing communities is Ratana Chuenpagdee, a Thai professor in the geography department at Memorial University in St. John's Newfoundland. She brings together expertise in governance, marine science, and sustainability to weave together an integrated vision of coastal fisheries management that considers the culture of small-scale fisheries—family history, indigenous knowledge, community, emotional connection to the sea—as well as large-scale commercial fisheries that tend to control governance of the oceans and fisheries.

"We know that the majority of our fishers are small-scale, maybe not in terms of total catch, but in terms of the people involved," she says. In part to collect the large amount of data on small-scale fisheries that her field needs to make its voice heard, and in part to start a grassroots network, in 2012 she helped found a movement called "Too Big to Ignore," which involves grant-funded research and a partnership with the Food and Agricultural Organization (FAO). Too Big to Ignore connects with national, regional, and local food organizations and researchers and includes eight hundred members in fifty countries. Frequent meetings generate discussions and findings on topics ranging from gender equity in the fisheries to a set of small-scale fishery guidelines.

Another concept, "Blue Justice," emerged as a defense against the potential displacement and marginalization of small-scale fisheries as governments tout the coming "Blue Economy," an idea developed by the World Bank that promotes "sustainable" fisheries, maritime transport, wind energy, and gas and mineral extraction. "In the Blue Economy, there's not going to be a lot of space for small-scale fisheries. We needed to come up with a way to bring some sense into the conversation," says Chuenpagdee. "Blue Justice is about recognizing that some of these sustainable development goals could actually hurt the people who really need to be protected."

In Newfoundland and Labrador, Chuenpagdee is leading on-the-ground dialogue to process some of the difficult emotions that linger following the 1993 collapse of its cod fishery. Efforts to engage young people, particularly women, in the industry and to change local regulations have been successful. One example is Chuenpagdee's former student Lillian Saul, who, along with her business partner Nova Almine, has launched Roots and Wings Fish Co., an enterprise that promotes and markets the traditional dried fish of Newfoundland.

In 2015, in part because of a Blue Justice study on the subject, the province of Newfoundland and Labrador instituted a regulatory change allowing consumers and restaurants to purchase directly from fishers for the first time—a significant and unexpected victory that makes possible what Sonia Strobel is doing in British Columbia. "We have a regulatory framework that may not align with what people would like to see, but changes have been happening," says Chuenpagdee.

What she is doing for small-scale fishers is what I hope to see the growing alt food system do for small-scale indigenous, local, and regional seafood producers around the globe. Groups like Skipper Otto, Iliamna, and Thailand's Pla Organic have done this in their own realms, while GreenWave is demonstrating a low-impact, peaceable way to harvest the sea. As consumers, we can seek out our local CSF or similar low-impact direct trade seafood supplier and reject the takeover of the industry by exploitative private equity and distant foreign ownership. We can help the small fishers of the world once again make a living wage. We can apply Ratana Chuenpagdee's approach not just to the alt seafood system, but to every sector of the alt food system and show that, in the aggregate, these growing networks of local, transparent, and far more ethical food systems are "Too Big to Ignore."

BELIZE AND GUATEMALA: UNTANGLING AND SHORTENING THE CACAO AND COFFEE SUPPLY CHAINS

THWACK. THWACK. THWACK. CACAO PRODUCER Maria Cal, wearing a red ochre shirt the same color as the cacao pod she holds in her left hand, rhythmically hits it with a long, straight knife. Barely pausing the action of the knife, she deftly flips the pod lengthwise like a football to hack into the other side. She makes seven cuts in all, then separates the halves and moves on to the next. Not only is she practiced enough not to slice her hand open, she exerts just the right amount of pressure to allow her to pry the pod open into two neat pieces—without damaging the precious pulp-covered seeds inside. White and slippery, they look like rows of large insect larvae and give off an alluring floral and fruity scent. Their soft, smooth flesh tastes both sweet and brightly acidic, like a cross between mango and lychee.

The matriarch of a family of ten, Cal, dressed in baggy jeans and rubber slides over thick socks, oversees one thousand cacao trees here in San Antonio village, Southern Belize, while her husband works on another farm. She is one of four hundred fifty smallholder farmers in this region whose harvests are collected by the social enterprise Maya Mountain Cacao (MMC). Harvest days are long, beginning at 5 a.m. with a cup of coffee and a bicycle ride to her farm two miles away. Her lunch might consist of some *jipijapa* palm hearts wrapped in a tortilla. Today her son, Cecilio Cal Jr., and her father, Ramon Balaam, are helping Cal with the harvest and seeding of the pods. Six years of farming with MMC has given Maria a measure of stability—fair, up-front cash payments, and the confidence to begin replacing plantain trees on her farm with cacao seedlings. Properly cared for, they will take about four years to mature and begin bearing fruit.

As you know by now, I am all for supporting local and regional supply chains as fully as possible. But there are some things that enhance life that cannot, at least not yet, be grown locally. Most experts will tell you that "food miles"—the distance a product travels from its source to your mouth—are not the worst part of a long food supply chain; that dishonor belongs to lack of transparency and equity in worker treatment, environmental impact, and disparity of pay and profit along the chain. "Everyone agrees we've become overdependent on long supply chains, and there are a lot of reasons to buy local, but if you're doing it because of the reduced carbon footprint, it's probably not as true as you think," says Susan Bridle-Fitzpatrick, a food systems consultant who teaches sustainable food systems and global food and nutrition security at the University of Denver. "For example, chickpeas grown in Mexico are way more sustainable than beef from Fort Collins. It depends on what the food is, and how it's produced; those things are more important than the transportation miles."

For me, two nonnegotiable quality-of-life-enhancing imports are chocolate and coffee. And this holds true for many people, including the Ukrainian soldier on the front who brought his coffee grinder with him, or monthly bean-to-bar chocolate subscribers exploring the single-origin cacao flavors of the world. The small things that infuse our daily lives with outsized amounts of joy are worth pursuing, but pursuing in ways that support smallholders and regenerative, climate-friendly agricultural practices. As in the other categories of food and drink that I have covered, it takes stepping outside industrialized food chains to do this; Big Chocolate and Big Coffee are especially notorious for their extractive labor and agricultural practices. I want to see what an agroecological approach to growing cacao and coffee beans and more direct, equitable supply chains look like.

Which is how I find myself this humid February morning trundling down a road out of Punta Gorda, Belize, riding shotgun with Serapio Chun, cacao operations officer at MMC. The organization aggregates and ferments cacao from member farmers in the Toledo and Stann Creek districts, supplying small-batch, bean-to-bar chocolate makers around the world, including Dandelion Chocolate in San Francisco; Ritual Chocolate in Park City, Utah; and Dick Taylor Craft Chocolate in Eureka, California. MMC cacao—roasted, winnowed, ground, and tempered into bars by small artisan makers—has amassed dozens of awards globally; its beans were named among the top twenty in the world at the 2019 International Cocoa Awards.

Although a burst water main left my hotel with no running water, plenty of it showered down in the middle of the night, a torrential downpour that awakened me with its roar. In its aftermath, the roadside vegetation steams lightly in the morning sun. We pass traditional Mayan homes thatched with palm fronds as we head northwest, toward the Guatemala border.

Here, as I will later find in the Guatemalan highlands, the Mayan culture remains dominant. Most Belizeans I meet speak three languages: English, the language of their country's one-time colonizer (when it was known as British Honduras); Kriol, an Afro-European hybrid born of colonization and the slave trade; and one of three different Mayan dialects, primarily Q'eqchi' and Mopan, and less so Yucatec Maya.

Belize, about twice the size of Jamaica, is a bit player in the global co-coa industry (the terms "cacao" and "cocoa" mean the same thing but tend to reflect the culture of the speaker: "cacao" is the Spanish adaptation of the indigenous word *cacaua*, while "cocoa" seems to be a European adaptation); its 136 metric tons a year production (86 metric tons of that from MMC) is dwarfed by giant West African industrial producers such as the Côte d'Ivoire and Ghana (producing 2.2 million and 750,000 metric tons, respectively, in 2022). Cacao's contribution to the Belizean GDP is so small that it is not even recognized as an official export, to the chagrin of growers who would like to see more government support. I was drawn here because MMC is part of the Uncommon Cacao network, a specialty cacao trader representing more than ten thousand smallholder producers around the world and dedicated to radical transparency.

Half an hour later, we arrive at the Maya Mountain central fermen-tation center, where the nine-member crew is preparing to pick up the day's harvest from Maria Cal's farm and others, a ritual repeated every two weeks. Petrona Diane Coy, MMC's managing director, and Anna Chun, administrative associate, are also there to greet me. As each crew member stands up to introduce him or herself, I learn that most are from the nearby towns of San Pedro Columbia and San Antonio and have left jobs as mechanics, construction workers, or similar vocations. The south-ern Toledo district, of which Punta Gorda is the capital, has few jobs to offer; MMC provides a chance to work closer to home. Launched in 2010, MMC also provides farmers with stability and equitable treatment, where fickleness and dashed hopes have been the norm.

After the ritual snapping of group photos, I hop in the truck with Chun, Coy, and Chun (no relation; there are a handful of names that are ubiquitous in the region, and Chun is one of them) and head into the field. Knowing the topic of my book, Coy has arranged visits with Cal and another of the forty-eight women farmers in the MMC network. Although their number is growing, the woman-led cacao farm is still an anomaly in Belizean culture.

LISTEN, LEARN, DISRUPT:
PETRONA DIANE COY AND EMILY STONE

COY AND THE FOUNDER OF both MMC and Uncommon Cacao, Emily Stone, are powerful women who now anchor the two organizations. Coy grew up in the village of Big Falls in the Toledo District, trained as an accountant, then worked for a marine conservation nonprofit before joining MMC in 2020. She fought the objections of male teammates to her appointment and proved that she could both lead and shoulder the heavy physical demands of the job. "The mentality of the society here and especially in the Mayan culture is that the males do the agricultural work," she explains. "Men aren't used to seeing a woman leading an organization like this. So yes, there were some challenges." Stone hired Coy despite the objections and is glad that she did.

Stone came to Belize in 2010 as a twenty-five-year-old with a background in environmental organizing and shareholder advocacy. During an internship with the consumer advocacy organization Global Trade Watch, she learned how under the terms of the Central American Free Trade Agreement smallholder producers had to compete against subsidized American agribusinesses. She saw how some trade agreements allowed multinational corporations to sue governments if they felt their policies were unfair; one example is the Spanish tech firm that won $40 million from the Mexican government after the tech firm's construction of a hazardous waste facility was shut down because it threatened a UNESCO World Heritage site and surrounding Indigenous communities.

Although many such investor–state dispute settlements are ruled in favor of the state, costly judgments like this example can be harmful to a nation's public health and ecosystems. "I learned how international trade agreements could be a secret weapon that corporations use to maintain systems of oppression," says Stone. She wanted to figure out how international trade could instead put money directly into farmers' pockets and build community wealth.

At a meeting with Alex Whitmore and Kathleen Fulton, founders of Taza Chocolate and champions of ethically sourced premium cocoa, Stone learned about the combination of promising cacao forests and disgruntled small producers toiling under the thumb of Big Chocolate and its local enablers in Belize. The couple was interested in buying cacao from Belize but its quality needed to be elevated via a central fermentation facility. This was the opportunity to make change at the local level that Stone was searching for.

"When I got to Belize, I heard all kinds of stories about how pissed off farmers were with the existing (cacao) association, and the abuses of power in that organization," she recalls. Her community organizing background told her that she just needed to listen to what the farmers had to say, learn what challenges they faced, and then figure out how to build a better, more transparent supply chain.

She took buses and hitchhiked on the backs of motorbikes through the countryside, meeting growers at their homes and piecing together the area's post-colonial cacao history. From 1984 to 1985 the U.S. Agency for International Development (USAID), along with the Belize government and the Hershey corporation, funded an ill-fated development program using conventional agrochemical pesticides and fertilizers. Hershey pulled out in 1993 when the bottom fell out of the global cocoa market. The British company Green & Black's arrived in 1994, touting Fair Trade practices, an organic premium, and training for farmers in management and accounting. It was purchased by Cadbury Schweppes in 2005, which was in turn acquired by Kraft. Today it is owned by Mondelez, the result of Kraft splitting into two companies.

By the time she arrived in 2010, says Stone, "There were fifteen hundred families supposedly producing cacao, but the total export of the country was only two containers. It didn't make any sense." The tiny "Fair Trade" organization, TCGA, she adds, "was selling cacao to Mondelez for super-low prices. It was a system in total need of disruption." Farmers were so frustrated many talked about cutting down their cacao trees and planting something that might prove more profitable. Their farms might be located as far as an hour by foot from their homes, which meant long trips hauling wet cacao seeds home on their back to process. The work of fermenting and drying the beans typically fell on women, on top of their household and childcare responsibilities. They struggled to keep pigs, chickens, and bugs out of boxes filled with sticky wet pulp and gauged by touch when the beans were dry enough to sell.

Many of the cacao trees were rife with the dreaded Monilia (*Moniliophthora roreri*), a fungus that causes pod rot. Taking the dried beans to market could involve up to a two-hour round trip, and if the beans were in any way defective, they would be rejected then have to be hauled back home, where farmers would attempt to sell to neighbors for a much-reduced price. Most relied on "coyotes," or local middlemen, who came around the farms offering to buy the beans at low prices, often to smuggle over the border into Guatemala.

Stone saw, as Whitmore and Fulton had told her, that it made no sense for individual farmers to be doing the fermenting and drying and selling their beans for such a low price. Farmers thought fermenting and drying cacao themselves would add value to their product, but this notion was misguided; most do not have the kind of education, resources, and remuneration scheme that would allow them to. In fact, selling wet cacao could bring them the same or higher prices, and save them the work of processing. Stone also knew that as a young White woman who had never been to Belize before, her words held little currency among farmers there: "They had had multiple experiences with gringos who promised the moon for spices or cacao crops, then disappeared after two years."

At that point Stone made a commitment to herself to "never promise what I couldn't deliver, and to be as transparent as possible." She made a crucial ally in a farmer named Gabriel Pop. Nearly the same age as her, he was one of a family of fifteen children. One day, he overheard Stone speaking to his family about her idea of selling wet cacao, and pulled her aside to tell her that he, too, thought this was the way to go, but that she would never gain the trust of the Mayan-speaking farmers without communicating to them in their language. He became integral to the formation of Maya Mountain Cacao.

Stone and Pop began buying cacao in January 2011 and figuring out how to centralize fermentation and drying. Stone had seen how cacao-producing community associations had formed in Guatemala after the civil war ended in 1996, creating centralized fermentation facilities. In Belize, the problem was finding the money to establish such a fermentation center, which could aggregate the production of smallholders and strengthen the local economy. Taza founders Whitmore and Fulton, along with an American entrepreneur in Belize named Jeff Pzena, put up the money for the fermentation center; several months later, Stone herself invested, becoming an equal partner.

In their first year, they exported a partial container, between four-and-a-half and five-and-a-half metric tons of beans. What Stone thought would be a one-year process of getting Maya Mountain up and running would clearly require more time. "I felt so committed, and I just didn't want to let anyone down; the farmers were really betting on this to work," she says.

After a year, she briefly returned to Boston, where she had been living, broke up with her boyfriend, and stayed in Belize for a total of four years. By 2013, MMC had built a social enterprise company working with smallholder farmers, its staff carrying out high-quality cacao fermentation in a centralized facility. In addition to supplying Taza, Raka, Dandelion, and Dick Taylor, MMC found itself with a waiting list of thirty companies who wanted in on their product. Sadly, Gabriel, who became field director, was diagnosed with cancer and passed away in 2019.

Today, MMC is staffed entirely by Belizeans, with Coy at the helm. Stone, meanwhile, began adding depth and reach to the more direct and transparent supply chain she was building. In 2016 she acquired a specialty cacao brokerage that had been operating under Taza, allowing it to connect directly to smallholders and source cocoa for many more bean-to-bar makers. Taking over and growing this segment of the business, which she named Uncommon Cacao, was a way to de-commoditize the cacao industry on a larger, albeit still small, scale. Uncommon Cacao serves as both MMC's export broker and parent company. Today, the brokerage works in fifteen different countries with nearly ten thousand producers, approximately a third of whom are women. In 2021 it opened its European office.

MAKING RADICAL TRANSPARENCY WORK

CREATING THE EQUITABLE AND TRANSPARENT short supply chain that is Uncommon Cacao's goal requires grafting the same kind of vertical integration and single-minded efficiency that global commodity supply chains have perfected, but onto a financial structure based on equity and inclusion. Just how tall this order is becomes clear when you look at what Big Chocolate—which includes international brokers, national governments, local traders, and yes, many local cooperatives—pays the five to six million smallholders that produce more than 90 percent of global cacao harvests: poverty-level wages.

MMC pays its farmers $4.77 US dollars per dried kilograms, roughly double what non-MMC local cacao farmers would get from a commodity buyer. This is significantly more than what a Côte d'Ivoire farmer would earn, although it is difficult—especially in times of extreme price volatility (more about that later)—to directly compare the two very different systems. For a premium of this size, MMC needs to deliver a product that is worth every extra penny.

Hence its near-fanatical focus on quality control and transparency at every stage—from land use, agroecological growing practices, pruning, disease prevention, careful off-season tree maintenance, and each step of the fermentation process. Poor technique can ruin a sack of cocoa beans. The fragrant, fermented, dried beans must wow buyers when they perform the final "cut test," the slicing of fifty beans in half lengthwise for inspection and grading. Dandelion Chocolate's cocoa sourcing and quality manager Ron Sweetser says that of all the producers in seventeen different countries his company sources from, MMC keeps the most meticulous records.

It is not until I am back in the United States, though, that I track down bars made with Maya Mountain cacao from Dandelion Chocolate and Dick Taylor Craft Chocolate. Both exhibit the cocoa-centric, fruity- and floral-packed essence that Sweetser described to me, and a distinctly mouth-watering strawberry drop note. After Dandelion found success by adding local nutmeg during the fermentation process in a bar collaboration with its Indian partner, the company looked for other spice-enhanced fermentation opportunities. Since all of its products contain only two ingredients, cacao beans and sugar, to enable comparisons of terroir and cacao genetics, the spice is added at the fermentation stage.

Coy informed Sweetser that the combination of allspice and black pepper in cocoa beverages was a traditional Mayan drink that new mothers took to enhance lactation. Dandelion liked the added fresh allspice berries and black peppercorns in the fermentation so much it became part of a trio of spiced bars, along with its nutmeg bar from India and a cinnamon-inflected bar from Tanzania. (Purists may quibble that the addition of spice and other flavors mask terroir and genetics, but chocolate barsmiths, chocolatiers, and chefs will always want to experiment with and enhance the ingredient they are showcasing.)

In addition to alluring flavor and spice combinations, chocolate makers are searching for superior genetics, which has become a selling point for MMC. In 2015 its Belize cocoa was designated an heirloom by HCP (Heirloom Cacao Preservation, a public-private partnership of the USDA and the Fine Chocolate Industry Association), one of seventeen cacao farms in the world so selected, mainly for their product's superior flavor. The designation was created in response to the threats of environmental change and deforestation to the world's supply of high-quality cacao, as well as economic pressures the commodity cocoa market exerts on smallholder farmers. Without a concerted effort to prioritize flavor and preserve genetic diversity, the world's most genetically important cacao groves could very well be abandoned as growers seek higher pay elsewhere. HCP's project is a proactive effort to protect genotypes and varieties that ancient civilizations have safeguarded for centuries.

Radical transparency, more equitable wages for workers, increased genetic diversity, and more delicious chocolate sounds like a win-win, and in some ways it is. But it is important to note that for the farmer, all of this comes with inherent, serious risks, which as we will see in Belize's own cacao-growing history, have burned them in the past. The commitment to quality that MMC and the entire high-quality cacao and coffee worlds hold—more care in tending their forests, in pruning and weeding, more careful harvesting, etc.—raises costs to farmers considerably. If a buyer like MMC disappears, farmers who have made investments in these farming practices may or may not have alternative markets.

LUNCH BREAK: CALDO, TORTILLAS, COCO, AND CACAO

AFTER OUR VISIT WITH CACAO-TENDER Maria Cal, we walk down the hillside with her to meet the MMC pickup truck. Two crew members hook one of her sacks full of wet cacao seeds to a portable scale, which is attached to a long pole they place on one shoulder, each facing the other; another crew member notes the particulars of date, time, farmer, and weight, then hands Cal a receipt to sign and her cash payment.

A short drive away, passing chickens, a horse, dogs, and cats along the roadside, we pull into the front yard of Luciana Chun, Anna's aunt. The traditional Q'eqchi' Mayan palm-thatched home, which Luciana operates as a guesthouse, includes an adjoining patio area outfitted with a wooden xylophone-like Mayan marimba for musical gatherings. Inside the two-room kitchen, Luciana and several relatives are seated around a tall, cylindrical mountain of *masa*, from which they pinch balls of dough that they pat into tortillas to be cooked on the large flat-back *comal*, or griddle. There is chatter and laughter as Luciana's two-year-old granddaughter Jazlyn Chun assists; later she will insist she be paid for her services. The women have prepared a traditional Mayan lunch of *caldo*, a chicken soup made with the green, cilantro-like herb *culantro*, lots of orange annatto pepper, oregano, and garlic. On the side are boiled *coco*, the taro root that tastes almost exactly like the Japanese version that I know and love as *satoimo*. The agricultural product that has united us today commands a central place in the meal: a large, enameled pot filled with a delicious drink of warm ground liquid cacao, which sits next to a huge, cloth-lined pink bowl full of fresh tortillas. It is an everyday feast of a meal.

Sipping cacao predates even the Mayan culture, going back more than three thousand years[1] to the Olmec civilization of Mesoamerica and even earlier—as far back as five thousand years ago,[2] to Ecuador, Colombia, Peru. In both Olmec and Mayan civilizations, cacao played a central role in sacred ritual ceremonies, for medicinal use, and at all levels of society. Mayan families in Belize still grow, roast, and grind their own cacao on stone *metates* just as Chun has done for us today.

After lunch, we return to the MMC fermentation facility, where Serapio Chun explains the seven-day fermentation process, from the placement of the wet pulp into neatly lined up wooden boxes in a space sheltered from wind and direct sun. The boxes are an inch-and-a-half thick to ensure the ideal heat and humidity levels that will allow native yeast and microbes to complete fermentation, and will reach a maximum temperature of between 116 and 120 degrees Fahrenheit. Every two days the fermenting beans are mixed and rotated into new identical containers. At each step of the way, careful records are kept of date of harvest, farm, batch, and fermentation result. If somewhere along the supply chain flaws are detected, or if a batch is deemed especially good, Chun will be able to look back on these records and query or praise the farmer who was responsible for the result.

The wet smell of tropical lychee gives way to the alcoholic, vinegary funk of fermentation in progress (remarkably like chocolate-scented tanks of fermenting sake). When fermentation is completed, the beans will be dried, sorted, and blended before export.

FAIR TRADE: HOW FAIR AND FOR WHOM?

SHIPPED FROM ITS FERMENTATION FACILITY, MMC's beans will end up at one of Uncommon Cacao's three warehouses, two in the United States and one in the Netherlands. It pays farmers between 41 and 162 percent over commodity prices and claims to be the only international cocoa trader that publishes what it pays its producers as well as data on all transactions along the supply chain. "Transparency is the critical foundation for any claims for ethical sourcing in a de-commoditized environment," Stone tells me. "We want to provide farmers an opportunity to be entrepreneurs, to make stronger and more stable market connections."

To understand what it means to "de-commoditize" an agricultural product like cacao, it helps to look back in time to its development as an international commodity. Uniform, standardized quality, buying and selling in bulk, sales based on price and availability, and downward price pressure are the hallmarks of a commoditized product. Though cacao was stockpiled and used as currency by the Aztecs before the arrival of Hernán Cortés,[3] it was the establishment of the Spanish cacao plantation system in the seventeenth century and the bulk buying and selling of it that made it comparable to other agricultural commodities such as sugar, coffee, and tea. What began as luxury spoils of colonialism for the wealthy was transformed by plantation labor into massive influxes of cheap, low-quality versions of those products, whether in England, France, or the Netherlands. These markets brought a measure of addictive comfort to the working class of the industrial era and created miserable conditions for the peasant farmers who tended and harvested them. In the twentieth century, cocoa production and chocolate consumption exploded even further with the emergence of West Africa as the center for cheap, extractive cacao.[4]

De-commoditizing cacao means differentiating it in some way, usually in higher quality, so that it commands a higher price than its commodity equivalent. What Stone and other believers in direct trade, alternative trade, or fair trade do is unbundle their product from the commodity market by paying an above-market price to producers who meet certain agricultural, environmental, labor, and production standards.

Yet Stone is one of a number of direct trade advocates I meet who are disillusioned with Fair Trade–certified cacao and coffee products, asserting that both in claims of equity and quality, they are not upholding their promises. Most consumers assume that a World Fair Trade Organization (WFTO) or Fairtrade certification label on a product means that producers are getting paid well, far more than the commodity price. But that's not always true. Fairtrade International sets a premium that buyers have to pay above the commodity price. For organic cacao beans from Belize, that is a mere $240 per metric ton, and the Fairtrade minimum price for organic cacao beans is $2,700 per metric ton, about a 9 percent premium. However, as I revise this chapter in early 2025, a period of market volatility has seen the price of cocoa shoot up from a relatively steady level in the $3,000 range to as high as $12,000 per ton, now hovering at more than $11,500 per metric ton. The Fairtrade minimum—which was never enough to bring prosperity to farming communities—would now be less than a quarter of market price. Consumers' assumptions that they are getting top quality when buying Fairtrade, often not true in the past, is now even less true. Instead, says Stone, "producers are selling the lowest grade because they're getting a floor price."

Fairtrade premiums do not put money directly into the farmer's pocket, either; instead, they are placed in a separate bank account for a community development fund. At the end of the year, producers are supposed to vote on which projects to fund, such as technical improvements, facility upgrades, or education, healthcare, and gender-equal leadership opportunities. But what Stone saw in Belize was quite different: managers driving expensive trucks, or money going to a select few families with political connection to the leader. "There can be a lot of favoritism, and not a lot of transparency," she adds. In Belize, where families have to pay out of pocket for their children's education after the elementary school level, MMC's direct above-market, cash payments help them cover such expenses.

Jonathan Rosenthal of the Equal Exchange cooperative (see Chapter 3) agrees that much of the fair trade market has become a parallel commodity market, but adds that executed well, this model does what many direct trade organizations do not do: build power. "Fair trade supports the creation of farmer co-ops, secondary and tertiary co-ops, and national, regional and global networks," allowing them to understand the international marketplace and build power, both locally and globally." He wants to see the transparency of MMC but also ownership by the farmers themselves. These are the elements that can create long-term change and free farmers from short-term focus on prices and dependence on local and regional buyers.

CURRENT WOES AND AN UNCERTAIN FUTURE

THE GLOBAL COMMODITY CACAO INDUSTRY, which MMC and other specialty growers are trying to set themselves apart from, is controlled by a few mega-corporations and centered on the commodity futures markets in New York and London. Prices are driven by supply and demand, but as climate change, disease, rampant deforestation, and the incursion of illegal mining threaten productivity in Ghana and the Côte d'Ivoire, wildly oscillating markets and panic trading have ensued, opening the door to speculation by hedge funds and other market players, further distorting prices.

More than 80 percent of Côte d'Ivoire's forests were destroyed between 1960 and 2010, with unsustainable cacao production considered to be the top driver of this loss.[5] Meanwhile, most peasant cacao farmers, especially in Ghana, where a government agency sets national prices for their crop, still live near or below the poverty line. In both West African countries, farmers are so demoralized that they are abandoning their farms, sometimes to enter the more lucrative (and highly environmentally destructive) illegal mining industry.

As with other commodity supply chains, a handful of corporations are the biggest cacao and coffee buyers, factory farm owners, and processors, combining commodities for those products into ever-morphing farragoes of ultra-processed foods that line supermarket shelves. Cargill is the leading cacao buyer and exporter, sourcing from thousands of smallholder producers through intermediaries, providing them with seeds and agronomic advice (although apparently no good solutions when chemical fertilizer prices soared, putting more pressure on already stressed smallholder farmers). It has its own processing facility in San Pedro, Côte d'Ivoire, and can easily funnel products into its five chocolate subsidiary companies, and the five thousand different brands[6] under its umbrella. Like the ABCD traders of the commodity grain system (see Chapter 2), it is a giant player that is invisible to the average consumer and shares its global platform with a handful of corporate cacao brethren: Nestlé, Mars, Lindt & Sprùngli, and Mondelez.

At the origin of the supply chain is the peasant farmer, mired in an invisible, murky world of extreme poverty, labor abuses (including widespread child labor), and indentured servitude. Nearly three-quarters of smallholder cacao farmers in Ghana and the Ivory Coast do not earn a living income, meaning that more than a million cacao farmers cannot afford their basic daily needs. They earn on average $1.42 and $1.23 per day, respectively, compared to the living income benchmark of $2.08 and $2.55 per day.[7]

Yet Big Chocolate, along with Big Coffee, Big Sugar, and Big everything else—are only part of a much larger, multifaceted problem: the global, economic, and moral system of racial capitalism[8] (the mutually reinforcing practices of racialized exploitation and capital accumulation). In cacao (and perhaps typical for all commodity supply chains) corruption up and down the supply chain, from labor abuses and inspectors on the take to governments and marketers stretching the truth about the protections and standards they are upholding, contribute to the flawed system. And we, the consumers, who want to satisfy our chocolate cravings at the lowest possible prices, are unwitting accomplices.

All of these factors have fueled a relentless drive for higher yields and further deforestation in West Africa and the Congo and Amazon basins, which in turn exacerbates the impact of drought. Rainforests in Indonesia have come under increasing pressure by cocoa farming interests as well.[9]

The greed, hubris, and disregard for nature that precipitated the panic reminds me of the systematic destruction of one hundred million acres of American prairie grasslands in the late-nineteenth and early twentieth centuries, driven by the manic planting of dry land wheat as farmers, urged on by federal policy, chased record-high yields and ensuing riches. Both in the Dust Bowl of the 1930s, which drove four hundred thousand starving people off the Great Plains, and in today's ravaged rain forests, it's hard not to see the disasters as a form of divine retribution for crimes against nature, when they are in fact the predictable outcome of destructive, extractive growing practices.

The same pressures that affect commodity prices—especially lower production caused by climate change—threaten the specialty cacao market as well, says Stone. Scarcity in West Africa has led the biggest buyers to scour the globe for product and offer such high prices that traders are struggling to retain producer loyalty. And because they are not picky about quality for cacao that will be made into supermarket candy bars, producers may be tempted to quit the labor-intensive practices required to sell to specialty traders.

Bean-to-bar makers, meanwhile, worry about how much of a price increase their customers will bear. As David Laborde, director of the UN Food and Agriculture Organization, wishfully noted, instead of wealthy developed nations gobbling up sugar-laden commodity chocolate bars that exploit mainly West African and Indonesian smallholder farmers, it would be far better if they consumed less chocolate, but paid more for fairer, higher-quality products; that would direct more money to underpaid farmers.[10] My next visit is with a woman who is making just such products, and is an example of the kind of artistry and innovation that can be found at the value-added end of the alt food supply chain.

VISITING A CACAO SAVANT
ON FLORIDA'S TREASURE COAST

ONE OF TODAY'S MOST HIGHLY decorated bean hunters and chocolate makers—who sources a portion of her raw material from Uncommon Cacao—is Denise Castronovo, founder of Castronovo Chocolate in Stuart, Florida. A gifted chocolate maker who started experimenting with mail order cacao beans in 2011, by 2014 she was collecting international awards. She is not a maker who relies on sensors, high-tech devices, and formulas to dial in her bars; her intuitive approach relies on taste memory, tweaking, and careful note-taking—one reason that she has no interest in automating or super-sizing her production.

The wave of rich, pure chocolate aroma that hits me when I open the door to Castronovo's small storefront and production workshop makes me want to jump into one of her two-hundred-pound stone grinders to be one with the shining, silken cocoa turning within. The word "swoon" was probably first uttered, possibly onomatopoetically, for moments like these.

My visit to her shop comes as Castronovo is testing out a new batch of Puerto Rican–sourced chocolate, her most expensive to date because of its location and the cost of labor in the US territory, as well as its rarity. In a twenty-five-kilo test grinder, dark, broad ribbons of Puerto Rican cocoa have been rotating for three days. Next to that, Castronovo is tempering a batch of Colombian Arhuaco cocoa—a heating and cooling process that stabilizes the crystal structure of the mixture, giving it a shiny finish and when cooled, a satisfying snap. She sticks a spoon into the stream of chocolate pouring from the spout of a Gami Diva25 tempering machine to offer me a taste: at once light yet filled with tropical fruit aromas, nutty, and silk-textured, and I feel the pleasure centers of my brain lighting up in matching tropical colors.

Castronovo's chocolate-making process starts with a twenty-to-thirty-minute oven roasting of the fermented, dried whole beans. After they are cooled, they are placed in a noisy winnowing machine that separates the shell from the nibs. From there the nibs will go through a pre-grind in a peanut grinder before being ground in the two-hundred-pound machines, tempered, then poured into molds or made into truffles or other products.

Castronovo credits a childhood spent playing in the forests of then-rural Walpole, Massachusetts, and her teenaged fascination with the Amazon for leading her to environmental studies in college. A stint in the world of geographic information systems mapping followed, and—to feed her love of craft—studies with a Japanese ceramic artist. An interest in so-called superfoods that are dense in nutrients and antioxidants led her to the burgeoning bean-to-bar movement in 2010, and her life's work. That she has played a role in extending and strengthening the alt chocolate supply chain is an unintended but welcome outcome to her.

Castronovo's first home experiments drew on the content-rich website Chocolate Alchemy, founded by a cocoa-evangelist named John Nanci, who has been called "the godfather of kitchen-counter chocolatiering." She was struck by the distinct flavor profiles of beans from the Dominican Republic, and then Bolivia. The latter, she recalls, "had all kinds of cherry notes and was almost like port, it was incredible!" But her real breakthroughs came after opening her storefront in July 2013. Until then she had only made single origin dark chocolate, a form that can explore one region's wide expression of flavors. She was curious about how the addition of milk—without the copious amounts of sugar that usually characterize milk chocolate—would affect the flavors of the high-quality beans she sourced. While commodity milk chocolate usually lists sugar as its first ingredient, Castronovo's are 60 percent chocolate, with a much lower ratio of organic cane sugar. The results were stunning. "I still got the fruitiness, but I also got these beautiful caramel and nutty flavor notes. They were rounded out, more delicate," she recalls.

The second thing that happened was that she met a Colombian woman who worked at one of the shops near hers. Castronovo had stumbled across a bare-bones one-page website advertising beans from Colombia, which noted that there were five different cacao-producing regions in the country. She reasoned that a country so close to Venezuela, known for fine cacao products, must hold promise. Recently an eleventh genetic group of cacao from Colombia, Caquetá, was added to the previously known ten,[11] but no one knew of it back then. On a trip back to Colombia, Castronovo's acquaintance managed to source some beans from the company, Cacao de Colombia. The chocolate bar that resulted, Sierra Nevada Colombia Dark Milk 63 percent chocolate, won her an Americas Bronze medal and World Silver in 2014 from the International Chocolate Awards, the first in a long string of awards.

Castronovo continues to search for indigenous cacao from the rainforest, both to further her exploration and expression of single-origin beans, and as a way to fight deforestation and support the small communities she works with. She has been embraced by the Arhuaco people of the Sierra Nevada in Santa Marta, Colombia, whose transporting chocolate I have just tasted. Spiritual leaders of the Arhuaco, known as *mamos*, are the keepers of ancient ecological wisdom and the belief that the Sierra Nevada is a living being, and its base the seat of human consciousness.

After decades of armed conflict affecting the lower portions of the Sierra Nevada, the tribe has begun to regain some of its spiritual sites. During the COVID-19 pandemic, which they predicted decades before its arrival,[12] the tribe turned inward to focus on rites centered on healing the earth. In September 2020, Castronovo received a WhatsApp message from a mamo. He was at the top of the Sierra Nevada, he told her, reaching out to global friends of the Arhuaco during a spiritual rite to restore balance to the earth. She began crying with gratitude. Since then, Castronovo has been invited back and has helped raise funds to purchase a chocolate stone grinder and tempering machine for the community to support its local chocolate-making activities.

ETHOS ROASTERS AND CO-OP LA ASUNCIÓN:
DISRUPTING THE COFFEE SUPPLY CHAIN

ON A SUNNY LATE SATURDAY morning in mid-February, I find myself with a plastic basket strapped to my waist, my feet crunching on dried leaves as I trudge through a sun-dappled coffee farm in the Guatemalan highlands. Alongside me are three generations of Mayan female farmers, members of La Cooperativa La Asunción, which comprises thirty smallholder families, mostly from the village of Satiquacaj in the municipality of San José Poaquil. The starting point of a direct-trade supply chain that ends in central Florida with coffee-roasting entrepreneur Lisbeth Pacheco, this is a micro version of the kind of unglamorous, yet people- and planet-aligned alt food system that is the beating heart of this book.

My harvesting companions today are Octaviana Tubac and Noehmi Curruchich Quille, who has brought along her eight-year-old daughter Roció, along with Gerson Morales, a founder of and technical adviser to the co-op and an agriculture official with USAID in Guatemala City. They are lightning-quick compared to me, using one hand to pull red fruit–laden branches closer to them while the fingers of their other hand nimbly dance across the fruit clusters, picking coffee cherries off a branch from back to front while leaving still-unripe green cherries unbothered.

Dressed in a traditional embroidered *huipil* blouse, her face weathered under a floppy yellow hat, Tuvac, seventy-eight, tells me (in the Guatemalan Mayan Kaqchiquel language, which Morales translates) that fifty years ago, before coffee became one of the main agricultural products of the village, her brother-in-law brought her a sack of good-quality beans; she has cultivated them ever since on small parcels sprinkled across the village. For all we know that sack could have been the first Red Bourbon coffee beans brought to the region, the fruity, full-bodied variety that La

Cooperativa La Asunción is known for. Tuvac has endured the passing of two of her ten children and, just a few weeks earlier, her husband, but says she feels healthy and proud to still be able to pick coffee.

After the cherries are harvested, they are taken to the nearby mill and processing facility, which is owned by Nohemi's husband, José. There, the cherries are put through the hopper of a machine that washes them vigorously, then shakes them as they move slowly along a conveyor belt so that the skins separate from the seeds, which we know as coffee beans. A thirty-six-hour fermentation follows, after which the beige-colored beans will be spread out on large concrete beds to dry in the sun. We take turns walking across the bed with a wooden rake-like mixer to turn the beans, leaving a striped pattern that resembles raked Zen rock gardens.

While not certified organic, the co-op practices regenerative agrofor-estry techniques such as interplanting leguminous Chalum trees (a source of soil and plant nitrogen), and grevillea and banana trees for shade (their dead leaves also provide soil organic matter). Interplanting beans in the early stages of forest growth when the canopy is not too thick provides food for members. The coffee cherry skins and the pulp byproduct of the milling process are added to the fields as another layer of organic matter. These practices build habitat for animals, insects, and birds, enhance bio-diversity, and increase soil water retention.

Although they do not eschew them, La Asunción members try to min-imize the use of chemical fertilizers and pesticides, both to protect the land and ecosystem, and to save money as their costs continue to rise along with that of oil and natural gas—a consequence of supply chains disrupted by war and climate instability. In addition to being more cli-mate friendly and equitable, the creation of shorter, more direct supply chains is a matter of national security for Guatemala.

Like everywhere else I visited, climate change is upsetting the normal order of things. Yet in the Guatemala highlands, it is only one of the many causes of the deforestation that threatens coffee harvests; the others include creeping urbanization, and farther north the ravages of palm oil production (lately brought into check by more stringent regulations), cattle ranching, and narco-trafficking. The latter is often accompanied by slashing of the rain forest to start income-generating cattle ranches, or to build air strips for illegal transport of drugs.

Both climate change and deforestation are exacerbating the water shortages that are becoming increasingly acute. The cooperative built a reservoir to catch rainwater during the rainy season, which will be used to water the trees during the dry season, or for processing in the wet mill. Labor shortages, too, especially during harvest time, loom larger and larger.

Coffee trees in this part of Guatemala begin flowering with the first rains in May or early June and take from seven to eight months to mature. Harvest begins in January. On this mid-February visit, some cherries are already withering on the trees for lack of water, and Morales knows that by November, underground wells will run dry. He hopes that the newly elected Bernardo Arevalo government will follow through on its progressive promises to support smallholder farmers and develop reliable irrigation systems.

Early that morning, Morales had given me a ride from Guatemala City to his home village Satiquacaj in the larger San José Poaquil region, after which La Asunción's coffee is named. Following a two-hour ascent past two of the four visible volcanoes from Guatemala City, Volcán de Acatenango and Volcán de Fuego—there are thirty-seven volcanoes throughout the country—and into the tree-covered highlands, we arrived at the home of his mother and the family compound where five of his six siblings live. Morales's mother, Francisca Cutzal, smiling and dressed in a brilliantly colored woven huipil and skirt, welcomed me with a hot fava bean beverage, flavored with cinnamon and sugar, toasty and a little reminiscent of Ovaltine. A plate of scrambled eggs, fried plantains, beans, and homemade tortillas followed, then a cappuccino from Cutzal's café-bakery next door.

Afterward, we walked along the main street of Satiquacaj, teeming with Saturday market vendors and loud, brightly painted buses that travel back and forth to Guatemala City. During the Guatemalan Civil War, which spanned the better part of four decades, more than two hundred thousand mostly Indigenous people, sometimes entire villages, were massacred under a series of military dictatorships, tragedies that followed centuries of colonial oppression and dehumanization.[13] Many villagers were killed in skirmishes between the military and guerillas. Morales's father and uncles were targeted, and his grandmother Asunción (for whom the cooperative is named) was assaulted. But today, I see signs of new construction and bustling activity all around me, and no traces of those violent, fearful times. Morales tells me that the current prosperity is a recent phenomenon, one fueled almost entirely by remittances sent home from family members who migrated mostly to the United States and some to Canada.

At one small table filled with butchered whole chickens and cuts of pork and beef, we find Thelma Morales, Gerson's cousin, and the past president of the La Asunción cooperative. Like him, she is a second-generation coffee farmer, and for six years served as the president of the co-op. The most challenging aspect of her tenure, she tells me, was navigating the legal permitting around direct exportation. I had heard from other Guatemalans about the country's famously infuriating bureaucracy; in the co-op those hurdles were exacerbated by the fact that for some shadowy reason, properties in this region were never officially registered. To become a member of the co-op, farms had to legally register, but many potential members feared that going on the books would somehow lead to the loss of their land.

As in Belize, the dominance of the Mayan patriarchy is visible in this 98 percent indigenous municipality, where leaders like Thelma have had to transcend their traditionally gendered roles to embrace leadership. Lisbeth Pacheco, the roaster who imports La Asunción's coffee and a fellow Guatemalan, recalls that though co-op members were hesitant to elect a woman president; she lent her persuasive powers, believing that Thelma was best suited for the job. As the co-op's biggest independent buyer, her voice mattered. The funds that Thelma and Nohemi Curruchich Quille, my coffee-picking companion, procured include 12,000 Quetzales (about $1,500 US) in microloans to women members of the co-op to invest in coffee plots and start small textile businesses. Thelma also applied for and received a small Food Producer Network grant from humanitarian chef Jose Andres's World Central Kitchen to start a small pig farm, whose nose-to-tail products we see on Thelma's table. Despite growing its membership from twenty to thirty farmers and tripling production since it began selling to Ethos, Pacheco's company, La Asunción members still must put together a patchwork of incomes and revenue streams like these to survive and build resilience into their livelihoods.

HATCHING THE ETHOS IDEA IN MASSACHUSETTS

TWO MONTHS AFTER MY VISIT to Guatemala, I travel south to Lakeland, Florida, to meet the woman at the other end of the Cooperativa La Asunción/Poaquil supply chain, Pacheco. I was drawn to her business by its impact-driven sourcing from smallholders in Central and South America, and I knew that she had gone from being a food scientist working for some of the biggest Big Food companies to running her scrappy, direct-to-consumer coffee roasting business—step one in de-commoditizing the coffee supply chain. I needed to find out how this transformation came about.

Lakeland is a graceful town in central Florida between Tampa and Orlando that is indeed dotted with lakes and wetlands, as well as swans and swan imagery, the latter a reference to the descendants of the original pair gifted to the city in 1957 by Queen Elizabeth. First European contact happened here much earlier, however. When Spaniard Juan Ponce de León arrived on what is now the Florida coast in 1513, he was so smitten by the beauty of the land he called it "La Florida," "the place of flowers." Native tribes then farming the rich soil and harvesting edible catch from the waters of Central Florida included the Tocobago, Timucua, and Caloosa.[14] Within two hundred years they were eradicated by wars, slave trade, and disease;[15] it took another one hundred years for their successors, the Seminoles, to be driven west to US government designated "Indian Territory" in Oklahoma.

Today Pacheco and her husband, Jolian Rios, natives of former Spanish colonies Guatemala and Colombia, respectively, have settled in a former North American *colonia* to help create a new kind of supply chain. Instead of siphoning off the natural resource riches of the developing world and keeping producers in poverty for the sake of profit, they are putting more money in the hands of smallholder farmers.

In the fourteen-hundred-square-foot roastery that she and Rios built in 2017 and stocked with state-of-the-art roasting machines made in Israel, England, and the United States, Pacheco, a slight, curly-haired woman dressed in jeans and an Ethos baseball cap, brews us a Poaquil Chemex pour-over, filling a mug bearing a photo of her with my coffee-picking companion Nohemi Curruchich Quille. She seats us so that we can both gaze out the window at serene Lake Beulah directly across the street.

Born and raised in Guatemala City, Pacheco's dream was to eventually make her way to the United States. Although both her parents are medical doctors, salaries in her impoverished country did not provide them anything near a send-your-child-abroad income. By chance, late in her senior year of high school, a recruiter from the Zamorano Pan-American Agricultural School in Honduras,[16] a selective private university that accepts students from across Latin America, came to visit her school. She applied for a scholarship and emerged with the top score among all entrants from Guatemala. Though she was not interested in agriculture, she was fascinated by food.

At Zamorano, Pacheco earned a degree in agro-industrial engineering, the equivalent of food chemistry. It was in Massachusetts, after earning a PhD in food chemistry in Texas and while enrolled in an MBA program at the University of Massachusetts at Amherst, that Pacheco reconnected with Gerson Morales, her former schoolmate at Zamorano in Honduras, who happened to be studying for his MBA at Brandeis University. Pacheco had been trying to come up with a business she could start that would make an impact. It would be a food business, because she was fascinated by the topic and her scientific background was in food. Business school taught her enough about supply chains and strategy to know she wanted her company's raw materials to come from developing or third-world countries to be consumed in the more developed world. Coffee, she realized, is one of the very few products "that checked all the boxes; it was a perfect fit. People drink it every day, even multiple times a day." There is more competition in the category than in chocolate, but, she adds, "It's a business that allows you to move the kind of volume needed to make a difference." Morales, after earning his bachelor's degree in agroindustry, was similarly interested in supporting small producers.

As they talked, Pacheco discovered that Morales's family grew coffee in Poaquil. He did not think it was any good; at the time, the family kept the second- or third-grade quality for its own daily consumption and sold the higher grades to coyotes. Coffee is ubiquitous in Guatemala; Pacheco says that parents even put a diluted form in baby bottles to feed to infants. Gerson had no idea his family's coffee could fetch a higher price.

The Moraleses put their coffee through a two-step standardized evaluation: First a physical exam of the unroasted green beans for uniformity of size and absence of defects. The second step, which determines the price, is a tasting via what is known as the "cupping" process: beans subjected to a medium light roast are ground and placed into small bowls, over which hot water is poured. The taster breaks through the layer of floating grounds that forms on top to sample the brew and evaluate its aromatics, acidity, flavor, body, and balance. The Morales's family coffee scored well above the 88 minimum that specialty coffee shops look for.

Morales formed the co-op in 2015, and it made its first sale to Ethos in 2016. The first year they purchased from La Asunción, Pacheco and Rios brought several hundred pounds to Florida with them in suitcases, roasting the beans with a two-kilo roaster at a rented space in Haines, Florida, and improving the logistics of their partnership each year. Pacheco remembers the exact date of their first sale: March 8, 2016, noting "That's our official anniversary." Now sales to Ethos tally from thirty to forty thousand pounds per year.

Ethos, as they do with all of their farmers, pays the cost of shipping and transportation. It is a cost typically folded into the price craft roasters pay large importers who then pass on this cost to the farmer in the form of lower pay. Shouldering transportation costs on top of the premium she pays, Pacheco explains, frees Ethos's suppliers from dependence on exploitative big importers, allowing them to pocket nearly twice the market price of coffee that Ethos pays them.

In the beginning Pacheco paid 100 percent of the grower's fees in advance, because the members of Co-op La Asunción, like most coffee producers, had no working capital to pay for things like equipment repair and other unforeseen expenses. "What keeps coffee producers in the cycle of poverty is that they're in need of cash now, because they need to pay for their supplies," Pacheco explains. Over time, she gradually lowered the percentage of their fees paid in advance, to the current 50 percent deposit at the beginning of the year, then payment in full upon delivery.[17]

Instead of tacking a small Fair Trade premium onto the farmgate price and giving that to the farming cooperative leader (corruption may be involved, but often co-op financial reserves are so thin that leaders are pressured to pay out all premiums to cover farm costs), individual Ethos producers receive a money transfer for their crop based on the amount of coffee they produce and its quality, which is assessed by the importer before shipping. Pacheco buys only coffee with a rating of 85 or above; the higher the score, the greater the share of a farmer's harvest will go to Ethos rather than being sold to other buyers for a lower price.

Its ongoing relationship with Ethos and its other value-added activities, says Morales, have helped La Cooperativa La Asunción purchase equipment for its coffee mill, buy fertilizer in bulk, and provide more training to members, all of which resulted in increased production and higher-quality coffee. Education and community support is what will help buttress their relationship with Ethos and their other small enterprises and help build self-sufficiency. Yet Ethos still purchases less than half of the cooperative's total production and members still struggle to cover the costs of harvests. Which means sometimes taking out loans from financial institutions or from members themselves.

A BIG COFFEE INTERLUDE

THE SAME HISTORIC PROGRESSION WE'VE seen in other food systems—from sustainable indigenous practices to Green Revolution–influenced industrialized farming and commoditization—has occurred in coffee. Native cultivation of many varieties in a biodiverse, multi-storied, managed polyculture gave way to increasing intensification, first with shaded monoculture areas, then unshaded monocultures of lab-bred varietals managed with synthetic fertilizers and herbicides.[18]

Vertical integration followed: conglomerates that controlled the entire supply chain—from smallholder producers and coyotes, to large plantations with mechanized harvesting, processors, and exporters, as well as the intermediaries that handle the logistics of warehousing, packing, international shipping, and trucking—all required to get coffee to roasters, supermarkets, cafés, restaurants, and you, the consumer.

The biggest producers in the coffee commodity market—Brazil, which produces Arabica coffee, and Vietnam, which produces Robusta (higher in caffeine, lower in lipids, less sweet)—dictate global prices. Because those countries' plantations are large-scale, automated, and use chemical fertilizers and exploited, poorly paid labor, the benchmark price of coffee in the international marketplace often drops below the cost of production for smallholder producers in the highlands who harvest by hand.[19]

Unethical labor practices are hard to trace since so much commodity coffee is aggregated to supply large buyers such as Nestlé (whose brands range from Nescafé and Nespresso to Blue Bottle and the Starbucks at Home brand). In 2022 the U.S. Department of Labor identified seventeen coffee-producing countries whose plantations have been implicated in forced and/or child labor.[20] One study of Guatemala's coffee industry revealed illegal child labor and forced labor under armed guards, confiscation of identification documents, and placing workers into debt spirals, noting, "Pricey, high-quality coffee is apparently no guarantee against violations."[21]

Starbucks, after touting its "100% ethically sourced" coffee, was sued in 2024 by the National Consumers League, which cited human rights and labor abuses in coffee and tea farms the company sources from in Guatemala, Kenya, and Brazil. Starbucks has since adjusted its claims to "99% ethically sourced coffee."

Sometimes it is hard to tell the difference between beans aggregated from smallholder farmers by large multinationals or by small-batch "ethical" roasters who have forged direct relationships with growers. Pacheco says those heartwarming profiles of smallholder producers that you see on a lot of craft roasters' bags these days often come to the roaster via the large distributor they buy their green beans from; in some cases, the roaster has never traveled to the highlands of Guatemala or Colombia to meet them. "People think the roaster and the farmer have a relationship and that the farmer is being paid well, but we don't really know, and I'll bet you money that farmer doesn't know his picture is on the bag," says Pacheco. "A lot of the time they'll even get the names wrong. That kind of thing just makes it a little harder for us, it blurs the line."

COMPETING WITH BIG COFFEE IN LAKELAND

PACHECO'S FOCUS NOW IS ON increasing the volume of coffee that she sells so that she can support more small producers and siphon off a bigger share of the $462 billion in coffee sold annually in the United States into her shorter, more ethical supply chain. Rather than the inefficient model of placing her craft coffee on supermarket shelves (where it "just sits on shelves and is not as good"), she and Rios are planning a brick-and-mortar café, scheduled to open in spring 2026, on South Florida Avenue, the commercial thoroughfare that bisects Lakeland. A drive-thru window, they know, is a must to capitalize on the popularity of suburban drive-thru convenience. They are ready to test their brand against the $36 billion-a-year global chain Starbucks, which operates three stores in Lakeland, one of which is directly across the street from Ethos's planned café.

While she can't compete with Starbucks on the national stage, Pacheco is betting that she can in Lakeland, where she has built up a loyal following through her values-driven direct-to-consumer model, her unbeatable freshness, and her steady presence at the Lakeland Farmer's Market. Ethos broke even in its second year of operation and started turning a profit in its third year. In eight years of business, sales have increased eightfold.

As we wind up our visit, Pacheco gives me a tour of her roasting room. She offers to roast a personal sample of green Marcala Honey from Honduras in her small British Ikawa machine, used for test batches. After pouring green beans into a funnel at the top of the machine, she sets the roast profile on her phone app and watches them whir and spin while applying heat. Their sweet aroma gradually turns tantalizingly toasty, cocoa-laden, and savory as the beans darken from green to brown.

The superpower of Ethos is that three times a week, on Mondays, Wednesdays, and Fridays, Pacheco collects the orders that have come in before 8 a.m. that morning, then roasts, packs, and ships each one that same day. "When the coffee goes straight from farmer to roaster to your door, you not only get fresher, higher-quality coffee, you also enable us to pay life-changing prices to our farmers and above-average wages to our team." Currently, Ethos pays staff between seventeen and twenty-two dollars per hour, in this respect, successfully competing with Starbucks.

Pacheco and Rios installed solar panels last year, closing in on energy self-sufficiency. They have no children, but she thinks about the future of the business and is intent on leaving a solid foundation for the next generation of Ethos leaders. Returning to her core purposes, she says, "If we cannot pay our farmers well, then we're no different from Starbucks, and if we're no different from Starbucks, then why are we doing this?"

WHAT CAN WE CONSUMERS DO?

MOST COFFEE LOVERS TODAY (AND the same goes for chocolate), Pacheco believes, fall into three categories: the customer who looks for the cheapest product, the customer who wants to buy ethically and sustainably but feels "too small to make a difference," and the customer who opts for unreliable certifications.

If you fall in the second category, knowing and trusting your farmer and your roaster is the key to eating ethically. Know and accept that it is not possible to be 100 percent ethical but do your research. As Rosenthal says, direct trade can paint a comforting "small-is-beautiful" picture, but without a macroeconomic strategy in place to empower farmer communities and give them agency, real change will be elusive. Look for enterprises that are trying to effect change on a deeper level.

As for those unreliable certifications, do your homework here, too. In October 2021, after finding child labor on Rainforest Alliance certified farms, the Chicago-based Corporate Accountability Lab (CAL)—a group of labor, environmental, and human rights experts working to hold companies legally accountable for harm done to people and the environment—filed suit against Rainforest Alliance and Hershey for false advertising. Part of the suit, against Rainforest Alliance, was dismissed on procedural grounds in 2023, but the case against Hershey continues.

It is easy to throw our hands up in the air and give up, but Charity Ryerson, founder and executive director of CAL, advises consumers to apply pressure on the local levers of power, whether it is their local Whole Foods manager or institutions such as schools, faith centers, hospitals, or city governments to change their purchasing patterns to more regional, sustainable, and ethical food and farm purveyors. At the Karma Food Co-op, which I belong to in Toronto, our food issues committee writes articles about the sourcing and farming practices of our selected suppliers, and members can challenge purchasing decisions or suggest better ones.

When shopping for any product, Pacheco looks for transparency and level of detail offered. The more specific the marketing information, beyond "sustainably sourced," for example, the more likely it is that the company proves trustworthy. Pacheco says, "There are many people and small companies doing amazing things, you just need to look for them—and be willing to pay a bit more. If the price of a product and its marketing claims seem too good to be true, it absolutely is!"

CHAPTER EIGHT

WOMEN OF THE GRAIN, GRAPE, AND AGAVE: REGENERATIVE BEVERAGES

FOR A MOMENT IN JULY 2017, craft beer brewers Sandy Boss Febbo and her husband, Jay, were the leading tip of the Kernza perennial grain movement. It was the second night of the Kernza Conference and about eighty researchers from the University of Minnesota, The Land Institute in Kansas, Patagonia Provisions, Portland's Hopworks Brewery, and General Mills, as well as researchers from as far away as Sweden, had gathered at the couple's brewery, Bang Brewing in St. Paul. The highlight of the evening was to be the unveiling of their first effort at brewing beer with the semi-mystical experimental grain.

They christened the blond ale "Gold," both a reference to the maroon and gold colors of their alma mater, the University of Minnesota, and because for them, discovering Kernza was like striking gold. A local chef, Erica Strait, had prepared a tabouleh-like salad with Kernza, chickpeas, tomato, cucumber, onion, and herbs. Like the beer, it showed off the nutty depth of flavor of Kernza over other varieties of cracked wheat, plus a satisfying chewy bite. The event was a combination craft beer fest and grainiac convention.

Agroecology advocates have been broadcasting the coming Kernza revolution for forty years now, and here, finally, was a marquee event: the culmination of a multifaceted effort by public, private nonprofit, and government funding, bringing together farmers, researchers, brewers, consumer product good manufacturers, and chefs—the entire supply chain.

To the assembled people, Kernza is a way of bringing back the perennial grasses and grains that had once made the American prairies rich, biodiverse ecosystems teeming with life both above and below ground. Unlike annuals, which have to be replanted each year, perennial grains emerge from the land on their own every spring. Topsoil does not have to be disturbed to plant seeds, and Kernza's twelve-to-thirteen-foot-long root systems help soil retain water during flooding, prevent soil erosion, sequester carbon, and soak up nitrogen runoff from chemical fertilizers, purifying waters that pass through the land. In addition to these ecosystem services benefits, Kernza has the potential to bridge the polarizing organic vs. conventional divide, since even when grown conventionally it requires just one application annually of an herbicide known as 2,4-D, which has been used since the 1940s. It returns both lost flavor—Kernza products are prized for that deep nutty, graham- or rye-like taste—and soil-building superpowers to the land. To be able to cultivate and harvest a grain like Kernza—with such powerful soil-building and climate change–mitigating powers—at the scale of even a small percentage of commodity wheat production would move the alt food system forward by leaps and bounds.

From the day they founded their brewery in 2013, the Boss Febbos' core mission was to participate in environmental stewardship through brewing. "It's about managing our food system with fewer inputs and more consideration," Sandy Boss Febbo says. It was not easy sourcing all organic grains, hops, and malted barley, but the couple persevered, building a handsome low-environmental-impact brewery that looks like a squat silo, surrounded by a native prairie grass and rain garden in an industrial area of St. Paul, and slowly expanding through word of mouth.

"So often people are overwhelmed and think their actions and opinions don't matter. But they do. Everything you do benefits the collective, it resonates," she adds.

Kernza's journey from promising wheat grass to the first perennial grain to be available commercially in the United States was inspired by the vision of Wes Jackson, a plant biologist, plant geneticist, and astute observer of prairie ecology. In 1976, along with his then-wife, Dana, he founded The Land Institute in Salina, Kansas, dedicated to developing a perennial grain-based agriculture as a way of healing land that had been impoverished by seventy years of destructive agricultural practices, moving away from the yearly tilling and planting of annual row crops to perennial production of grains, legumes, and oilseed varieties.

Attracted by Kernza's versatility (it can be used in beer, baked goods, and as a whole grain like barley or rice), ecosystem services, and nutritional profile, the Land Institute launched its breeding program in 2003, starting with seeds isolated in 1984 by a researcher named Peggy Wagoner at Pennsylvania's Rodale Institute. In 2011 it was dubbed "Kernza," a cross between the word "kernel" to emphasize the role this small wheat grass can play in human diets, and "Konza," the name of a Kansas prairie biological station, which is in turn a reference to the Indigenous Kaw Nation of those prairies.

That same year the University of Minnesota, followed by several other university research centers, began their own Kernza trials. By 2013 the grain was on the menu at the Birchwood Café in Minneapolis in the form of a savory Kernza, kale, and Fontina waffle topped with an apple shallot compote. In 2014 General Mills partnered with the University of Minnesota and The Land Institute on Kernza research that led to a half million dollar donation to the effort in 2017. Sandy Boss Febbo had also read about the Kernza beer collaboration between Patagonia and Portland, Oregon's Hopworks Urban Brewery.

So in the beginning of 2017, when the Boss Febbos were delivering a keg of beer to the Birchwood Café and chef Marshall Paulsen casually asked if they'd like to try their hand at brewing with Kernza, their answer was an immediate and emphatic yes.

Through Paulsen the Boss Febbos connected with the University of Minnesota's Institute for Sustainable Agriculture (MISA), which is part of a coalition of partners called Green Lands Blue Waters (GLBW). The group takes a holistic approach to agriculture and conservation in the Upper Mississippi Basin, working with farmers and food producers to coax profits from landscapes and waterways while strengthening the entire ecosystem, somewhat similar to Mimi Casteel's vision for a unified regional ecosystem in Oregon's Wallowa Valley.

One of MISA's mantras is "continuous living cover," which expands on a basic tenet of regenerative farming, cover cropping. Conventional summer annual cropping systems cover the land only three months of the year, leaving it vulnerable during the winter to erosion and loss of nutrients like phosphorus and nitrogen, which kill fish and other forms of aquatic life. Perennial crops, along with winter annuals, extend their roots into the soil to bind, stabilize, and enrich soil particles. This makes them highly effective at building soil organic matter and protecting the soil surface from wind and water erosion year-round. These crops can play key roles in a state agriculture dominated by environmentally destructive industrial corn and soy production. While most cover crops, such as rye and oats, are annuals, Minnesota's most progressive farmers are focused on keeping the ground covered year-round with a mix of perennial and annual crops.

When I drop in on MISA's offices at the University of Minnesota to visit executive director Helene Murray and local writer Beth Dooley, they ply me with coffee, local raspberries, and packets of popped Kernza.

Dooley's contribution to the MISA effort is her cookbook, *The Perennial Kitchen*, centered on Midwestern perennial grains, nuts, and seeds, and regeneratively farmed vegetables, poultry, and livestock. Murray tells me about efforts to increase Kernza's small seed size, which will make cleaning and threshing much easier, and to address the five-foot-tall plant's propensity for "lodging" or toppling over. While Kernza gets most of the attention, she points out that there are many other grains the institute is researching and promoting. To counter some of the hype around Kernza as the poster grain for regenerating soil and ecosystems, she adds, "there's no silver bullet."

This is why the MISA Forever Green initiative is diversifying its small grain efforts among fourteen new perennial and winter annual crops that will promote clean water and healthy soils *and* produce income for farmers. Hybrid perennial hazelnuts are delicious to eat out of hand or to use as a healthy oil, while annual winter camelina and pennycress—members of the mustard family—can be used for healthy edible oils, or for biofuels, biodegradable plastic, packaging materials, and lubricants. Aaron Reser, associate director of GLBW, says, "If you talk to anyone working on Kernza, you'll find the same thing: a bunch of holistic thinkers" who view land and water, agriculture and conservation, farming for both profit and ecosystems services as "one inclusive and mutually beneficial effort." The crops they are promoting are not a replacement for commodity soy and corn farming, but as add-ons with co-benefits.

One day, a small contingent of MISA and GLBW members visited Bang Brewing. "It was hilarious," Sandy Boss Febbo recalls. "They came through the tap room to chat and try some beer. They asked us questions about our focus on the environment. We were totally being vetted."

The couple impressed the researchers with their passion and commitment, but they weren't prepared for what came next. The Land Institute was planning its second annual conference in Minneapolis in 2017: Would they be up for brewing a Kernza beer to serve for the occasion? "It was a little stressful, but we felt confident in our brewing, and to have the opportunity to brew with an experimental grain, a perennial was just stunning."

They connected with Christian Ettinger, owner of the eco-conscious Hopworks Urban Brewery in Portland, and then-head brewer Trever Bass, who created the first Kernza beer, for some tips. Bass advised the Boss Febbos to treat Kernza like they would any raw wheat, and to keep it to 15 percent of the mash to ensure that their mash grain bed does not get "stuck," or prevent the wort from easily filtering through. They selected two-row barley, the variety they used for their favorite SMASH (single malt, single hop) recipe, and a yeast they knew to be nice and clean. The goal was to keep a soft hop profile so the taste of the grain would not be obscured.

At the first opportunity to do a sensory appraisal of the new brew, recalls Sandy Boss Febbo, they knew: "Oh boy, this was going to be something special, and really fun." Kernza was a delicious grain; they just needed to get out of its way and let it shine. As they brewed repeat batches, the only thing they changed was where the Kernza was sourced. As with wine, each different field, whether south of the Twin Cities or north, or from Kansas, reflected a unique terroir.

The process of working with a multi-state team of agricultural researchers from the nearby St. Paul campus of the University of Minnesota and The Land Institute in Kansas was one of the most rewarding of the couple's lives. Their partners kept Bang Brewing supplied with enough Kernza to brew multiple one-hundred-pound batches of Gold, sourced from organic university research fields and Land Institute test plots. Since there was no cleaning or dehulling machine that had been optimized for Kernza, each batch had to be processed by hand, a herculean task that grad students and researchers helped with. "Everything you hope for when you want to work locally and regionally was happening with that one ingredient," says Boss Febbo. "It was such a personal process."

KERNZA CO-PARENTING:
THE LAND INSTITUTE'S RACHEL STROER

LIKE THE UNIVERSITY OF MINNESOTA, its Kansas partner, The Land Institute (TLI), is looking at a number of perennial grains that will usher in a more regenerative and sustainable form of agroecology. Kernza is not even the primary focus of current work, says TLI president Rachel Stroer, but just one of five different breeding programs that include perennial versions of sorghum, legumes, oilseed, rice, and a different breed of wheat.

One promising feature of TLI's Kernza work addresses the chief criticism of Kernza: low yields. The institute has dramatically increased the speed at which advances in crop characteristics like bigger seeds, higher yield, and threshability are happening. One cycle, or generation, of improvement has gone from taking five years when the program started in 2003, to six months with the use of infrared genomic techniques. Lead scientist in the Kernza domestication program Lee DeHaan believes that in the next fifteen years, Kernza yields will equal that of annual wheat.

In addition to the creation of perennial versions of all of the major row crops, the institute wants to return genetic diversity to the land by planting multiple species in one field, the "polyculture" that Wes Jackson outlined in his seminal 1980 text *New Roots for Agriculture*. It is also encouraging more diversity in the number of crops that the world's population eats. Instead of the same five to ten, a nation or region might eat fifty different crops, based on what is most suited to the landscape, geography, and climate of a place.

"The easiest play at scale is probably in beer," says Stroer, "and Sandy is a beer wizard. We can elevate the ecological and environmental benefits of Kernza, but Sandy has really helped elevate its taste profile." Thinking back to that moment in 2017 when the collective Kernza community first tasted their deeply nutty and delicious Gold Kernza beer, Boss Febbo says, "To be in that moment, pouring the beer for everyone and sensing the vibe of shared excitement and pride, was a tangible reward for so much work. There is so much potential for Kernza."

TRACKING MINNESOTA'S INDIGENOUS PAST AND THE KERNZA COMMUNITY NETWORK

IN EARLY SEPTEMBER, I SET out for the Twin Cities to meet a few of the key players on Team Kernza. I wanted to learn more about Bang Brewing and MISA's work with Kernza and other perennial grains to help build an interconnected, regional, more resilient food system. What I found was one of the most cooperative, intertwined, and exciting food systems networks of my travels, thrilling in its growing complexity and interdependence. Although this is a chapter on regenerative beverages, the nature of the alt food systems I am exploring means that I end up following my Kernza beer meanderings into an interconnected grain community that includes farmers, millers, and bakers, as well as brewers, maltsters, and distillers.

Unlike the commodity food system, where corporations aim to get a single product from producer to consumer as cheaply and as efficiently as possible, the key word in "alt food system" is the word "system." It is predicated on networks that mimic nature in their diversity, complexity, and mutually beneficial arms and nodes. Often, we need only to look at ancient indigenous food culture for a glimpse at what we've lost and what we might return to.

My first stop was lunch with baker and grain activist Michele Huggins, at Indigenous chef Sean Sherman's restaurant Owamni. Located in a modern development on the banks of the Mississippi River, it is a conscious reclaiming of Indigenous identity and foodways lost to colonialism. The name of the restaurant derives from the Dakota name for the sacred site Owámniyomni ("the place of the falling, swirling waters").[1] Twelve thousand years ago, a powerful waterfall as thunderingly majestic as Niagara Falls roared close to present-day St. Paul. As the force of the water eroded the bedrock limestone, large chunks of the sandstone beneath it crashed into the river, and the falls slowly migrated upriver and became shorter in length. Nearby, Waná i Wíta (Spirit Island) was a sacred ceremonial site to which Dakota and Anishinaabe women traveled to give birth to their babies.[2]

St. Anthony Falls, as the waterfall was renamed by mid-nineteenth-century White settlers, was a picturesque tourist destination for a short while, but soon a crush of sawmills, and then flour mills cluttered and despoiled the landscape and river. By 1880, twenty-seven flour mills producing more than two million barrels of flour annually made Minneapolis the leading flour producer in the country.[3] Owamni is housed in the nineteenth-century shell of the former Columbia Flour Mill. Just across the Mississippi River, atop the historic Pillsbury A Mill's red tile grain elevator, I spy large red letters that read PILLSBURY's BEST FLOUR. A five-minute walk down river from Owamni, a yellow sign that reads GOLD MEDAL FLOUR in ten-foot-tall letters sits atop a tall white grain elevator. The city is also the birthplace of General Mills.

It is fitting that Huggins and I have met on this site, once the center of an industrialized grain hub that fed America and the world, now a restaurant whose servers wear T-shirts that read #86COLONIALISM. Owamni eschews all colonial ingredients, including wheat flour, cane sugar, and dairy products, returning to a cuisine that relies solely on the surrounding land and native flora and fauna. Its menu expresses the land's original grain and foodshed in the form of heritage (not hybrid genetically modified) corn and wild rice, squash, sweet potato, elk, bison, and walleye. This spot is where the two systems rub up against each other to create something new; the excitement that surrounds Sherman is in part due to the hope he offers of a more holistic epoch emerging based on tribal foodways of the past.

Huggins and I, too, are here today to discuss the emergence of this new, local food economy that considers land, water, people, plants, animals, and insects to be one complex, interdependent network. Although there are many perennial and winter annual species that will help in this transformation, she, too, has been captivated by Kernza as the supernova of the bunch. She arrives at our lunch bearing a gift bag filled with Kernza maple cake, a small bag filled with whole Kernza wheat, which I will later mill, and another with Kernza flour she milled herself.

Over glasses of citrusy and mildly sweet staghorn sumac, clover, and hawthorn iced tea, she recounts the long, winding road that led her to Kernza. A former teacher and financial services worker, she took up baking when she moved to southwest Minnesota and became curious about what was growing around her. Her interest in fermenting foods led her to sourdough, and her exploration of the small local grain economy led her to Kernza and other heritage grains. As one of the few African Americans in her one-stoplight town of Granite Falls, Minnesota, she proclaimed her identity with her business's name, Doughp, which reflects the fresh beats of the 1990s hip hop she grew up with: The Fugees, Wu Tang Clan, a Tribe Called Quest. "During my slap and fold, when I'm making bread, I beat to whatever I'm listening to, whatever that beat is, and I feel like whether it is a faster beat or slower, it kind of changes the results for my bread," she explains. Working with whole grain local Kernza requires being an intuitive baker, because of variation between harvests and sources. She'll adjust hydration based on whether her dough feels too dry or wet, often related to fluctuations in weather. "When it's cooler outside, water absorption, length of the rise, and even mixing times can vary," she says.

To be an evangelist for local, organic whole grains alone puts farmers and bakers outside the mainstream culture in Minnesota, but to be Black and do that is another level of remove. Although she has forged strong ties in her community through her work volunteering at a local arts center and donating weekly free loaves to a community mutual aid program, after the murder in Minneapolis of George Floyd, Huggins tells me, "I actually felt scared. There were no protest parades here, there were no support groups. There were all kinds of things going on in Minneapolis, but nothing in my community. The silence was scary." No one commented on the murder to her, but she did see signs go up all around her home defending the police force.

Finding a place in this rural community has come in tandem with her deepening role as a community and local grain activist. Over time, she learned that there were different varieties of wheat harvested at different times of year and that behaved differently in the baking process. She learned that if she aged unwashed organic eggs for a few days at room temperature (washing can break down the "bloom" or protective bacterial coating that keeps them fresh), she could get just the right moisture content she needed for her French macarons. The white flour content of her breads slowly decreased, to zero for most and to 15 percent for Kernza bread, which needs to be balanced by flour with lower protein and high gluten content in order to attain a level of oven spring that will satisfy customers.

By forging relationships with local small grain and Kernza farmers like Luke Peterson of A-Frame farm, and Ben Penner of Ben Penner Organic Farm, she can pick up a hundred or two hundred pounds of wheat berries, grind them at home, and offer her customers the freshest bread possible. She's also learned a few things about the challenges of creating an alt grain supply chain in the breadbasket of the country.

By now we're well into one of Owamni's classic dishes, sweet potatoes with ancho chili crisp and maple syrup, and earthy poblano peppers stuffed with wild rice, mushrooms, and aji amarillo chili. Like Sandy Boss Febbo, Huggins is a stickler for buying whole grains as locally as possible. But when you are building an alt local grain supply chain that connects farmer, miller, brewer, baker, and other retailers, it takes time for all the pieces to fall into place and for inefficiencies to be smoothed out. Recently, on a drive-around to look at local farms, Huggins discovered that the organic Einkorn wheat she has been ordering from Wisconsin—and feeling some guilt over the distance—is grown on a farm just a five-minute drive from her home. The farmer has to have it hauled to Wisconsin to be cleaned and dehulled because that service, which he needs on a small batch rather than industrial scale, is not yet available closer by.

It is local supply chain problems like these that keep Alyssa Hartman, executive director of the Artisan Grain Collaborative (AGC), up at night. AGC's goal is to make inroads into the hegemony of corn and soy production, which have become so predominant that small grains or cereal crops such as barley, oats, rye, and wheat have virtually disappeared from the landscape, now accounting for only 0.7 percent of total field crop production in the Upper Midwest.[4] Hartman was drawn to the job in 2019 she says, "because it was an exciting opportunity to explore what value-added grain agriculture could look like in America's historic grain basket."

"Value" can be added in many ways: the deliciously nutty Kernza beer that Sandy Boss Febbo brews; the hand-folded and slapped loaves of naturally leavened Kernza sourdough bread Huggins makes; the Kernza naan of Artisan Naan Bakery in St. Cloud, Michigan; Perennial Provisions' Kernza crackers; the single-barrel, three-year-aged Kernza whiskey from Minneapolis's Tatersall Distillery; or the local heritage grain pasta dishes that chef Gavin Kaysen offers guests at Spoon and Stable in Minneapolis. All of them are participating in building Minnesota's alt-grain shed.

MATERNAL INSTINCTS: PROTECTING CHILDREN AND LAND: NOREEN AND MELANY THOMAS, DOUBTING THOMAS FARMS

THE NEXT DAY, I DRIVE out to meet one of Bang Brewery's local grain suppliers at Doubting Thomas Farms in Moorhead, Minnesota, about two-hundred-and-fifty miles northwest of the Twin Cities. GPS and cellular are unreliable out here so I am unable to find the farm among the vast GMO soy, corn, and sugar beet farms. Co-owner Noreen Thomas and I finally arrange to meet at an intersection in nearby Kragnes. "My hair looks a little like Albert Einstein's," she tells me, by way of helping me identify her. Her hair is more auburn than Einstein's salt-and-pepper do, but similarly untamed, and a clue to a different kind of genius.

At the farm, she sits me down in her kitchen with daughter-in-law Melany, and offers me coffee from BernBaum's, a Jewish deli located a five-minute drive to the west, in Fargo, North Dakota. "Our well water is okay for us, but it can affect other people's stomachs," she says. Bern-Baum's chef Andrea Baumgardner is a longtime fan and buyer of Doubting Thomas's organic products; the farm's wheat flour is the secret to the deli's tender focaccia and superior bagels.

Noreen and Melany are fourth- and fifth-generation farmers in a line that stretches back to the great-great-grandfather of Noreen's husband, Lee. A tireless marketer, in addition to being an educator, ecologist, and seed breeder, Noreen reached out to Sandy Boss Febbo at Bang Brewing in 2019 to tell her that she was growing and malting her own organically grown barley and oats. "That was a watershed moment that we had been waiting for since 2013," says Boss Febbo. The industrialization of Midwest grain farming had left a giant hole where she hoped to find midsize producers like the Thomases. But she found repairing the hole slow going: "Building that local grain system back is a very focused exercise, taking a full community and network." In March 2020, Bang was able to release its first beer made with all-Minnesota ingredients, including the Thomases' barley and malted oats, the latter of which Febbo says brought a creamy haziness and smooth mouth feel to her SUDS cream ale, balanced by fruity esters and a refreshing hop bitterness.

But the Thomases are outliers in their region and state, among the one percent of certified organic farms in Minnesota. Her husband Lee's Swedish roots run deep in an agrarian culture where "as soon as your foot can reach the pedal you're put in the tractor" says Noreen, whose own background is a mix of European with a "splash" of Native American ancestry. The Thomases were strictly conventional in their farming methods.

Going organic was Noreen's idea from the beginning. Before marrying into the Thomas family and farm she worked as a lab technician in pesticide residue testing at the USDA's state lab in Fargo. "There were a lot of women in the lab, and a lot of conversations that were very frank, very open," Noreen says. "We could see the residual effects of DDT that was still in the environment" as well as those of newer classes of agricultural chemicals. "They were doing studies with things that kind of glow in the dark that I thought could be very dangerous to children. So I just opted out."

When she and her husband moved to the family farm in 1991, she went from being surrounded by smart, driven women scientists to a life of relative isolation. She worked in hospital education for a while, then on the marketing side of the farm while raising the couples' three sons.

Then her headaches started, migraines that came after her husband sprayed the crops with herbicides in the spring. Studies conducted by researchers at the University of Minnesota showed a higher frequency of birth defects between 1989 and 1992 among children of the Red River Valley—where Doubting Thomas is located—than other major agricultural regions, and that children born to male pesticide applicators had the highest risk. Conceptions in the spring, when herbicides are sprayed, resulted in significantly more children with birth defects than in any other season.[5]

In the late 1990s, Noreen coaxed Lee to attend a meeting of the Midwest Organic & Sustainable Education Service (MOSES). Seeing the "hippie-looking person with a tie-dyed shirt and tinted round glasses on," recounts Melany, made him want to walk out immediately. But Noreen pleaded for him to stay, saying "I'll take you out for supper. We'll go have shrimp. Just hang in there." There were about three hundred people in attendance at the meeting. Today the same group, renamed Marbleseed, attracts upwards of thirty-five hundred people to its annual conference. Against the steely opposition of Lee's father, they forged ahead with the farm's conversion to organic.

But she said, "The pushback was hard." Her father-in-law did not speak to her for months, and her children were taunted on the school bus. As the farm transitioned to organic in the late 1990s, she struggled to find buyers, relying on selling bulk non-GMO soybeans to wholesalers at low cost. Thomas finally landed Baumgardner, her first chef client, in 2022. A 4H pig project that the Thomases' son Evan was involved in had gone awry and the farm's pig population ballooned from two pigs to eight. Without the storage space for the processed pigs, Lee was convinced the family was going to lose its collective shirt on the project. Noreen had the idea of going to Baumgardner, a supporter of local sourcing. Much to the family's shock and relief, the chef bought all of the Thomas's pigs and asked, "What else do you have?"

Chef, food systems change advocate, and *The Third Plate* author Dan Barber (see Chapter 2) visited the farm, and Noreen became a grower for his groundbreaking Row 7 Seed Co., which seeks to broaden the diversity and deepen the taste of vegetables, but also to democratize the spread of organic seeds. She was invited to conferences, began consulting for farms converting from conventional to organic, and was eventually awarded a Bush Fellowship, which is bestowed on individuals with a radical vision of change in their community. Her tireless marketing efforts led not only to the Bang Brewing collaboration, but another beer partnership with Bow and Arrow Brewing Co. in Albuquerque, founded by North Dakota–born Indigenous entrepreneur Shyla Sheppard. Under its Native Land label, Bow and Arrow and Minneapolis brewer Arbeiter Brewing Co. used Doubting Thomas's blue corn to create an organic Mexican-style lager.

When none of the Thomases' sons wanted to take over the farm, Melany, eldest son Evan's wife—who was deeply invested in the farm's organic mission—volunteered to step in. With a degree in animal science but little hands-on farming experience, she has been learning how to harvest with a combine and just purchased a larger-capacity and more efficient seed cleaner. She has also become a policy advocate, and chair of the policy committee for the National Farmers Union, joining the group's annual "fly-ins" to Washington, DC, to lobby on its behalf. In 2022, after three years of on-farm experience, Melany was named the Minnesota Farmers Union's Rising Star.

Sadly, the organic, vertically integrated malting business that Noreen started closed during the COVID-19 pandemic, hurt by the subsequent downturn in craft brewing in the region. But malted oats, Noreen confides, "are fabulous in cooking," and a much more nutritious substitute for rice or oat groats.

BRINGING MALTING BACK TO THE MIDWEST'S REGIONAL GRAIN NETWORK: HANNAH FRANCIS

WITHOUT A LOCAL ORGANIC MALTSTER, Boss Febbo went back on the hunt. She was able to once again turn to the growing midwestern knowledge network for local, organic, or regenerative food systems. At the University of Wisconsin Madison's Organic Grain Resource and Information Network (OGRAIN) program she met outreach specialist Hannah Francis, who acts as the conductor of an orchestra of farmers, researchers, and educators centered at the University of Wisconsin and connected by a passion for growing organic small grains. A robust eight-hundred-member listserv chews over questions ranging from how to tackle worm infestations to connecting buyers and sellers of rice seed.

"All of this grain activity," says Francis, "feels like its snowballing. People are really excited and there is a desire among innovative farmers doing cool regenerative practices with Kernza or other small grains in rotation to diversify their landscape and find value-added components." Their knowledge network is also connecting to like-minded grains systems around the country, in university agricultural departments in New York, Vermont, Oregon, and Minnesota.

At one of the field days she organizes, a trip to the USDA cereal lab in Madison, Francis noticed that barley breeding research was underway in partnership with a malting lab. "Wisconsin used to be a huge barley producer many years ago, before corn and soy took over," says Francis. And the art of malting has been practiced in these parts since the turn of the twentieth century. Today, however, most of the state's large maltsters, including Breiss Malt & Ingredients Co., bring in barley by the train carload from the northern and western regions of the United States, including Idaho, Montana, and North Dakota. Francis wanted to fill that void in the local supply chain.

A farmer member of both OGRAIN and AGC, Willie Hughes bought a small-scale pilot malting machine and he and Francis began teaching themselves to use it. She hauled a tote bag full of barley from the farm to friends at the Michael Fields Agricultural Institute, a nonprofit based in East Troy, and used their very old, small Clipper 1B grain cleaner, the same machine that Melany Thomas was so excited to find used on the market. After feeding the grains through the machine, which consists of two stacked trays that sift and separate the grain from the chaff, she took the cleaned bags back to Janesville to feed to Willie's malting machine.

There, they poured the cleaned barley into a stainless-steel cylinder, filled it with water and drained it repeatedly, then injected some oxygen and began agitating the seeds. "At this point they've grown tiny rootlets which extend outside the seed but don't fully emerge. You're just barely germinating the seed and stopping that process by applying heat," Francis explains. "It's similar to a coffee bean where you can roast it to different levels to get light, medium, or dark-roast coffees. This activates the enzymes and sugars of grains, which will in turn, with the addition of yeast, be fermented to create delicious beer sweetness, acidity, and flavors.

After a lot of trial and error, they now have some malted barley they are sharing with local brewers and their grain community. But the question remains: Can this be grown sustainably and profitably on a regional grainshed scale to feed craft breweries like Bang? Boss Febbo has not yet had the chance to test brew with Francis's and Hughes's malted barley. Although craft malting is one area of craft brewing that is growing, Francis says, one barrier is that Wisconsin's climate is not ideal for small grain growing because of its slightly higher humidity rates, and its large swaths of corn crops can be host to mycotoxins that can make it hard for barley farmers to meet maltsters' specification levels. The other is infrastructure. Producing profitably at the craft malt scale requires a big investment, of time, of land, and about $100,000 worth of equipment, says Francis.

Craft beer brewing and all of the ancillary crops and infrastructure it requires are filling a void and diversifying an agricultural and beverage landscape that has been flattened by the agricultural monocropping, but Francis has made it abundantly clear how many such voids remain in this regional foodshed. "We're looking to de-commoditize our agricultural system and that is tough when you're up against really big players. Most large-scale breweries will source grains from out west, malt and brew in-house, skipping a lot of the steps of a small system."

"Still," Francis adds, "it's kind of fun grunt work to figure it out, and we will see the emergence of these regional facilities."

ONE FOR THE ROAD: PARTING KERNZA THOUGHTS

THE NIGHT BEFORE I DEPART, I am witness to the web of relationships, the warm, tight-knit community that the Boss Febbos have built around the principles of climate resilience, regenerative grains, and really good beer. As the sun gilds the bluestem, switchgrass, blazing star, and echinacea in the brewery's native grass and rain garden, I sit at an outdoor table with the couple, who greet their entering and leaving customers: Atom, who designed their furniture, Marcus, the coffee merchant who designs Bang's herbal and fruit mixers, folks from the nearby letterpress and design shop who do all the brewery's design work.

Over steins of crisp "Perennial Percent" Kernza IPA—part of a Bang Brewery series of beers introduced in 2020 that include one percent of Kernza—we feast on naturally leavened, woodfired pizzas from the Bang's pizza makers in residence, Pastel Artisan Pizza. There is Kernza in this, too, in the form of the 3 percent rye-Kernza crust topped by three cheeses, blue potato, red onion and garlic cream. One and 3 percent; these are not huge percentages of Kernza. But the idea is that when you can model recipes with just a small amount of Kernza—especially for a classic, universally loved duo like pizza and beer—the potential for moving the needle and building ecosystem resilience on a wide scale is enormous.

A year after my visit, that needle took a big leap forward. In late 2024, The Land Institute took Bang Brewery's one percent and ran with it, launching its own trademarked "Perennial Percent" label, announcing that the Minnesota-based company Sturdiwheat would be adding a perennial percent of Kernza to every product in its lineup, which already included a Kernza muffin and a Kernza pancake mix.

The initiative validated something Boss Febbo had said to me during my visit: "I'm a huge believer in the idea that individual actions matter, and Jay shares that. It is within our ability to make things happen, to effect change."

GROWING WHAT SHE FERMENTS,
WITH ANIMALS: ALICE ANDERSON, ÂMEVIVE WINE

THE FIRST THING I SEE when I arrive at the ten-acre Ibarra-Young Vineyard in Santa Barbara County, California, is a line of chickens and ducks waddling, with purpose, in a line from their wooden coop straight into the rows of vines in front of them. It is a gloriously sunny and mild mid-March morning, and the dark silhouettes of the pruned old vines, ropy and gnarled, stand out against the blue sky like skeletal scarecrows. What is striking is that I cannot see their feet because they are covered by the lush, foot-tall grassy understory, which keeps the herd of sheep that grazes here during the winter months happy.

"It's organized chaos, for sure," says grape grower and winemaker Alice Anderson, who has pulled up to the vineyard in her car right after me, her face framed by long, wavy sun-streaked auburn hair and matching tortoise-shell glasses. "But the whole idea is to have all of the soil covered at all times, whether that means matted dead grass or something living." The chickens, ducks, sheep, and thick carpet of green are all part of her regenerative farming system. Maintaining cover crops year-round, enriched by a cycle of grazing, manure, and robust composting builds soil resilience and increases moisture retention.

Since 2019, this emerald scrap of land has been Anderson's canvas, which she tends to with a miniaturist's attention to detail, making lean, juicy, and elegantly aromatic wines that express this piece of the Santa Ynez Valley and her holistic vision for it. Five vintages into growing and fermenting for her own Âmevive label, she has received national attention for her alluring wines, the results of her climate-sensitive way of grape growing and winemaking. Here, every element of nature—including the human hand—works in concert to capture the energy of the earth in a bottle of wine.

During her time on this land, which she manages along with her business and life partner, Topher De Felice, Anderson has covered it with more than two hundred tons of organic compost, forty different cover crops, fowl and sheep, creating a lush biodiverse ecosystem teeming with microbes, insects, pollinators, and animals. Many of them—like the egret, the western fence lizard, the California native Crotch's bumble bee, the western bluebird, and the black-tailed jack rabbit—appear on the delicately rendered watercolors that adorn Âmevive wine labels. They are the work of Anderson's mother, Eileen, who has done this professionally for more than thirty-five years; Anderson herself does the smaller back-label illustrations.

On our way into the vineyard, we pass a long, plastic tarp–covered compost windrow that is just one source of energy that powers her no-waste vineyard. A one-year ferment of microbe-digested vineyard prunings, animal waste, and tree trimmings, its fungal-rich microflora nourishes the vine root system. Anderson uncovers the pile and thrusts both hands into the mass, bringing up the equivalent of black gold, a mound of dark brown humus studded with pieces of woody grape vine canes and twigs. To feed it, she has created a compost "mother" made of fresh manure, eggshells, and stinging nettle, all of it inoculated with several different microbial biodynamic preparations. Before-and-after photos she has taken of the vineyard chart the land's journey from spare and dry to dense, lush green.

To rebalance the land from above ground, Anderson has focused on tightening up the pruning of the vines to achieve a new happy medium: less pushing for grape yield and more encouragement of leaf growth, which enables the plants to store more carbon for the next season. "Making great wine is all about the balance between vegetative growth and fruit," she explains. "Every growing season presents different challenges, so we want to guide our vineyards to make the best wines with the cards that the growing season has dealt. We need to observe and react differently every year, with the same basic vine management principles in mind."

Increasing biodiversity has also allowed Anderson to wean her vines off the systematic—and to her mind—overly rigid schedule of organic spraying they had become accustomed to. She walks the land regularly and knows where the "hot spots" are that need more of the biodynamic sprays that she alternates or uses in conjunction with biologicals (pest and mold deterrents derived from natural materials such as plants, animals, minerals, and microbes) and essential oils. She is lucky that she is not growing on the coast, but inland, protected from the moist marine air and powdery mildew pressure by the Santa Ynez Mountains; this makes it easier for her to rely mostly on the natural biology of the vineyard to maintain its resilience against fungal pathogens.

Her old vines, planted in 1971—making Ibarra-Young one of the oldest vineyards still in production in the county—add another layer of resilience. They are so well-adapted to this climate that they can withstand just about anything nature throws at them, from water stress to extreme cold or heat. In the summer of 2020, they saw a five-day run of 110-degree Fahrenheit days, and then five days later, two straight days of 118 degrees, yet sailed through without any loss of fruit. The vineyard's newer block of Graciano—organic but planted in late 1990—was nearly wiped out. Anderson does wonder what the wines from her old vines would taste like if they had never been subjected to herbicides, but even grown organically since 1993, she says, "there's a lot of feeling and emotion," in the wines she makes from these grapes, "an energetic expression of a place tended with a lot of love."

Her vineyard is way ahead of most in preparing for an increasingly dry future, and water is an issue here because the vineyard's sandy, gravelly, and loamy soil does not have a high water-retention capacity. Building lots of soil organic matter has helped, and moisture meters help her calibrate her water needs with some precision. The vineyard's location in the Los Olivos flood plain means rainfall in the surrounding San Rafael and Santa Ynez mountain ranges will drain into the valley floor, providing enough water for irrigation. At least for now. Irrigation, which Anderson says, "is really freakin' expensive," will only become harder to come by as climate change advances.

AN INDUSTRIAL WINE INTERLUDE

ALL OF THE PRACTICES I have described illustrate the alt regenerative winemaker's way of hewing to the ancient *vigneron* tradition of both growing grapes and making wine, but also incorporating the latest in soil science and regenerative agricultural practices. Alt wine's industrially produced counterpart typically leans on copious amounts of herbicides, pesticides, and fungicides in order to maximize yield. These practices, as we have seen, affect entire ecosystems and work counter to biodiversity and species retention. Whereas a small producer like Anderson can be nimble and tailor her spraying (organic or not) regimen to changing circumstances, most wineries, she notes, spray according to a preset schedule and formulas, "just because that's the easiest thing to do." All of Anderson's wines are low intervention: unfined (fining is a process that removes yeast cells and other particles), unfiltered, fermented with ambient yeast and minimal sulfur (used to help preserve the wine and keep fermentation on track), and stored in neutral French oak.

In response to consumer demand, even the biggest vineyards are working toward increasing sustainability on many different fronts: high-tech precision agriculture that helps minimize water use and inputs; turning to renewable energy sources; seeking more climate-adapted varieties of grapes, and looking at more sustainable forms of packaging. Yet industrially produced wines, natural wine advocate Alice Feiring points out, can still select from any of seventy-two approved additives allowed in winemaking,[6] from sulfites and coloring agents to preservatives and animal-derived fining agents. It is impossible for consumers to know exactly what is in these wines.

CREATING A QUINTESSENTIALLY CALIFORNIAN WINE, BY WAY OF NEW ZEALAND AND FRANCE

A CALIFORNIA NATIVE WHO GREW up in Modesto crazy about horses and riding, Anderson figured out that winemaking combined her love of nature, animals, science, and growing things. After pocketing a degree in 2014 from California Polytechnic University, San Luis Obispo's wine and viticulture department, she lit out for New Zealand's cool-climate Central Otago region in search of wine-making experience and good skiing. At the family-owned, biodynamic wine producer Rippon, she learned to love the communal practice of pruning every day (even in freezing weather) and building compost. She also followed with interest the family's integration of animals into the vineyards.

A stint in the Northern Rhône Valley followed from 2015 to 2017, as *caviste* for winemaker Pierre Gaillard, whose list includes traditional big, full-bodied Marsanne, Roussanne, and Viognier wines. She spoke no French and was offered a job only after agreeing that after the first day, no English would be spoken (she coped). "It was my first experience in viticulture," she says, where long days in the cellar, complemented by time in the vineyard, taught her how various grape-harvesting and fermentation decisions lead to certain styles of wine. When she returned to California, she deployed those skills to fashion fresher and more energetic warm-climate wines, a little higher in natural acidity and lower in alcohol—a style more to her taste that also matches the lighter style of foods that Californians, especially, tend to eat.

The Rhône Valley was also where she came to understand the basic tenets of French food and wine culture: that everyone grew their own vegetables, that small local farmer's markets were the heart of the local food system, and that winemakers grow their own grapes. Those that did not "were not necessarily that well respected," she recalls. She couldn't "unlive" those years or unlearn those lessons, she adds: "That's where I truly understood that I wanted to grow what I make."

In 2017, she moved to Santa Barbara County to take a string of positions with respected Central Coasts winemakers Justin Tyler Willett at Tyler Winery, Angel Osborne (maker of A Tribute to Grace), and Graham Tatomer of Tatomer Wines. She was also ready to start her own project and began looking for some land to lease and farm. She was in her mid-twenties by late 2018, beset by the urgent feeling that she had to prove herself. "I must have been giving out some sort of I'm-looking-to-farm-a-vineyard energy," she recalls, because several friends sent her an advertisement for a vineyard for lease with a 1970s-era photo of a woman riding a mule through a vineyard; her friends knew she was obsessed with the idea of farming with draft horses. The woman was the property's late owner Charlotte Young, who planted six acres of Ibarra-Young vines between 1971 and 1973 with Jalisco, Mexico–born vineyard manager Miguel Ibarra. When Anderson began leasing the land from the Young family in 2018, it had been farmed since 1986 by vintner and advocate of Rhône varietals, Bob Lindquist, who in the late 1990s planted the last four acres of young vines, which he farmed organically.

While Âmevive ("lively soul" in English) is Anderson's creative outlet and shot at making wine exactly as she wishes, she also works part-time for a local vineyard management company that farms 130 acres of organic grapes and deploys sheep and pigs to forage the vineyard rows during the winter months. Her job is to scout for parcels and manage and implement the organic spray programs.

At the far end of the vineyard, we stop at a picnic table to taste the wines Anderson has brought with her: a 2021 Syrah made with old-vine grapes grown on the Ibarra-Young vineyard; a 2021 Ravie Grenache, Syrah, and Mourvèdre blend sourced on other vineyards in Santa Barbara County; and a 2021 Mourvèdre, also estate-grown at Ibarra-Young. Anderson produces just under three thousand cases per year, and the length of grape skin contact in her fermentations varies. Skin-contact wines employ an ancient method popular with natural winemakers in which the skins of white grapes are left in contact with the fermenting juice, amplifying tannins and texture and resulting in hues ranging from slightly tinted to amber or orange. A percentage of the grapes in her reds are whole cluster-fermented (also a return to pre-modern wine techniques, before grape crushing and de-stemming were automated) for the textural component and age-ability that they bring to the bottle. Native bacteria fermentation—as opposed to using commercial wine yeast—is aided by the addition of a *pied de cuve*, a natural fermentation starter Anderson makes from grapes in her vineyard or in the cellar.

The gorgeous Syrah is from one of the original 1971 plantings, typically light and lean yet bursting with ripe fruit: an elegant, energetic expression of the soul of the vineyard. The Ravie is vibrantly fruity, crunchy, and alive, a romantic ode to the gentle landscapes of Santa Barbara County. All are beautifully aromatic explorations of the rich biodiversity of her vineyard and the others she sources from.

In Anderson's ideal, blue sky future, she will be farming all of the parcels her wines are sourced from and using draft horses to help with both harvest and spring cultivation. "As somebody who doesn't have millions of dollars or a lot of family capital, it's a slow progression," she says. She doesn't mind waiting, though, because she loves every part of her job, from the monotony of pruning all day to moving her sheep and watching them graze, to fermentation management, to fine tuning in the cellar, to taking photos and marketing her wines. "I love following the story, watching these little buds sprout out of these old vines, tending them all the way to finished wines." Her favorite part is how all the knowledge she has gained so far synthesizes into a holistic vision, "a complete understanding of where everything came from, and how what starts on the vineyard floor ends up in our wines."

Her world view reminds me of the Minnesota systems thinkers running the Forever Green and Green Lands Blue Waters initiatives, and of Ratana Chuenpagdee's creation of an interlinked network of small- and medium-scale ecosystems, fishers, and coastal economies. One field or patch of ocean is a microcosm of the local and regional foodshed. Each system looks helplessly small compared to its industrial food system counterpart. But its power is in the aggregate, and the vision we can each hold of that aggregate as an ideal we aspire to. My next foray, into the world of regenerative mezcal, is yet another small piece of that vision.

THE RADICAL BIODIVERSITY
CHAMPIONS OF MEZCAL: FABIOLA TORRES
MONFIL AND DIANA PINZÓN MONCADA

THE IDENTICAL CAMOUFLAGE GREEN T-SHIRTS that Fabiola "Faby" Torres Monfil and Diana Pinzón Moncada wear telegraph the nature of their business and the beliefs it is built on. On the front, the name of their Puebla, Mexico–based small-batch mezcal label ZIN-ACANTÁN appears in flowing white cursive. The back features a raised brown fist wreathed in different species of agave plants, and the slogan ¡NO ES SOLO UNA SEMILA! NUESTRA LUCHA ES LA CONSERVACIÓN DE LOS AGAVES ENDÉMICOS DE MEXICO. PROTEJAMOS NUESTRA BIODIVERSIDAD NUESTRO PATRIMONIO BIOCULTURAL. Translation: "It's not just a seed! Our fight is the conservation of the endemic agaves of Mexico. Let's protect our biodiversity, our biocultural heritage."

We are sitting in the outdoor cabana tasting room at Torres Monfil's home and *mezcalería*, anchored by the sturdy trunk of a live mesquite tree in one corner and shaded from the scorching sun by a thatched roof of rope-bound palm fronds. The cabana has replaced Torres Monfil's bedroom as the guest tasting room. Birds coo and chatter loudly, and every fifteen minutes we hear the solemn tolling of the church bell. Most of the five hundred inhabitants in this village of San Diego la Mesa Tochimiltz-ingo—located in the Atlixco Valley about a three-hour drive southeast of Mexico City—are involved in making mezcal. Only hers, however, has remained small batch in the style of her forbears, while other producers sell to large brands for rebottling, out of facilities run by engineers rather than *mezcaleros*.

THE UNSUSTAINABILITY OF BIG MEZCAL

LIKE OUR OTHER ALT FOOD system heroes, Torres Monfil and Pinzón Moncada stand outside the mainstream, in this case, the exploding global mezcal market, the ramping up of agave cultivation it has caused, and the destructive effects of those farms on the ecosystem. In Oaxaca, especially, where 90 percent of mezcal is produced,[7] the wild agave, a keystone species to ecosystem diversity, has been overharvested. To meet demand, producers have planted vast monoculture fields of agave. Deforestation—a result of both clearing land to plant agave and the use of large quantities of firewood to roast the agave hearts or *piñas* (pineapples)—is another problem.

What makes mezcal especially unsustainable is that the harvesting of the piña, typically just before the plant develops its *quiote* (the stalk from which the flower will emerge), is not an annual happening in the agave's life cycle. It occurs just once, when the plant reaches maturity and maximum sweetness. In Puebla, it takes about twelve years for the agave to reach that point. And it takes a lot of agave to make just one liter of mezcal, between twenty-two and fifty-five pounds of espadin agave.[8]

Mezcal is the name applied to any spirit distilled from the agave and encompasses the huge (nearly six hundred million liters produced in 2023) tequila market, which in the United States dates back to the turn of the century and has its own history of extractive agriculture and boom-and-bust commodity price cycles. While tequila is solely distilled from the blue agave of five west-central Mexican states, the biggest producer of which is Jalisco, mezcal is distilled in nine states, three of which (Puebla not included) are also tequila-producing states. Annual production of distilled agave spirits marketed as mezcal morphed from less than one million liters to more than fourteen million in just over a decade,[9] and according to Pinzón Moncada, far more than that for agave distillate not labeled as mezcal.

The unhurried ritual of peasant farmers harvesting a few of the spiky succulents per year to distill enough mezcal for their own celebrations—weddings, funerals, to bring with them to their mountain *milpas* (cornfields) as a fortifier, or to use in place of currency to trade for other goods—is rapidly disappearing. Escalating prices, too, have put local mezcal out of reach of villagers. To offset this trend, after each distillation Zinacantán offer villagers over age sixty a *mescalito* (small glass of mezcal) or two on the house.

DEFENDING MEXICO'S AND PUEBLA'S BIOCULTURAL INHERITANCE

THE BUSINESS PARTNERS GUFFAW AND giggle incessantly—especially Pinzón Moncada, who is more prone to laughter—but they are also deadly serious comrades in insurgency against Big Mezcal and the draining of Mexico's biocultural inheritance. "We are losing the genetic diversity and richness of our agave culture and selling out to a handful of global beverage companies. And for what? Short-term monetary gain. The dark side of mezcal," Pinzón Moncada likes to say, "is very dark." In a few short years, consolidation and takeover by the industry (the latest are Bacardi's 2023 purchase of the artisanal Oaxaca brand Ilegal for $130 million, and before that, Diageo PLC's purchase of George Clooney's tequila and mezcal brand Casamigos for one billion dollars) have left six multinational drinks giants responsible for roughly 90 percent of all mezcal production.

Torres Monfil is a fourth-generation *mezcalero* (master mezcal distiller) and the first woman to bear the title in her family's three-hundred-year history of making mezcal. The ninth of ten children, she says that women have always taken part in the mezcal distilling process, they simply were not given credit for their contributions. It was her mother who told her she could do the work if she wanted.

Pinzón Moncada is a Colombian-born forest engineer who divides her time between her home in Albuquerque and her second home in San Diego la Mesa Tochimiltzingo. The duo met through Pinzón Moncada's husband, Richard Chad Young, who was doing research for his master's degree in watershed sciences while volunteering for the Peace Corps in Puebla. Young discovered that the local agave populations in that region were in decline and launched a volunteer project in 2013 to grow agave from seed in an attempt to replenish their numbers and retain their genetic diversity. He tapped Torres Monfil to be the leader of the ten-member, all-women project; when Young returned to work in the United States later that year, he asked Pinzón Moncada to take over the group. She traveled from Albuquerque to Puebla three or four times a year to oversee the seed nursery group, and she and Torres Monfil became fast friends.

Around San Diego la Mesa Tochimiltzingo three wild varieties—*Agave potatorum, Agave angustifolia silvestre,* and espadilla (a hybrid of *Agave angustifolia* and *Agave rhodacantha*)—are all in decline. Big Mezcal (including tequila), in its rush to production, simply relies on "clones," cuttings, or offshoots of existing plants, which create fields of genetically identical plants. To protect and expand the genetic diversity that monocropping agave diminishes,[10] Torres Monfil and Pinzón Moncada select and plant seeds from agaves that offer the best expression of their variety and are most disease- or drought-resistant. But unlike clones, agaves grown from seed are dependent on their most important and effective pollinators, two endangered bat species that have co-evolved with the agave for millions of years.

One of them, *Leptonycteris nivalis,* is in danger of extinction. Also known as the Mexican long-nosed bat, it migrates north, up to seven hundred fifty miles every spring, chasing the flowers of the agave. The bat's long nose is ideally engineered to pull the sweet nectar from the agave flower, which resembles the long, sheathed spear of an asparagus tip. The nectar will fuel the bats' journey to the southwestern United States, where the females will give birth to a single pup. Because of the bat's central role in the agave ecosystem, Torres Monfil and Pinzón Moncada chose the name "Zinacantán," meaning "land of bats" in the Indigenous Nahuatl language.

LAUNCHING AN ECOSYSTEM-ALIGNED BRAND

WHEN TORRES MONFIL INVITED PINZÓN Moncada to witness the mezcal distilling process in 2015, it was a little like Sonia Strobel (see Chapter 6) learning about how the fishing industry worked: Pinzón Moncada couldn't believe so much work, tradition, and craft went into a product that sold for so little.

After political and financial tensions led to the dissolution of the women's agave seed planting group in late 2014, Torres Monfil and Pinzón Moncada joined forces to launch Zinacantán, with Pinzón Moncada contributing a thousand dollars, and Torres Monfil providing the 1.2-acre space for the mezcal factory.

Torres Monfil and Pinzón Moncada's goals were to create as close to an ecologically sustainable mezcal as possible, from organic seed collection and planting, sustainable harvests that support native bat populations, identification of "mother" agaves whose seeds they would save, and reintroduction of genetically robust and diverse plants to their regeneratively farmed fields. It was a way of preserving the traditional agave spirit of Puebla. The duo opened their current factory adjacent to the Torres Monfil home in 2021.

Torres Monfil leads a team that includes her brother Silvestre, and three or four other family members. Though the men were at first skeptical, now they refer to her as "Doña Faby," a term of respect and deference. She hews to the ways of her forebears, putting her annual January harvest through a seven-week, late-January to early-May single distillation process that relies on ambient yeast, a clay oven, and the burning of the indigenous *guaje* (river tamarind or white lead tree) wood. She also follows the tradition of high ABV (alcohol-by-volume) levels—47 to 51 percent—to allow the best, most nuanced expression of each agave variety.

A SINGLE VARIETAL TASTING

ZINACANTÁN MEZCALS ARE CHARACTERIZED BY a gentle sweetness and floral complexity, with just a hint of burn instead of the raging smoke of many commercial brands. Pinzón Moncada pours us a flight, starting with espadilla (known in Oaxaca as espadin), the most commonly distilled variety, a distillation of 47 percent alcohol *Agave angustifolia*. The hand-drawn label (by an artist friend in Monterrey) depicts a bat flying above the revered active volcano of Puebla, Popocatépetl, named for a warrior of Aztec mythology, who forever faces his beloved, the princess Iztaccíhuatl, embodied in another volcano.

Its concentrated floral bouquet becomes even more potent after Pinzón Moncada places a few drops on my forearm and lets it oxidize for seven seconds. Its perfume is soft, exotically floral, and only slightly smoky, spreading and wafting from skin to breeze. Next, she pours from a 720-milliliter export bottle of 48 percent ABV single distilled papalométl (the local Nahuatl name for *agave potatorum*) mezcal, even more delicate and floral; since it is for export it is, as required by law, labeled as "agave spirit."

Torres Monfil and Pinzón Moncada are unable to export it labeled as mezcal because they have opted out of what they consider the corrupt and overly expensive process of procuring the Denomination of Origin for Mezcal (DOM) label they would need to do so. The DOM is supposed to act like France's *appellation d'origine contrôlée*, letting consumers know it has been produced in a way specific to a certain geographic region using specific traditional methods. But the federal government has repeatedly sanctioned and fined the primary DOM regulatory body, the Mezcal Regulatory Council, accusing it of deceptive and abusive practices.[11] Torres Monfil and Pinzón Moncada have made a proper mezcal according to age-old tradition, they just haven't paid for the legal right to label it so.

The wood tank–fermented papalométl mezcal is followed by Torres Monfil's latest creation, the black-label 200-millileter papalometl mezcal fermented in a leather cowhide vat, intense and wilder than the last. The bottles will be aged for six months before shipping, to allow their natural acetic and lactic acid notes to recede, and the spirit to attain balance.

On May third each year, the end of the season and the anniversary of the label's founding, Torres Monfil makes one more type, a small 80-liter batch of *pechuga* mezcal, in which a whole turkey, marinated in Torres Monfil's family recipe for mole poblano, is placed in a basket and hung in the distillation pot. The result is a complex, balanced mezcal with the aromas of wood, red mole, and vanilla. Pechuga mezcal has become trendy in recent years, but for Torres Monfil and Pinzón Moncada, it is an important celebration of biocultural heritage.

Their mezcal should never touch any type of mixer; first, as a sign of respect to the eight-to-twenty-five-year agave lives that have gone into making it, and second because small-batch, organic mezcal has a richness and complexity that are pure expressions of their agave varietals and poblano terroir. Each bears the mark of a true artisanal mezcal as well, with the lot number, bottle number, date of distillation, and number of liters produced handwritten on the back label and signed by "Maestro Mezcalero," Torres Monfil herself. In the year after I take a bottle of both the wood-tank and cowhide-fermented papalométl Zinacantán home with me, their subtle, multilayered allure will transform my previous curiosity toward single-varietal mezcal to a near-obsessive love, one small sip at a time.

Zinacantán only produces 1,500 liters of mezcal per year, not even a drop in the bucket compared to well over twelve million per year produced by Big Mezcal, because that's what they can sustainably harvest from their two fields. To help educate other small producers about the importance of agroecological practices and sustainability, two weeks before my arrival they, in partnership with Sonora Silvestre Collective, a Sonora, Mexico–based company, launched an agave seed bank called Fondo Agavero. It will be another vehicle to help spread their agave management protocol.

A VISIT TO THE AGAVE FIELDS

TO GET A LOOK AT this system up close, we jump into the partners' Nissan Frontier four-wheel drive—a reduced-price cash deal sourced on Facebook from a seller in Chiapas—and head to the closer of Torres Monfil's two fields, this one about a ten-minute drive from her home and factory. Their twelve-acre plot is an *ejidos*, a piece of communal land held in trust and parceled out by the government, mainly for agricultural use. The system, which harks back to pre-Hispanic collectivist land-ownership systems, was adopted during land reforms of the Mexican Revolution (1910–1920).[12] Recently the duo took out a loan to purchase their first parcel of land, five acres located about a thirty-minute drive away in the San Bartolomé Chimalhuacán part of San Diego la Mesa Tochimiltzingo municipality.

To my untrained eye, this field appears rock-filled and desolate, in part due to the fact that a portion of it was once used by Torres Monfil's mother, Luisa, to graze sheep. When she and Pinzón Moncada point out signs of their holistic management plan in action, I begin to see their influence on the land. To deter rabbits from devouring the agave, they reintroduced native nopales and cacti as alternate foods. They decided to leave untouched the ground cover of dry weeds to retain moisture in the soil during the four-year El Niño cycle (periodic atmospheric warming caused by a shift in the trade winds) that is just starting. The leafless, skeletal trees dotting the land, too, are there by design, to hold and maintain soil health and prevent evapotranspiration (loss of moisture from plant to air caused by overheating) among the young agaves they have planted from seed. To keep the field sustainable, Torres Monfil only harvest 80 percent of the crop each season; the plants that produce the highest levels of sugar (measured by digital refractometers) are preserved as mother plants.

The most prominent signs of green are from low-lying fan-shaped palms, which Pinzón Moncada tells me are invasive. The ground is so poor here, it is only suited to the fastest growing of agave species, espadilla, which does not have the deep root systems that their other species, the gorgeous silver-gray agave potatorum (butterfly agave), have. We will see those in another, sandier portion of the property along with the endemic but endangered convallis variety of agave that the duo are helping to save.

The biggest enemy of the agave plants are the *picudos*, or weevils, an infestation worsened by the importation from Oaxaca of up to fifth-generation monoculture agave clones and their weevil hitchhikers. In a well-functioning forest ecosystem, the weevil's role would be to attack sick plants, while healthy agave would have strong enough immune systems to fight them off. But clone monoculture agaves lack those defenses and their numbers become an all-you-can-eat buffet for weevils unless staunched by chemical pesticides. So the pressure on this pesticide-free field, surrounded by monoculture agave fields, is intense. Still, through a two-pronged defense plan, Torres Monfil and Pinzón Moncada have brought the presence of the pest from rampant to minimal in their fields.

First, they remove affected agaves and bury them in another area of the farm, treating the infected areas with lime or diatomaceous earth and leaving it fallow for a year. The hard-edged surfaces of the diatoms—the fossilized remains of minuscule aquatic organisms made of silica—scrape the insects, their eggs, and larvae, causing them to dry out and die. Second, they attract weevils with a pheromone-baited trap mixed with molasses and soap in a one-liter plastic bottle.

Torres Monfil also uses an ancient, low-tech way of finding and marking the contours of her land—where and how it is sloping—so that she can plant in a way that best reduces water runoff and nourishes the soil: a wooden "A frame" that looks like a large compass with a string and a stone attached to help find the ground's level point. Stakes placed two meters apart allow her to see contour lines where the land is level, and she plants agave plants and trees along these lines. They will act as barriers to soil and water runoff and help restore the degraded ecosystem. Giant, 1,100-liter plastic drums capture rainwater that will be used for emergency irrigation in April and May if drought conditions become severe.

NEAT AS A PIN AND COMPACT, TOO: THE MEZCAL FACTORY

BACK AT THE MEZCALERIA, THE co-owners give me a tour of the compact production facility, which is as neat as a pin and highly organized. Torres Monfil says that her strengths as a woman and master mezcalero include cleanliness and organization, which allow her the freedom to pay close attention to the distillation process. "It's like cooking. When you put all of your attention, care, and energy into the details, the final result will be very tasty," she says.

Not only does Torres Monfil work in batches that are a fraction of the size of the modern factories in her village, she is also deliberately trying to recapture the most hand-crafted methods still extant in her family's collective memory. One is the leather tank, fashioned from one of the family's own bulls, which she cut and tanned herself. Another is her latest building project, the re-creation of a still mysteriously named "The Filipino."

Before we get to those, however, she shows me the basics: the four-ton-capacity brick oven, which looks like a large firepit. This is where logs of *guaje* firewood are lit, topped by volcanic rocks. The oven heats up for at least six hours, after which the agave *piñas*, which have been soaked in water, are added, covered by wet palm fronds, soil, then wood to keep it all in place. The addition of water extinguishes the flames and slowly steams the piñas over five days, concentrating their aroma and flavors. A cross, always facing west in the direction of the setting sun, is placed on top of the pile to bless and protect the cooking piñas.

Once they are softened, the pineapples are cooled, chopped up by machete, and put through a mill, which reduces them to the fibers that will be placed in the wooden or leather fermentation vats. Torres Monfil leads us to a one-ton pine tank, covered with agave fibers and weighed down with rocks, which is in the ten-to-fourteen-day dry fermentation period, aided by ambient, wild yeast. It emits a tantalizing smell a little like fermenting corn, or pineapple mixed with smoke. When it reaches a Brix (dissolved sugar content on a refractometer) reading of eight, it is ready for the next ten-to-fourteen-day wet fermentation, when water is added. I can hear the active bubbling of the wet fermentation tank, feel the heat of the fermentation, and smell the sharp alcohol. These are the sensory cues that Torres Monfil and her brother Silvestre will be attuned to when they determine the exact moment to stop the fermentation.

The nineteen-hour single distillation of the *tepache* (the low-alcohol mixture of water and pulp) in their hardwood-fueled 350-liter copper still usually starts at 2 a.m. and ends the following evening. "I smell, listen, and taste, to choose the correct moment," Torres Monfil says. She takes care to sustainably reuse both of the waste products that result from the mezcal-making process. They use the *bagazo*, or fibrous waste, for animal feed or compost; Torres Monfil also makes adobe bricks out of bagazo, soil and water, some of which she used to construct the walls of a small seed bank.

She neutralizes the *viñaza*, or acidic water that results from the distilling process, by mixing it with lime (calcium hydroxide) and uses it for compost. The wastewater also went into plastering for the walls of the seed bank. Zinacantán's batch sizes are small enough that this recycling of waste products works. But for industrial mezcal production, large amounts of viñaza dumped in waterways is lethal to aquatic life.

Next, we walk over to the 1,500-pound-capacity leather tank, protected from the open air and sun only by a loose tarp and a sheer length of dark fabric. Resembling a sagging trampoline lashed to hand-hewn logs with the fibrous dried leaves of the canna plant, this is Torres Monfil's recreation of the tank style her great-great-grandparents used, long before the federal government began encouraging the use of wooden tanks.

Her latest challenge is to re-create the aforementioned "*destilador Filipino*,"[13] or "Filipino still." The style, I learn, was first introduced by Filipino slaves and sailors in the late 1500s and early 1600s, who toiled away on the galleons of their conquerors. All too happy to jump ship when the opportunity arose in the New World, they settled in Indigenous communities as allies in resistance. The newcomers introduced their own crops to the Mexicans, including tamarind and coconut, as well as their distilling culture, although it is unclear if distilling was practiced from earlier times, in pre-contact Mexico. Torres Monfil's family used a Filipino for its single-distillation method up until about forty years ago. She has slowly assembled the parts she needs to re-create it: a 100-liter clay pot to hold the tepache and place over the fire, a hollow *colorin* (coral tree) cap, condensation coil, and a copper pot cooling hood.

A strong believer in the need to protect against evil spirits and, as Pinzón Moncada puts it, "bad vibes," there are a number of talismans found throughout the factory: A small cross handmade from two strips of red paper is affixed to one leg of a wooden tank. A whole bulb of garlic tied with a red ribbon hangs above the fermentation tanks to summon good vibes and banish the bad ones—like those that accompanied the engineer from a large maker contracted to another mezcaleria in town. One day, he and an inebriated coworker entered Zinacantán's factory and began trash talking Torres Monfil's methods. She summarily ejected him and his toxic vibes.

The spiritual center of the factory is the small brick shrine with a peaked concrete roof, which holds the figures of three saints: the Virgin of Guadalupe, Mexico's own version of the Virgin Mary; San Judas Tadeo (Saint Jude, of difficult circumstances); and San Dieguito (an affectionate diminutive) de Alcala, the patron saint of the village. In front of the saints are three miniature glasses filled with mezcal, the equivalent of the flasks of sake found in the wall-mounted shrines in sake breweries across Japan—gifts to the gods in hopes of a good production season.

In less than a month, along with hundreds of others, Torres Monfil and Pinzón Moncada will make the annual pilgrimage up the slopes of the volcano Popocatépetl to make offerings to "Popo," or "Don Goyo," as it is known in Nahuatl, which they hope will protect them in the year to come. Some hope that an appeased Don Goyo will relieve the water shortages and skin conditions that have plagued the region recently, possible consequences of exposure to chemical pesticides and other agro-chemicals, and possibly from water pollution as a result of marble mining in the region.

The power of religion, spirits, and Indigenous myths remain vividly alive in the daily life of this small village, even as—or perhaps because of the way—they collide with the present-day reality of ecosystems degradation caused by extractive mining, Big Agriculture, and Big Beverage. While most pilgrims will climb the mountain bearing gifts of flowers, candies, and song, Torres Monfil and Pinzón Moncada will come bearing bottles of regenerative Zinacantán mezcal.

Like Sandy Boss Febbo's savory and nutty Gold beer brewed with Kernza, or Alice Anderson's romantic, electrically charged expression of California Central Coast terroir, the duo have opted for a type of agriculture that honors the land and natural ecosystems. They give back as much as they take out of the land, keep capital in the local and regional economy, and build regional knowledge networks that will strengthen the alt beverage system. They show how humans can symbiotically weave their lives into the local ecosystem, coaxing beverages of sublime beauty out of its grasses, fruits, and plants.

For consumers, it will be "flavor that flips" the switch, as Dawn Woodward says it does for customers of her Toronto whole grain bakery. They may be lured in by flavor, but it is narrative that has the power to make alt beverage fans supporters of the alt food system. These women makers' stories remind us that we, too, can be part of that narrative, that "individual actions do matter."

SOWING THE SEEDS OF THE ALT FOOD SYSTEM FUTURE: VISITS WITH INDIGENOUS AND DIASPORIC WOMEN

SEEDS HOLD WITHIN THEM OUR ancient past and the keys to our uncertain future. They embody resilience in their ability to adapt to new environments, climate shifts, and deep, dark ages in which they may have to go dormant, only to burst into leaf when the time is right. Depending on who is bringing them forth into the world, seeds can be instruments of empowerment, inclusiveness, justice, and climate adaptation. Or they can be bits of intellectual property fenced off from the commons by patents and regulations, designed to make farmers indentured servants to the line of products they have been hogtied to, and the agrochemical monopolies that own them. Casting about for the most hope-giving and forward-looking note to end on, I realize that it has to be seed saving.

"Seed saving" or "seed keeping," as it is sometimes called, is the long and laborious process of selecting superior plants—standouts because of their exceptional taste and flavor, advances in climate adaptation, or resistance to pests or disease—and growing them out over generations to stabilize their seeds before sharing or selling them to others.

Seed saving requires the kind of care and patience needed to raise a child, plus a lot of scientific note taking: it takes a good ten years of careful tending and selection before a seed saver can amass the volume needed to both save enough seeds and conduct tests on them. During the first two years of this process, California heirloom wheat farmer and seed saver Mai Nguyen plants seeds in trays in a greenhouse environment to protect them from birds. Once they have reached the tillering stage (when leaves have appeared, but no stem), Nguyen transplants the seedlings into moist field ground in the greenhouse and monitors their growth, meticulously noting the number of leaves, when the shoot "heads" (when the next-generation seed head emerges from its sheath), and its different stages of ripeness. They also note ambient temperature, amount of rainfall, and soil moisture.

In the beginning of the third year, Nguyen plants the seeds they have selected directly into the ground, half in fall, and half in late spring—some need a period of dormancy in deep cold—and continues to monitor and record their growth. After another four to five years of growing out, harvesting, and replanting seed, they will have enough to send to the California Wheat Commission lab, where the seeds will be tested for extensibility, elasticity, enzymatic activity, and protein, as well as undergoing a test bake. This traditional method of seed selection, breeding, and saving looks like the quaint relic of a bygone era compared to the scale and technology of the commodity seed supply chain.

For the home seed saver, by contrast, who will not be selling saved seeds on the commercial market and therefore is not subject to USDA rules (which monitor percent germination, acceptable weed seed thresholds, and accuracy in variety descriptions), simply saving the seeds of your favorite plants each season and improving upon the seed you save from year to year will help increase resilience and biodiversity in your garden.

A BIG SEED PRIMER

MUCH LIKE THE OTHER BRANCHES of the food system we have toured, the need for an alt system of smallholder seed savers stems from the commodification and monopolization of a global industry. For more than ten thousand years,[1] in civilizations around the world, farmers like Nguyen have saved and bred seeds from the tastiest and most resilient among their crops, improving traits they liked, adapting them to the local climate, and preserving regional and cultural food traditions. In the United States, the first step toward the privatization of seeds came after the federal patent office was opened in 1839 and began mailing millions of free packages of seed to farmers every year.[2] Seeds were considered an important public resource to be managed collaboratively. After the USDA was formed in 1862, the agency took over the collection and dissemination of seeds, and the protection of the country's germplasm, or plant genetic material.[3]

The USDA worked with land grant universities (designated by state legislatures or Congress to teach agriculture, science, and engineering to members of the working classes) to adapt plants to regional environments. From the beginning, though, the paternalistic government handling of seeds was based on theft: Each state was given thirty thousand acres of federally controlled land it could endow to these universities—land acquired through the violent seizure of nearly eleven million acres of Indigenous land.[4]

Government, public land grant institutions, and private industry formed the main cast of characters in the hundred-year story of the consolidation of the seed industry, which in turn is closely tied to the story of the commodification of our food system. It began with the development of high-yielding hybrid corn seeds in the 1920s, and continued with the

Green Revolution, the 1950s-to-1990s-era movement that boosted yields and ensured even greater profitability with its emphasis on chemical fertilizers, the development of hardier, shorter, much easier to machine-harvest varieties, and intensive monocropping.

One of the traits of hybrid varieties is that their own seeds will not grow "true to type," meaning they will not be exact replicas of their parent seeds. Farmers who planted these seeds thus lost the ability to save seeds and instead had to buy seeds every season, providing a new income stream to seed breeders and encouraging the rapid growth, consolidation, and commoditization of the private corn seed industry.[5]

In 1970, the passage of the Plant Variety Protection Act made patented intellectual property (IP) protection possible for seeds, and in 1985 genetically modified (GM) crops were introduced and deemed to be among the biotechnology innovations that could be patented IP.[6] The full patent protection given to GM crops in the 1990s meant that farmers who grew them were no longer able to legally save seeds, and in fact could be prosecuted for doing so. But the process of applying the principles of intellectual property—once limited to nonliving, immutable inventions—to living organisms (seeds) has resulted in overlapping, ill-defined IP systems, making it difficult for seed savers who want to promote biodiversity and resilience to craft a counter-intellectual property rights strategy.[7]

While seeds were increasingly being moved from the public commons to patent-protected corporate ownership, a landscape once populated by farmers who saved seeds and thousands of independent seed companies has been drastically altered by a frenzy of acquisitions and mergers. Today more than 60 percent of the $58 billion global seed market is controlled by four multinational pharmaceutical and chemical companies: Bayer, Corteva, ChemChina, and BASF.[8] Patented, genetically modified seeds now form the bulk of this commodity.

The seeds these four companies produce bind farmers who buy them in a cycle of dependence and threaten those who do not. Two GM seed developments illustrate this like no other. Monsanto's "Roundup Ready" crops are genetically modified to be resistant to Roundup, an herbicide that Monsanto produces and sells. There is little that farmers who choose not to grow Roundup Ready seeds can do to protect their crops from the drift of herbicide from other farms onto their fields. (See Chapter 4 for more on this, and the billions of dollars in damages Monsanto has paid in connection with Roundup herbicide.)

Another challenge associated with drift is cross-pollination of GM crops with non-GM crops. This can result in decreased biodiversity and threaten certification for organic farms, since they can no longer guarantee that their crops are all grown from organic seeds, a requirement under the guidelines for USDA organic crop certification. Sales of entire harvests have been lost due to the presence of GM traits found in organic crops that likely resulted from cross-pollination. Yet in 1988, when a Canadian farmer looked for a loophole in this web of encroaching IP protection and tried growing out his own seed contaminated by Roundup Ready GM seeds, he was sued by Monsanto and found guilty of patent infringement.[9]

In the 1990s a partnership of government and private research developed a technique called Genetic Use Restriction Technology (GURT), resulting in Monsanto's GM "terminator" seeds, created to be fertile in the first generation and sterile in the second generation. This modification would be another method of making it impossible for farmers to save these seeds from year to year, instead being forced to buy seeds annually. Monsanto provided a Kafkaesque rationale for these terminator seeds, asserting they were designed to prevent the genetic contamination of non-GM plants on surrounding fields.[10] While in 1999 Monsanto pledged to never release terminator seeds,[11] it takes constant vigilance on the part of those opposed to terminator seed technology who support open-source seeds as an alternative to patented seeds.

Just as in farming or grocery store retailing, vertical integration and economies of scale—of breeding, producing, and marketing of seeds—has led to a monopolistic diminishment of variety, taste, and biodiversity, and have made crops more vulnerable to drought, climate change, and pests. These shifts also brought lower pay to those working in this consolidated industry and higher seed prices for farmers who are increasingly shackled to the large multinational companies that control all of their inputs from seed to fertilizer, to the right to repair their own farm equipment.

An example of just how far removed farmers and gardeners are today from the sources of their seeds came in 2023, in an episode known as "jalapeñogate," in which gardeners across the country planted what they thought were one type of pepper seeds, only to be unpleasantly surprised when a variety of peppers other than what they had bought began popping forth from their plants: wax peppers instead of jalapeños, yellow banana peppers instead of bright orange and red carnival peppers.[12] Because of the complexity, opaqueness, and consolidation of the global, multitiered seed supply chain, it was difficult to figure out exactly how this had happened, or where to get accurately labeled pepper seeds—large numbers of wholesale nurseries across the nation that source their seeds from overseas suppliers received faulty shipments. Many made good on customer losses, resulting in significant lost revenue and serving as a wake-up call to just how seriously Big Seed threatens our food security and food sovereignty.

We have come a long way from the days of seed diversity and wide availability from a multitude of breeders, when government and academia played a more active hand in protecting plant diversity and farmers' access to it. But all is not lost. In a landscape seemingly controlled by Big Seed, there are still those trying to reclaim and democratize access to plant diversity and their ancestral culture—seed savers.

REBECCA WEBSTER: RE-LEARNING ANCESTRAL WAYS, ONE HARVEST AT A TIME

THE ORIGINAL SEED SAVERS WERE the citizens of the Indigenous First Nations who have stewarded our lands for millennia. They predate the Age of Enlightenment, the Age of Discovery, the Green Revolution— those optimistically named eras that turned out to have their dark sides, too. Many have been removed from the ecosystems they helped shape and manage, to the great detriment of those ancestral lands. For many First Nations people, seeds represent the most elemental reconnection with their culture, perfectly engineered packages of DNA that represent millennia of adaptation, and the cultivation of taste that today's generation longs to reconnect with. Remember that Indigenous people make up only 6 percent of the world's population, but they safeguard 80 percent of its remaining biodiversity.[13] Rebuilding food and seed sovereignty in the broader Indigenous diasporic culture is one way to begin shifting that balance.

One of the most touching, and telling, parts of the YouTube video "Indigenous Seed Exchange Etiquette" is the way it opens: "It's okay to be nervous about attending a seed exchange or trying to acquire seeds through a trade. We have to remember that we are the product of generations of removal, relocation, colonization, and assimilation. Our ancestors had to lay down much of their traditional knowledge, and many of us are just now picking that knowledge up and reestablishing our relationships with our food, language, history, and culture."

The reassuring voice that soothes the insecurities born of deep-seated trauma and separation is that of Rebecca Webster, enrolled tribal citizen of the Oneida Nation west of Green Bay, Wisconsin, cofounder of the nonprofit Ukwakhwa, Inc., and associate professor in the department of American Indian studies at the University of Minnesota, Duluth.

Growing up on the reservation, she and the boy who would eventually become her husband, Steve Webster, were both interested in their tribal culture, customs, history, and language. In 2015, with their daughters Grace, eleven, and Mia, nine, the family harvested and tied its first traditional white corn braid (a way of braiding together the husks of corn and then hanging them to dry) and became hooked on reclaiming its ancestral white corn culture. The next year—with a group of like-minded Oneida families—the Websters started a nonprofit cooperative called Ohe-láku, which means "among the cornstalks." When she was offered a tenure-track position at the University of Minnesota Duluth in 2016, Webster accepted, on the condition that she could stay on the reservation and teach remotely. In 2017 Webster convinced Steve to quit his job, sell their house, and buy ten acres of land on which they could build a new house, continue to grow corn with the cooperative, and homeschool their daughters. "It was the best decision I ever made," Webster tells me.

With help from friends and family, they built their own house. Ohe-láku gradually added beans and squash, which are grown together with corn in a system of mutual support that is the foundation of Indigenous agriculture: the Three Sisters. The cornstalks provide a support for the beans to wind around and climb, away from the sprawling squash vines on the ground. The beans, in turn, fix nitrogen, making this important nutrient available to the entire family, and strengthen the cornstalks against winds. The squash vines and their large leaves shade the ground, enabling it to retain moisture while warding off weeds and other invaders with their prickly leaves and vines.

Between 2017 and 2022, the growth of their homestead and cooperative was astounding. Ohe-láku added seed keeping, maple syrup tapping, food preparation, food storage, toolmaking, and crafting to its activities. After consulting with their Wolf Clan faithkeeper Leander Danforth, an Oneida language speaker responsible for carrying out many community ceremonies and giving members their Oneida names, the Websters and their community named their space Ukwakhwa: Tsinu Niyukwayayʌthoslu ("Our Foods: Where We Plant Things"). USDA and other grants provided the funds to build two high tunnels (a kind of tall, lightweight, flexible greenhouse), a gazebo, commercial kitchen, trading post, storage building for farm equipment, and pavilion and attached shed for larger events. The trading post they erected is filled with jars of beans, corn, wild rice, jams, pickles, fruit, maple syrup, and loose-leaf tea. They trade those, as well as dry goods such as beadwork, books, hides, and blankets by barter system, as was the custom of their ancestors.

Because seed saving is central to rebuilding their food system, the community did not taste the beans it grew for the first five years, instead focusing on being able to save and share seeds. "There's a lot of shame and embarrassment in our community over not knowing our traditional ways or having relationships with our seeds. We wanted to provide a space where people can come and learn, with no expectations that they be experts. Our seeds and our foods are really a way back to our culture—they bring us back together as a community," says Webster. "Our ancestors had to lay down a lot of our practices just in order to survive during colonization, assimilation, removal, the boarding school era, all of that."

A few members of the Oneida community are longtime seed keepers, one in particular a well-known bean seed keeper. But most of the seeds they began with—including Oneida yellow-eyed and Haudenosaunee true red cranberry beans—were shared with them by Indigenous seed savers in New York state. Angela Ferguson, a Tuscarora tribal member who works for the Onondaga Nation—where Webster's tribe originated and lived before being forced to relocate to Wisconsin by the federal government in the early 1800s—was one of her first seed mentors.

"There have been certain key people and key families that have held on to our seeds and nurtured them, often in secret because these aren't always things that mainstream society respected or even allowed," Webster says. Before the passage of the 1978 American Indian Religious Freedom Act—which protects the rights of Native Americans to practice their traditional religions on spiritual sites, to possess and use sacred objects, and the freedom to worship through ceremonial and traditional rites—seed saving was not expressly forbidden or outlawed. But Native Americans were persecuted for conducting tribal ceremonies[14] and engaging in broader cultural practices that connected them to their ancestors and the land; it is not hard to see how tribal members might have felt that this custom, too, had to be kept secret.

The secrecy around seed saving was why people like Webster and her husband, despite growing up on the reservation, did not have access to these ancient practices. Now, she notes, "more and more people are joining in this adventure of trying to relearn and reconnect to our seed relatives."

The concept of seeds as relatives to humans is one that is threaded through Webster's 2023 book, *Our Precious Corn: Yukwanénste*, which tells stories of corn and its integral role in the daily and ceremonial lives of the Oneida and other Haudenosaunee people. She writes of corn, "If we truly perceive her as the spiritual being she is, we can also see how she has been our nurturer and educator." One prelude to seed selection Webster describes in the book are the "husking bees" during harvest time, when the entire tribe gathers to help with the harvest and husking of corn, and today "continues to be a time of great celebration and storytelling." As one Seneca elder she quotes, the archaeologist, historian, and folklorist Arthur Parker, said of the husking bees, "Work was play in those days when mutual helpfulness made money unnecessary." The husking bees were also the time when the women of the community would decide which cobs were suitable for keeping as seed for future planting and which were for eating.

At Ukwakhwa, too, it is the women who select seeds for saving, nominating the cobs they think have the best potential for passing on their genes to the next generation of corn; Webster makes the final decision. With the Tuscarora white corn, which is the primary variety they grow, they look for long, straight cobs eight rows across, uniform color, and nice plump kernels. More than eight rows, yellow kernels mixed with the white, or dimples are all signs of cross-pollination.

Corn, too, Webster writes in *Our Precious Corn*, tells the story of trauma that the Yukwanuhsyu-ní (formerly known as the Iroquois Confederacy or Six Nations, today as the Haudenosaunee people) have endured. In the late 1700s, as the colonists geared up for the revolution that would free them from British rule, the Iroquois Confederacy attempted to stay neutral but inevitably became swept up in the conflict. The Oneida and their Tuscarora "guests" (cultural and linguistic cousins the Oneida had adopted into the Confederation after they warred with southern Colonists and were driven north out of their native Carolinas) sided with the revolutionaries.

In the winter of 1778, Oneida warriors walked hundreds of miles south from central New York to Valley Forge, Pennsylvania, carrying hundreds of bushels of white corn to share with Washington's starving troops. Among the delegation was a woman named Polly Cooper who showed the soldiers how to improve the taste and nutritional content of their inadequate diets. She prepared a corn soup by husking the ears, grinding the kernels into meal, and mixing the boiled soup with fruits and nuts. After the war, she and the warriors refused to accept payment for their aid, explaining it was their duty to help friends in need. As a token of her appreciation, Martha Washington sent Cooper a shawl and a bonnet, which her descendants safeguard to this day.

The humanitarian actions of these two tribes—and the Indigenous custom of sharing and gift-giving as a way to cement alliances—stands in stark contrast to the profit-driven, patent-protected seed fortresses of Big Seed. Yet the Oneida warriors' good deeds hurt their allies in the end. In 1779, when Washington ordered Major General John Sullivan to attack the four confederacy nations that had sided with the British, the Oneida did their best to avoid participation in this campaign, and even shield their fellow Confederacy members. "Journals of Sullivan and his officers provide insight into the breadth of their damage," Webster writes. Sullivan's men destroyed forty Iroquois Confederacy towns and hundreds of homes, uprooting or felling thousands of fruit trees and destroying nearly ten million pounds of corn, as well as untold amounts of beans, squash, and other vegetables. Often residents of the pillaged towns had to leave in such haste that they left food cooking over their fires.

In a passage of her book titled *The Corn Remembers the War*, Webster writes of one elder who taught younger members that the red dots that appear on the shells of their white corn are not bad, they are remnants of the blood of their ancestors that had seeped into the soil and made their way into the corn. The spots, he said, are "a reminder that we need to remember our history and appreciate our resiliency." For Indigenous communities today, seed exchanges are a way to regain some of that resiliency and seed-saving knowledge.

In 2019, Ukwakhwa hosted a highly successful seed exchange for more than one hundred people who gathered from across the country. The first round was for participants who brought seeds to barter or sell, and the second was for the remainder of attendees. "What happens a lot during a seed exchange is that people will lose their minds, be so excited to see all these seeds and they get grabby about it. So, we wanted people who brought seeds to have an opportunity, and then when trading is done, see how generous we can be to those who didn't bring seeds," says Webster.

Just as the history of mutual aid and resilience of the southern African American agricultural cooperatives can serve as a road map to growing and strengthening the alt food system, so can the story of Indigenous reclaiming of their seed-saving heritage.

KAITLYN WALSH AND SPRING ALASKA SCHREINER: UNFURLING THE WELCOME MAT FOR RETURNING SEED RELATIVES

KAITLYN WALSH SEES HER ROLE in the story of Indigenous seed saving as being a conduit for seeds returning to her community, part of the sixty-thousand-member Indigenous diaspora in and around Minnesota's Twin Cities. She and Spring Alaska Schreiner, another mixed-race Indigenous seed saver, are examples of seed saving both as a way back to one's own culture, and as a way to return control of seed sovereignty and biodiversity to individuals: farmers, gardeners, anyone who has an interest in re-democratizing seeds.

As a child, all Walsh knew was that she, Kaitlyn Eve, had been named after her Indigenous great-grandmother, Eva Katie Pequette, a member of the Minnesota's Fond du Lac Band. To Walsh, the name was a treasured gift and link to her Indigenous past. Yet she knew little about Eva Katie.

After the death of her cousin's father in 2019, old black-and-white photos of Eva Katie surfaced during the funeral-planning process, depicting Eva Katie holding a birch basket and winnowing wild rice. Walsh learned that both her uncle and her cousin had in their possession some of these winnowing baskets that Eva Katie had woven out of birch bark, and that her cousin had inherited her large, cast-iron wild rice parching kettle.

The experience of seeing the framed photograph of her great-grandmother "ricing" (the process of harvesting and processing wild rice) called out to her in a powerful, visceral way. It was like discovering that your ancestor was a Jedi Knight. "I felt something waking up, like I could actually pursue tribal food sovereignty work and be more myself," Kaitlyn told me. She saw herself, her family, and her ancestors in those photos and artifacts. "It was the moment I knew I needed to shift my life drastically."

That same year, when Kaitlyn and her grandmother Temprance Debe, Eva Katie's daughter, attended an Indigenous food sovereignty gathering in Duluth, Temprance was overwhelmed by the wealth of Indigenous foods displayed, and after attending the event, suggested that before returning home they visit a wetlands area on the reservation, known as the Ditchbanks. This was a favorite spot where Temprance had taken her grandchildren to explore and hunt for agates. This time, though, influenced by what they had seen at the food sovereignty fair, the floodgates of Temprance's memory opened, and recollections from her early childhood—entire days spent at the Ditchbanks with her family, gathering and eating berries and nuts—returned. She was eighty, and Kaitlyn was thirty; the generational passing down of long-forgotten knowledge that Kaitlyn longed for was finally taking place.

Temprance regaled Kaitlyn with stories she had not told in years, sprinkling them with Indigenous insights into birch trees and high bush cranberries. Kaitlyn was shocked at her grandmother's demeanor, too; it was like seeing decades fall away from her as submerged memories float-ed to the surface. When they walked over to one of the rice lakes and its adjacent wooden overlook, built for use during ricing season, Temprance exhibited even more unusual behavior. "She's had mobility issues her whole life. But when we get out to the lake, she runs up to and hops up on this overlook. I was like, 'since when do you climb stairs like that, lady?'" Walsh recalls. According to Ojibwe tradition, they recited a prayer, then let some of the loose Prince Albert pipe tobacco that Temprance kept in the glove compartment of her car for just these purposes to waft down into the water—a prayer for a more bountiful harvest during a season that was giving poor returns.

Today Walsh's work revolves around her community, the Fond du Lac Band of Lake Superior Chippewa west of Duluth, where she is a supervi-sor at the Na'enimonigamig Cannery. During her off hours, she serves as network coordinator for the Native American Food Sovereignty Alliance Upper Midwest Indigenous Seed Keepers Network and works to grow out traditional varieties of seeds for the community. The act of "rematri-ating" seeds and facilitating intergenerational healing is an empowering process, yet also freighted with doubt.

"There's definitely that warm, connected side of things where I feel secure and taken care of, and accompanied by my ancestors," says Walsh, thinking of the gift of her great-grandmother's name that enabled her to ask scary questions. But there are also "intense feelings of grief, sadness and trauma around why grandma didn't get to learn these things, and why I didn't get to until now. It can feel very lonely." Being at Fond du Lac and reconnecting with family and the community there has helped. "It's something I try to remember when I'm struggling or feeling impostor syndrome. I never feel like I'm doing enough, and I don't know if I'm do-ing the right thing." During those uncertain times, she thinks of her late uncle Leland, and feels his hand on her shoulder, saying, 'Alright, alright. Let's go." The seeds, too, will talk to her during these times. "They do not let me forget."

One of the people in attendance at the 2019 seed exchange organized by Rebecca Webster's nonprofit Ukwakhwa was Spring Alaska Schreiner, a native seed keeper, farmer, native foodways instructor, and policy activist who runs her six-acre Sakari Farm in Bend, Oregon, and markets a line of botanical salves and tinctures to specialty food products. ("Sakari" means "sweet" in the Iñupiaq language.) Schreiner's long brunette braids and brightly beaded medallion earrings signal her heritage as a member of Alaska's Valdez tribe, an amalgamation of Native Alaskan tribes that includes the Sugpiaq, Inuits, Chugach, and Pacific Eskimos.

Arriving in Bend in 2006, she was a Native fish out of water. In Alaska, Indigenous communities did not share the same experience of war, removal, and relocation that tribes in the lower forty-eight states did, and a spirit of intertribal mutual support connected different tribes and communities across far-flung waterways. Feeling cut off from Indigenous culture and traditions, Schreiner wanted to re-create that sense of intertribal mutuality. She began seed saving in 2009, launched a native seed company, and started a nursery specializing in pre-contact "first foods" (foods that predated European occupation and colonization) such as sweetgrass and yarrow. Their use as botanicals led to her Sakari Botanicals line and later an intertribal seed bank and the nine-hundred-square-foot Niqi Native Kitchen. Here, she brings together the Native community, offering cooking classes to Indigenous youths and serving as an incubator kitchen for value-added products. She launched the Central Oregon Seed Exchange to encourage and teach seed exchange and seed saving, and forged ties with the Hopi and Oneida Nations to grow and save seeds for them.

On a tour of her facilities and farm, Schreiner shows some tobacco seed pods that she is helping to grow out for the Confederated Tribes of Grand Ronde in western Oregon, and gracefully curved, bright orange Native gete-okosomin squash that are two-to-three-feet long, which she marinates in maple sugar and then freeze dries into a snack that tastes more of sweet melon than squash. "Everything just tastes so different and so much better [than non-Indigenous varieties], with insane flavor," she says of these and other crops like Hopi tomatillos, black beans, and the Makah Ozette potato of the Pacific Northwest Makah Nation. She believes this is in part because the seeds are ancestral and unmodified, and in part because of Sakari Farm's healthy soils and practices ranging from cover cropping to composting, native burning practices, and the creation of a pollinator habitat.

In the fragrant drying room, bunches of White Buffalo Calf Woman hang upside down alongside sweetgrass, Hopi red amaranth, yarrow, and Hopi red onion; in one of seven greenhouses, seven-foot-tall, dried, already-harvested stalks of Hopi blue corn will soon be composted. In Oregon, where tribal relations can be territorial, Schreiner still does not always feel safe from intertribal criticism doing the work she has chosen. "I just have more courage now," she says.

PRESERVING AND SAFEGUARDING INDIGENOUS SEEDS: WHOSE RESPONSIBILITY IS IT?

ONE ISSUE THAT BOTH SCHREINER and Webster touch upon in our conversations is how to safeguard tribal seeds from the wider world. Already Schreiner points out, Indigenous seeds such as big horse spotted or Hopi pink flour corn varieties are part of the non-Indigenous Baker Creek Heirloom Seed Catalog.

Webster says that another commonly given example of Indigenous varieties co-opted by White seed companies is a squash variety grown by the Haudenosaunee called buffalo creek squash, "a beautiful, really giant variety that's delicious and plentiful. It is now available commercially under the name Boston marrow. What happened is some folks from seed companies came into our communities, got hold of our seeds, grew this out and slapped their own name on it. So now that seed in that plant is out there in the world wearing somebody else's name. It's a really unfortunate situation because it's another example of erasure of our seeds and our seed relatives, who they are and what communities historically took care of them."

Nevertheless, her approach is not to wall off Indigenous seeds from the rest of the world. "We don't have razor wire around our gardens. If somebody really wanted to get access to our seeds, grow them out, and call them their own, there's not a whole lot we can do to stop them." Instead, she advocates for documenting her tribe's heritage seeds, noting their characteristics, and letting others know that these are their seed relatives, should Monsanto or any other entity try to claim them. "We've learned that every time an Indigenous person plants a seed that is an act of resistance, an assertion of sovereignty, and a reclamation of identity," Webster says.

There are cases in which the very erasure of seed ownership and stewardship caused by colonialism has led to cross-cultural efforts to preserve some important varieties. Heather Darby—the University of Vermont extension agronomy specialist I spoke to in Chapter 4—has a deep love for corn and an interest in the nutritional value of northern flint corn. Her interest is the type cultivated for both humans and livestock by Indigenous communities from the northern part of the United States up to the Gaspé Peninsula of northern Quebec. Were the different-colored flint corns nutritionally superior to dent corn, the most common variety grown in the United States? To investigate this and other pressing corn questions, two decades ago Darby began working in partnership with the corn-breeding researcher Frank Kutka at the College of Menominee Nation in Minnesota, a land grant institution chartered by the people of the Menominee Nation. More recently, she has begun working with Kutka in collaboration with New England's Abenaki Indigenous community.

Darby's fear is that the northern flint is in danger of being lost, "not just because of the impact of being taken from their Indigenous caretakers, and the cessation of their careful selecting and saving of seed over time, but also because of the impacts of climate change." Her ongoing partnership with Indigenous communities—which can help elevate traditional knowledge to the place of respect it deserves—involves studying northern flint's susceptibility to climate change and breeding new varieties that can withstand climate change yet still feed Indigenous communities.

Darby's work is an example of the kind of allyship that is open to scientists, researchers, and anyone who gardens—offering support to Indigenous or other keepers of culturally relevant seeds, rather than appropriating them for their own use. While finding Indigenous sources of such seeds can still be difficult, you can more easily purchase the seeds products of the Korean, Indian, Palestinian, and Vietnamese seed keepers we will meet next.

KRISTYN LEACH: A KOREAN ADOPTEE FINDS CULTURAL CONNECTION

KRISTYN LEACH, A LEADER IN the movement to save seeds that are culturally relevant to diasporic communities, recalls how her dad, a Long Island, New York, policeman who worked a catering job on the side, would come home late from a gig bearing leftover food. Even if Leach and her two brothers were already in bed, they would come downstairs to try whatever the dish was, "corny stuff like Hawaiian chicken with maraschino cherries." Food was central to her family, and whether it was working in their large vegetable garden, helping her grandmother cook, going grocery shopping, or—outside the family—working part-time shifts as a short-order cook, her fondest memories revolve around food.

It wasn't until she moved to Olympia, Washington, at nineteen and began working small-scale farm jobs, however, that Leach, a Korean adoptee, encountered Asian vegetables such as Korean perilla or Korean radish through the Kitazawa Seed Company catalog. The encounter was an early intimation of what she would later term "an existential longing for ancestral connection." It launched her journey deep into seed keeping as a way to learn about her own diasporic heritage, as well as a path to keeping biodiversity and cultural traditions alive.

Those early farm jobs in Washington, managing a specialized commercial lettuce farm and later working for tomato breeder Fred Hempel in California also reawakened her childhood interest in science. She became absorbed in challenges like how to clip basil in a way that would yield a continual harvest. At one of her jobs, she asked a farm manager who also taught in the agriculture department at Evergreen State College in Olympia, Washington, for reading recommendations. He offered her a reading list, and she set out on a path of self-study using that as her guide, pulling the books and resources she needed at the local library. She haunted free cooperative extension field days, took copious notes, and returned to the library to flesh out her knowledge.

Her move to the Bay Area and time spent working in restaurant kitchens—from intern to pastry station and prep—she says, "was eye-opening for me: seeing the food culture that existed there, meeting a lot of young

Asian American cooks." Despite her extensive farm experience, she realized that the culinary perspective and produce of the farms she had worked on was predominantly Eurocentric. During a stint working at Camino Restaurant in Oakland, she also came to understand the appeal of specialty produce. Annabelle Lenderink, then farm manager at the pioneering organic Star Route Farm, became a mentor and inspiration to Leach. "She was growing lots of Italian heirloom vegetables and was introducing all these interesting chicories to chefs. I started to see this zeitgeist of small-scale agriculture, and how people craved things that aren't just the standard stuff."

These discoveries expanded her interest in Asian vegetables that had been kindled the first time she opened the Kitazawa catalog; she began growing Korean vegetables as a side hustle. "It was a way to carve out a niche for myself that was personal and genuine," she explains. Her exploration into Korean perilla was complicated because she had no childhood taste memories to call on to tell her what was "authentic," or what was a departure from the classic taste profile. She could make meaningful seed selections for heat and drought tolerance but felt at sea when it came to flavor, texture, and aromatic compounds. Since she lacked the confidence of that "overt taste memory," she relied on her self-taught botanical skills, and her belief in her ability to grow viable seeds.

When she met David, Dennis, and Daniel Lee of the Namu Restaurant Group—Bay Area favorites beloved for their takes on Korean hot pots and California–Korean fare—and saw their "cool, visceral," and very positive reaction to her Korean vegetables, it was the validation that she craved. They discovered a shared interest in preserving their cultural identity through exploration of Korean vegetables, but also in going beyond the commercial, chemically treated cultivars "predominantly owned by Monsanto" to look for native varieties that predated commodity seeds. In 2011, the Lees and Leach launched Namu Farm on two acres of leased land in Winters, California; she relocated to live there in 2017.

Leach wants to both satisfy Korean Americans' "sentimental longing for the familiar," and to strive for continual improvement in seed and plant breeding via community input and conversations around taste and memory. And she wants the process to be bottom-up instead of top-down, driven by citizen seed savers, farmers and chefs, not corporations.

In 2016 she launched Second Generation Seeds, a collective of growers that encompasses East Asian, Southwest Asian, and North African diasporas, and the plants that have evolved in them. Members share seeds and knowledge, adapting their chosen heirloom varietals to their local climates. The next year, Leach, along with community organizer Yong Chan Miller, started a Korean American *nonghwal*, or rural volunteer group, to help connect members to South Korea's agricultural roots, its democracy movement of the 1960s through 1980s, and encourage the growing of heritage vegetables. In 2023, Leach launched a national Seed Fellows network, selecting ten growers whom she mentors through monthly workshops, community engagement, and technical and financial assistance.

Second Generation Seeds' tagline seems especially relevant to Leach's own background, and, as I'll come to learn, to other members' diasporic histories as well: "By preserving, adapting, and breeding beloved crops, we affirm that culture is rooted in our imaginations, not just our memories." Even as an apartment-dwelling home gardener, I can support Second Generation Seeds' work by visiting its online shop and trying my hand at growing its crops.

ZEE LILANI AND NADIA BARHOUM: CROWD SOURCING TASTE MEMORIES, PUTTING HANDS IN DIRT

TO ROUND OUT MY JANUARY trip through the Bay Area, I meet with two Second Generation Seed Fellows, Zee Lilani of Kula Nursery in Oakland, and Nadia Barhoum of Thurayya Seeds in El Sobrante, Contra Costa County. Though their roots are in different parts of the world—Gujarat, India, via Pakistan for Lilani, and Palestine for Barhoum—for both of them, saving seeds is a way to salve the generational trauma of conflict and displacement, and create a living bond with their ancestral countries through taste, stories, seed saving, and collective memory.

Kula Nursery is hidden behind a colorfully graffitied and razor-wire topped fence in a densely populated section of West Oakland. Lilani, dressed in black jeans, a light down jacket, and holding a large bunch of keys, comes to the entrance to let me in. In this 972-square-foot greenhouse space decorated with a glittery silver disco ball and yards of traditional Indian yellow-gold marigold garlands ("I don't like to promote fake flowers, but they're fake," says Lilani), she grows more than a hundred different varieties of what she calls "heritage plants," most of them important to the South Asian cultural traditions, rituals, and cuisine of her people. "Kula" means "family" or "ancestors" in Sanskrit. It is the off-season now so the bulk of her offerings are finished and what is left are rows of curry plants, two lengths of sugar cane that she is trying to propagate in a bin of soil, some night-blooming jasmine grown from cuttings, and a tamarind tree.

Lilani's seed growing and saving takes place on a half-acre plot in Petaluma, about a forty-minute drive to the north in Sonoma County. There, she stewards a dozen different South Asian varieties—eight of them commercially available as seeds and through her Kula Nursery website, including eggplant, okra, tomato, and Tulsi basil. Her goal is to adapt these culturally important varieties to the local climate and build resiliency over successive generations of saved seeds.

After earning her master's degree in international agricultural development at UC Davis in March 2022, Lilani thought she would work in policy to help bring about food system change. But the ongoing pandemic made finding work difficult, and she found herself doing what she loves most, farming and growing food in her Davis backyard. Her mother happened to visit one day, and Lilani witnessed the look of delight that lit up her face when she saw the okra and amaranth her daughter was growing, both so important in Indian cuisine and to her family's fraught history of double displacement.

Originally from the city of Surat in Gujarat, India, Lilani's family was forced to relocate to Pakistan after the end of British rule and the partition in India in 1947. The forced migration of Muslims to Pakistan and Hindus and Sikhs to India displaced between twelve and fifteen million people in what is considered the largest mass migration in human history. Lilani's family, so abruptly and painfully torn from its roots, did its best to retain its food customs. Although her mother was born in Karachi, Pakistan, she grew up on Gujarati-style home cooking. None of Lilani's family members, as Pakistani Americans, have been allowed to return to India due to ongoing political tensions between the two countries.

The family immigrated to the United States in 1991, when Lilani was a year old. On that pandemic-era visit to Lilani's Davis garden, her mother had not seen amaranth leaves—which she remembered eating every Friday in Pakistan—for close to thirty years.

The incident set Lilani to thinking about what other foods her family might not have tasted since leaving their country. She peppered her grandmother with questions: "What vegetables were important to you growing up? What vegetables do you miss?" The idea of a heritage plant nursery began to take shape.

Much like Leach, who didn't grow up with the taste of Korean vegetables, Lilani, who has lived in California her entire life, knew that community input was crucial. The Irvington Farmer's Market in the South Bay community of Fremont is not exactly local for her, but one she specifically targeted because it is the most important market for Bay Area South Asians and the specialty produce that they favor. "I just knew that I had to be there because they would be the ones to teach me what was missing in the food system." The tactic worked, too; by fielding its requests and demands, the Irvington market community helped shape her list of seeds.

When Lilani brought four buckets of her tomato harvest to the market and had her community sample them, she quickly identified a list of four taste and texture profiles she knew were important to zero in on. She dubbed the sour tomato that she developed "Desi Girl," an answer to Monsanto's Early Girl. Unlike the hybrid, patented seeds of Big Seed, which give no credit to the communities or cultures whose genetic material they are based on, and which will not reproduce, hers are open pollinated, meaning genetically diverse and able to grow out true to type year after year. It gives her pleasure to know her customers can steward, grow out, save, and share seeds that will enter or re-enter their lives and become part of their diasporic culture.

Each of the dozen heritage vegetables she grows on her seed farm, Lilani says, "is very special because it has either been given to me from a community member through the nursery or has been brought from a family farm in India." Passed down from generation to generation, such seeds are becoming scarcer as Big Seed dominance spreads. Lilani's seed varieties—a number of them from her grandmother's hometown of Surat—include a curved, spiky- and bumpy-surfaced Indian bitter gourd known as *karela*, both tasty and highly medicinal; the green bean *surti papdi*; the long bean *choli*; various peppers; and luffa gourds. For okra, her community favors dark, long pods that stay tender when cooked, so that is what she looks for when saving seeds.

Her seed farm also serves as a laboratory in which she can watch how each year, her seeds become more resilient and adapted to their Bay Area climate and the needs of the people who live there. "I tell people all the time that this curry plant is not going to grow to the ten-to-fifteen-foot tropical tree that you see in India; it really is meant to be a houseplant that will supply enough for your own consumption."

Like Lilani's family, Barhoum's familial history lends seed saving an extreme emotional resonance, so tied up it is with a sense of loss, heart-break, and longing for cultural connection to her homeland. Her ancestors were forcibly exiled from their country in 1948, during the mass displace-ment known as the Nakba, following the first war of the Palestine–Israel conflict. Her father was the lone member of his family to immigrate to the United States, where Barhoum and her two siblings internalized a fierce pride in their Palestinian identity.

Feeling a connection to her family's agrarian roots, from an early age Barhoum was drawn to work on the land: "Maintaining that connection to the land and our people is one of the keys to our collective liberation," she says. But she found it hard to go against the wishes of her college pro-fessor father, who had transcended his refugee status through education and who stressed academic achievement and a professional career.

She bided her time doing human rights and social justice work, then in 2018 entered UC Santa Cruz's Farm to College program. "[The program] was only six months," Barhoum recalls, "but just imagining a lifetime of working on a piece of land and then being forcibly expelled and you know, your family members killed . . . it brought up a lot of grief for me."

It was then that Barhoum hatched her plan of bringing seeds from Palestine, growing culturally significant plants, and building an archive of traditional knowledge and land-based traditions. During the program, she invited Vivien Sansour, the artist, conservationist, and founder of the still-operating Palestinian Heirloom Seed Library, to speak, and in 2019 was able to wrangle a two-week visa to Palestine. The visit was not easy: She was detained at the airport, questioned about her contacts, had her phone searched for suspicious numbers, and was denied exit via the Tel Aviv airport. From then on, she would have to enter and exit through Jordan. Yet she was able to visit the Palestinian Heirloom Seed Library and buy some seeds. At her home in El Sobrante, among terraced planter beds on a third of an acre, she has begun growing out those seeds, which include okra; Battiri eggplant specific to the village of Battir in the West Bank; a type of bottle gourd called *yakteen*; and a fuzzy, ribbed cucurbit that is eaten like a cucumber called *fakous*.

Barhoum is also growing a type of wild sage, *maramiya*, which is used medicinally or often mixed with black tea and sugar for the traditional drink *shay bi maramiya*. Her cousin sourced the maramiya from the family's ancestral village of Al Malha in West Jerusalem. The village was the site of bloody conflict in the 1948 Arab–Israeli war, when all of its Arab residents were either killed, wounded, expelled, or forced to flee.

"It's the first time I've ever gotten to feel or touch or smell the smell of my village, and when I think that my *teta*, grandmother, may have harvested from those plants, my soul feels happy, like I'm fulfilling some sort of destiny that I've been denied my whole life," she says.

The October 7, 2023, Hamas attack and Israel's brutal retaliation felt to Barhoum "like a continuum" in the violence and trauma. "People talk about PTSD, but we never got to have the 'post' part," she says. Fewer and fewer Palestinians have access to land and water, and the seeds they do have access to are Israeli seeds. All of these things have lent a heightened sense of urgency to Barhoum's task of preserving Palestinian seeds, and a need "to be in community, to not be on the defensive constantly but finding more spaciousness to be proactive." She is in touch with members of the Palestinian diaspora farming in Greece and sees potential for building a Palestinian seed community in exile there.

THE SEED ACTIVIST AND THE
SEED WHO WAS SAVED: MAI NGUYEN

IN A TIME WHEN BIG Seed is tightening its grip over the commoditization and privatization of seeds, the quiet, annual act of saving them is both subversive and, culturally, deeply resonant. But it is also, as heritage wheat farmer and seed saver Mai Nguyen reminded me, hugely practical.

It was during their time as an intern at the Mendocino Grain Project, a local grains and staples hub, in 2013 that Nguyen, the American-born child of Vietnamese refugees, learned how to save seeds. They were a heritage grain convert interested in starting their own farm, and the Project was involved in growing out twelve different varieties of wheat. "They weren't all necessarily older varieties, but the need to save seed was pragmatic because of our scale and remote location," they explain. It made no sense to continually truck in small quantities by grain farming standards, yet large by UPS shipping standards. Sending one hundred pounds of grain by UPS was not cheap, and saving seeds was free.

When they launched their own five-acre Cà Pháo Farm in Ukiah, Mendocino County in the fall of 2014, they wanted to fight climate change through the development of a climate-resilient farm system based on four varieties of organic heirloom wheat with good yields but low water needs; seed saving was an integral part of this effort. By grazing sheep on the fields to build and nourish soil, their crops could outcompete the weeds without any additional nutrients or synthetic fertilizers.

These heirloom varieties are much taller plants—they grow anywhere from five to seven feet tall—and are super carbon sinks, storing up to six times more carbon than modern wheat. "All of that grain stalk is carbon from the atmosphere," says Nguyen. The heirloom Chiddam Banc de Mars and Wit Wolkering wheat varieties, and dark, northern rye varieties Nguyen grows can easily justify their presence in their fields based on their ecosystem services alone. Yet they boast another, equally valuable, quality: delicious texture and flavor in baked goods.

As with heirloom cacao, however, taste and genetic diversity are not qualities that the commodity food system prizes. Global rye production, even before being pushed down by widespread droughts and the war in Ukraine, had been declining because farmers found it too cumbersome to harvest. Nguyen, by contrast, says they will untangle every long stalk of rye from the corner of their combine because each is worth its weight in climate benefits as well as flavor.

Since launching Cà Pháo Farm, Nguyen has leased between fifty and one hundred fifty acres in Sonoma County to grow their heritage wheat under their Farmer Mai brand, and continue their advocacy work in farm policy, climate change–mitigating grainsheds, food sovereignty, and land justice. Their growing renown as a public figure in organic farming (they were the recipient of a James Beard Leadership Award in 2024) has also made Nguyen a magnet for seed gifts, which has enabled them to amass a grain seed library of one hundred different varieties over the past thirteen years. After Nguyen gave a talk at the Cascadia Grains Conference in Washington state in 2016, a man came up to them, thanked them for their work, and thrust a paper bag filled with a perennial grain native to California and the Pacific Northwest in their hands. It turned out to be a native rye whose developer drew on the same gene pool as the vaunted perennial Kernza (see Chapter 8). There have been a number of other seed-gifting instances like this, involving total strangers and treasure troves of genetic material, which Ngyuen says "feel like magic." They didn't even have a chance to get the Washington man's name; he just ran off and melted into the night.

Other seeds have come to Nguyen through their work in refugee resettlement camps, or having colleagues who are refugees. The seeds have come to them from Syria, Afghanistan, Iraq, and the Horn of Africa. "As climate change advances, more and more people will be displaced, both within the United States and globally," Nguyen says, "and these heritage seeds will become increasingly important, not just because we are going to need perennial staple crops as sources of climate resilient food, but also because people crave the tastes of home and the sense of comfort they bring."

Nguyen plans to move their seed-saving efforts forward through a nonprofit they helped found, the California Grain Campaign, which is raising funds to purchase land, ideally in Sebastopol, Sonoma County, where they farm. There, their holistic vision includes creating, teaching, and funding all of the elements needed to create a resilient small-farm foodshed where grain is an integral component, both as cash crop and cover crop. It would include testing different organic farming systems that integrate grain, and training farmers on how to add grain into their crop rotation by teaching them the skills they will need to do so, such as small-engine repair and operating farm machinery. The labor a grain farmer needs falls somewhere between the large-scale mechanized harvest of mega-farms and the non-mechanized scale of small and mid-sized farms, so this is a hole in the supply and knowledge chain that Nguyen wants to fill.

"Many farmers of color I know grow vegetables because there's a lower investment in necessary tools compared to grain farming. Yet, they want to incorporate grains because it is a good cover crop and makes for a healthful farm ecology," they explain. The California Grain Campaign already supports equipment sharing but will add supply chain support to help give farmers access to tools, processing, and markets. To help develop those markets, they plan to create a commercial kitchen for test baking and educating food professionals and the public on using climate-adapted whole grains.

As we wind up our conversation, Nguyen and I pause to admire the seed as a symbol of hope in a dark time, bundles of life that can cross oceans and preserve culture, taste, and tradition. Nguyen themself, like the seeds that were entrusted to them by their Vietnamese community, is a bundle of DNA rescued from a culture ravaged by colonialism and war. "I'm one of those people, you know," they say. "I am a seed that was saved."

EPILOGUE

AS I COMPLETE MY TOUR of the alt food system, it is hard not to think about the sheer lopsidedness of the picture I am painting. On the one side, the audacious, idealistic woman leaders of the alt food system who are forging a way of feeding the world that is more climate resilient, transparent, nutritious, and equitable. On the other, much larger side, is the commodity food system that exhausts soil, fills skies with greenhouse gases, pillages oceans, and creates a race to the bottom in producer wages.

Of course, presenting the story as a binary of two stark opposites is a rhetorical mode that leaves out important changes that are happening in the middle that have nothing to do with greenwashing. More and more conventional farmers are embracing the tenets of regenerative agriculture because they work and they save money. Governments—in the United States, at least up until the installation of Donald Trump as president for the second time in 2025—were placing stricter regulations on deforestation and loosening their purse strings to fund climate-smart regenerative practices and encourage the development of resilient local food systems. In private industry, food corporations are increasingly aware that regenerative farming will benefit both their bottom line and the future productivity of their producers.

In addition to searching out local alt food system networks such as Red Tomato and its EcoCertified fruit, the chocolate of Uncommon Cacao, the seafood of Skipper Otto, and the pasture-raised meat of Carman Provisions, we can speed food system transformation by letting our legislators, store managers, schools, and public institutions know that funding the local alt food system is a top priority for us. When grocery shopping, "ask questions about where your food comes from," advises Jonathan Rosenthal, cofounder of the worker-owned fair-trade cooperative Equal Exchange. "Take time to learn about how brands deal with farmers, and make choices." Though it can be paralyzing to feel that you lack the information to make the best, most sustainable choices, Rosenthal urges consumers to make the best decision possible: "You can't be perfect."

Look for organizations that are working to connect land, farmers, agroecological practices, capital, and political systems to make the alt food system the dominant system: groups like Karen Washington and Olivia Watkins's Black Farmer Fund; the National Black Food and Justice Alliance (NBFJA); Mad Agriculture, the Boulder, Colorado–based organization that works with regenerative "stewards at the edge" to provide financing and many other services; and Zero Foodprint, a nonprofit that helps fund the transition to regenerative farming practices by channeling a percentage of sales (or other contributions) in the restaurant and hospitality sector to grants for soil-building and ecosystems-repairing practices.

Look to the Local Catch network to connect to local, community-based seafood sources.

If you are interested in learning more about seed saving, the Organic Seed Alliance, a nonprofit research, education, and advocacy organization, is a good place to start. Seek out and support organizations like Glynwood Center for Regional Food and Farming that are training the next generation of alt food farmers, or American Farmland Trust (AFT), which is accelerating the adoption of regenerative farming practices and the creation of farmland protection programs.

Cooperatives, like Karma Cooperative in Toronto, and those of the

African American Federation of Southern Cooperatives, can be sources of community, solidarity, and strength. They are another way to take part in your local alt food system and help us exercise political and economic control over our food. They are a way of opting out of Big Food and building local resilience.

Whether you are a student, apartment dweller, or part of a senior residential community, you can form your own alt food system. Noreen Thomas of Doubting Thomas Farms in Minnesota delivers organic produce to Macalester College in St. Paul, where a grant program allows food-insecure students to aggregate food from local farms. Noreen's son, Evan Thomas, along with a group of friends, dropped their college food contract and opted to buy food direct from farmers. They cooked and baked together in their residence hall.

Another way to make local organic food affordable, Thomas adds, is to form a relationship with a local farmer. "Looks for seconds, and ask the farmer if you can buy in bulk or start your own buying club. Making a big order from a farmer is so helpful to them."

Changes in political leadership—occurring now in the United States as I write this—always have the potential to set back food system change, and the near future in America threatens to be just such a period, when so many advances in the alt food system—from improvements in farm labor conditions, climate change mitigation, and science-based advances in regenerative agriculture—will likely be slowed and rolled back. Big Food lobbyists are likely to gain more power, farmworkers both illegal and perhaps even legal[1] will be deported, and trade tariffs will raise farmer costs even more. Efforts to end structural racism in the USDA and climate-mitigating federal farm conservation programs, too, will likely come under threat.

This makes individual efforts to grow the alt food system all the more meaningful. During troubling political times, being armed with a clear sense of what an equitable and regenerative alt food system looks like will help us combat efforts that threaten those systems.

As we work to rebalance the scales at home, smallholder farmers in developing countries are fighting to keep their small-scale agricultural systems—and the agency and self-determination that come with them. They are rejecting the chemical fertilizer– and pesticide-laden industrial model western countries have adopted and have tried to inculcate around the world, and instead augment their own traditional farming methods with the latest agroecological techniques. The alt food system can encourage these farmers and connect to them, as Lotus Foods is doing by promoting agroecological rice-growing methods around the world, and Maya Mountain Cacao and Ethos Coffee Roasters are doing in Central America.

My journey through the alt food system was one that for years I knew I wanted and needed to take, although I was not sure how it would all come together in the end. Meeting the incredible cast of characters in this book has validated that intuition, connecting me in unexpected ways to my Japanese heritage, younger versions of my parents and grandparents, and the experiences and memories they gave me—all of which helped to put me on this path in the first place. Everything has come full circle.

Taking our cues from the examples of the women we have met who are working at the forefront of food system change, perhaps the simplest lessons will take us the farthest: We are neither at the center of the food system, nor at its apex, but part of an interlinked whole. It is a system gravely out of balance, but by starting on the alt fringes, we can work our way back to the center as we strive to bring balance back to our land and ocean ecosystems. Our individual actions do matter.

ACKNOWLEDGMENTS

ONE OF THE PLEASURES OF writing this book was traveling to the workplaces of my far-flung subjects, whether farm, ranch, factory, greenhouse, vineyard, brewery, or fishing grounds. Each visit left me inspired and grateful for the physically and often mentally and emotionally hard work that they do. My heartfelt thanks go out to each and every one of the women and female-identifying subjects in this book for their vision, time, hospitality, and patience as I peppered them from afar with additional questions.

I thank my agent, Max Sinsheimer, for finding a home for this book at Melville House, and for being my best first reader and the reassuring voice of reason and encouragement. I am deeply grateful to my ace editor, Michelle Capone, for understanding the message I hoped to share with readers, and helping to hone and shape it to greatest effect.

A number of people whom I interviewed did not make it into this book, which—even with a generous word count—was not large enough to accommodate all of the strands of this story that I would have liked to tell. For that, I apologize and hope those conversations will make it into another publication one day.

I extend my respect and gratitude to the friends, colleagues, and far-flung contacts who helped guide me to many of my subjects, including Mary Cleaver, Kathleen Finley, Ashley Hollister, Kathie Arnold, Dharath Hoonchamlong, Niki Nakazawa, and Nicole Dooling.

This book reaped many benefits from the expert input of a number of readers: Mary Cleaver, whose combination of food system knowledge and editorial acumen was unbeatable, Michael Rozyne and Jonathan Rosenthal for their perspectives on cooperatives, fair trade, and certifications; Mark Christian and Antonie Fountain; Catherine Donnelley; Kara Leibowitz and Anthony Myint; and Micaela Colley for their respective expertise in cacao, dairy, regenerative agriculture, and seed keeping. A special thank you to Amy Grondin for reading both the seed saving and the fisheries chapters, the latter on her smart phone aboard a fishing boat off the coast of Alaska, then rushing to and fro on land to find a Wi-Fi hotspot through which to transmit her input. Thank you also to the women of the Pleiades Network for your environmental stewardship and leadership, which sets the bar high and is a source of inspiration. And to the women of Pine Meadow Center for Arts and Agriculture—Kathy Deggendorfer, Becky Lukins, Laura Rubin—for providing me a glorious month of quiet in a beautiful spot to begin writing this book, and to my fellow residents Sandy Honda and Collin Bell for so many interesting and nourishing discussions about work and art. To the North Coast residency in Woodstock, NY: I wish every writer had access to your brand of radical hospitality.

Finally, I would like to thank my family members and friends for supporting, sheltering, and feeding me, and keeping me company through the long, intense journey of writing this book: Grant, especially, and Sandy, Melissa, Sumi, Julie, Jon, Sophie, Laura, Charles, Kathy, Dennis, Mary, Sue, Corey, and Lynda.

ENDNOTES

INTRODUCTION

1   "Hidden Costs of Agrifood Systems at the Global Level," *The State of Food and Agriculture 2023: Revealing the True Cost of Food to Transform Agrifood Systems*, Food and Agriculture Organization of the United Nations, 2023.

2   "Food System Impacts on Biodiversity Loss," research paper, Energy, Environment and Resources Programme, The United Nations Environment Programme (UNEP), Chatham House, and Compassion in World Farming, February 3, 2021.

3   Ricardo Salvador, "Here's What Agriculture of the Future Looks Like: The Multiple Benefits of Regenerative Agriculture Quantified," *The Equation, Union of Concerned Scientists*, September 19, 2018.

CHAPTER 1

1   Aaron Mok, "The Preservation of Culture Begins with a Seed: Black Seed Keepers are Recovering African American History," *Sierra*, February 27, 2021.

2   Vann R. Newkirk II, "The Great Land Robbery: The Shameful Story of How 1 Million Black Families Have Been Ripped from Their Farm," *The Atlantic*, September 2019.

3   Pete Daniel, "African American Farmers and Civil Rights," *The Journal of Southern History* 73, No. 1, (2007).

4   Vann R. Newkirk II, "The Great Land Robbery: The Shameful Story of How 1 Million Black Families Have Been Ripped from Their Farm," *The Atlantic*, September 2019.

5   Shirley Sherrod, Catherine Whitney, *The Courage to Hope: How I Stood Up to the Politics of Fear* (New York, Atria Books, 2013), p. 93, Kindle edition.

6   Pete Daniel, "African American Farmers and Civil Rights," *The Journal of Southern History* 73, No. 1, (2007).

7   "Before the War: Japanese Immigrants Pursue the American Dream," Heart Mountain World War II Japanese American Confinement Site, 2013–2024, Heart Mountain Wyoming Foundation.

8   Lee W. Formwalt, "A History of Cypress Pond Plantation, Dougherty County, Georgia," n.p., p201.

9   Dina Umali-Deininger, "Greening the Rice We Eat," *World Bank Blogs: East Asia and Pacific on the Rise*, March 15, 2022.

10   Somini Sengupta, Tran Le Thuy, "Rice Gets Reimagined, From the Mississippi to the Mekong," *The New York Times*, May 20, 2023.

11   "Financing Sustainable Rice for a Secure Future: Innovative Finance Partnerships for Climate Mitigation and Adaptation," Earth Security Group, p. 4.

12   International Rice Research Institute, "IRRI Education: 60 Years of Empowering Women in Rice Science Production Through Education and Capacity Building," IRRI Education, April 8, 2024.

13   Miles Hadfield, "The Wartime Secret of the Second Largest Consumer Co-op in the USA," *Co-op News*, January 28, 2020.

14   Monica M. White, *Freedom Farmers: Agricultural Resistance and the Black Freedom Movement*, "Justice Power and Politics" series, (Chapel Hill, University of North Carolina Press, 2019), 65–88.

15   Federation of Southern Cooperatives, "Hearing from Wendell Paris on the History of the Federation (2009)," YouTube, July 31, 2013.

16   "Value-added," a term heard often in the alt food system, refers to a product that is the opposite of a commodity, a unique product that enables a localized food chain to compete with the massive efficiencies of scale that the commodity food system has created. Or it can mean taking a bulk commodity product and adding extra value to it, for example, by growing it organically, or creating a new product out of it, such as making farmstead cheese from milk.

17   Danielle Vermeer, "Redlining and Environmental Racism," University of Michigan School for Environment and Sustainability, August 16, 2021.

18   Alexis D. Vick, Heather H. Burris, "Epigenetics and Health Disparities," Current Epidemiology Reports, March 4, 2017 (1):31–37.

19   Lucy Fisher, "System of Rice Intensification Recognized for Climate Policy Impact," *Cornell Chronicle*, February 23, 2021.

20   Rose Jacobs, "Rising Corporate Concentration Continues a 100-Year Trend," *Chicago Booth Review*, August 15, 2022.

CHAPTER 2

1   M. V. Maffini, T. G. Neltner, S. Vogel, "We are what we eat: Regulatory Gaps in the United States That Put Our Health at Risk," PLoS Biol. 2017 Dec 20;15(12):e2003578.

2   Judy Campbell, B.Sc., et al., "Nutritional Characteristics of Organic, Freshly Stone-Ground, Sourdough & Conventional Breads," Ecological Agriculture Projects Publications, 35, 1991.

3   Mark Phillips, "Building the Value Chain for Local Grains in the Northeast: Talking with June Russell of GrowNYC Grains," *Hudson River Flows*, 2018.

4   Oldways Whole Grain Council, "Milling the Past," January 23, 2019.

5   Sophia Murphy, et al., "Cereal Secrets: The world's largest grain traders and global agriculture," Oxfam Research Reports, August 2012.

6   "The Farmer's Share," National Farmers Union, according to the USDA Economic Research Service, 2021.

7   Laura Valli, "The Rye Searcher," The Real Bread Campaign, November 2020.

8   Stephen Jones, et al., "Breeding, Farming, Milling and Baking within a Chaotic Climate," Washington State University Breadlab, *Bread Lines*, Spring 2022.

CHAPTER 3

1   Nancy Matsumoto, "Want to Get Back to the Land? You're Not Alone," *Yes! Magazine*, May 26, 2017.

2   "Imports Make Up Growing Share of U.S. Fresh Fruit and Vegetable Supply," USDA Economic Research Service, July 31, 2023.

3   Gloria Zarilla, Eurofresh Distribution, "Canada, A Market Where 81% of Fruit is Imported," January 24, 2023.

4   These changes, if widely adopted, can make a meaningful difference in mitigating climate change. Project Drawdown, a network of scientists and researchers focused on climate solutions, estimates that conversion to efficient trucks like VV's could draw down between nine and eleven gigatons of Co2 by the end of the century.

5   George Anderson, "Walmart Was a More Essential Retailer Than Target in Q2," *Forbes*, August 21, 2023.

6   "Price Discrimination and Power Buyers: Why Giant Retailers Dominate the Economy and How to Stop It," American Economic Liberties Project, *Anti-Monopoly Policies & Enforcement*, September 21, 2022.

7   "Food Prices and Spending," USDA Economic Research Service, November 29, 2023.

8   Eva Jacobs, Stephanie Shipp, "How Family Spending has Changed in the U.S.," *Monthly Labor Review*, March 1990, 20–27.

9   "Farm Share of U.S. Food Dollar Dipped Below 15 cents in 2022," USDA Economic Research Service, November 15, 2023.

10   Daniel Costa, "California is on the brink of enacting the first significant law to combat international labor recruitment abuses and protect 300,000 temporary migrant workers. Will Governor Newsom sign the bill?" Economic Policy Institute, *Working Economics Blog,* September 8, 2022.

11   Richard Marosi, "Desperate Workers on a Mexican Mega-Farm: 'They Treated Us Like Slaves,'" *The Los Angeles Times*, December 10, 2014.

12   David Lazarus, "When Companies Say a Merger Will Result in Lower Prices, Try Laughing in their Face," *The Los Angeles Times,* July 10, 2018.

13   Dana Cronin, "Walmart's Pandemic Port Squeeze," *Civil Eats*, December 13, 2023.

14   Jana Caracciolo, "The Fight Over Organic: An Update," Agricultural Marketing Service, The National Agricultural Law Center, September 27, 2022.

15   Dan Mitchell, "Walmarting Organics: Who Wins?" *Civil Eats*, April 17, 2014.

16   "Equitable Food Initiative Certification," National Farm Worker Ministry, *Take Action/Farm Worker Campaigns.*

CHAPTER 4

1   Dry matter forage does not include hay or silage (hay that has been compacted, fermented, and stored). For details see "Calculating Dry Matter Intake from Pasture for Ruminants," Oregon Tilth, Ohio Ecological Farm and Food Association, 2022.

2   The transition is made slowly, over several days, which is better for udder health and decreases the likelihood of the cow developing bovine mastitis, an inflammatory response caused by microorganism infection, trauma, or, in this case, change of milking schedule. DGDG members have made the transition in close discussion with each other to share information on what transition style worked best.

3   Poor soil health from purchasing feed grown from conventional farms engaged in monocropping and chemical inputs and/or conventional dairy farming practices that do not rotate cows on pasture and use chemical fertilizers and input.

4   Lee Rinehart, "Building Healthy Pasture Soils," Cornell College of Agriculture and Life Sciences, October 2, 2017.

5   Brad Heins, "Grass-fed Cows Produce Healthier Milk," University of Minnesota Extension, 2021.

6   Allison L. Unger et al. "Fatty Acid Content of Retail Cow's Milk in the Northeastern United States—What's in it for the Consumer?" *Journal of Agricultural and Food Chemistry*, March 25, 2020, 68 (2), April 2020.

7   Kirk Kardashian, *Milk Money: Cash, Cows, and the Death of the American Dairy Farm*, contributor, Bernie Sanders (Durham: University of New Hampshire Press, 2012).

8   Danielle Wiener-Bronner, "Why Dairy farmers Across America are Dumping Their Milk," CNN Business, April 15, 2020.

9   Kirk Kardashian, "Many of Vermont's Dairy Farms Have Shuttered, and the Forecast is for Still Fewer—and Much Larger—Operations," *Seven Days, May 31, 2023.*

10 Ibid.

11 Steve Raabe, "Colorado-based Aurora Organic Dairy to pay $7.5 million settlement," *The Denver Post*, September 7, 2012.

12 Maryellen Driscoll et al., "A Scoping Review of Safety and Health Interventions in the High-Risk Dairy Industry: Gaps in Evidence Point to Future Directions in Research," *Journal of Agromedicine*, 27(1), 51–63, November 14, 2020.

13 Hannah Dreier, "Alone and Exploited, Migrant Children Work Brutal Jobs Across the U.S.," *The New York Times*, February 25, 2023, updated February 28, 2023.

14 The women of the Dairy Grazing Discussion Group are not all against the use of antibiotics. Those who are not certified organic will use them sparingly and for specific needs. None use blanket treatments or metaphylactic (treating an entire herd after one member has been diagnosed with a disease) treatments.

15 "Feed Grains Sector at a Glance," USDA Economic Research Service, updated December 21, 2023.

16 "USDA Coexistence Fact Sheets: Soybeans," USDA, February 2015.

17 Maureen Farrell, "Years After Monsanto Deal, Bayer's Roundup Bills Keep Piling Up," *The New York Times*, December 6, 2023.

18 Mari Gaines, "Roundup Lawsuit Update January 2024," *Forbes Advisor*, November 3, 2023.

19 Peter Applebome, "The Morning the Milking Was Finished," *The New York Times*, February 3, 2010.

20 "Vermont Dairy Update: May 2024," The University of Vermont Extension, Vermont Dairy Data—10 Year Summary.

21 Hayden Stewart, "Plant-Based Products Replacing Cow's Milk, But the Impact Is Small," USDA Economic Research Service, December 20, 2020.

22 Hayden Stewart, Fred Kuchler, "Fluid Milk Consumption Continues Downward Trend, Proving Difficult to Reverse," USDA Economic Research Service, June 21, 2022.

CHAPTER 5

1 Kristi Allen, "Why Eating Meat Was Banned in Japan for Centuries," *Atlas Obscura*, March 26, 2019.

2 Richard Battaglia and Kakuyu Obara, "Japan Mandates Traceability for Beef," USDA Foreign Agriculture Service GAIN (Global Agriculture Information Network) Report, July 1, 2003.

3 Nicolette Hahn Niman, *Defending Beef: The Ecological and Nutritional Case for Meat*, 2nd edition (White River Junction, Vermont: Chelsea Green Publishing 2021), 5.

4 Dan Blaustein-Rejto, "Livestock Don't Contribute 14.5% of Global Greenhouse Gas Emissions: The total is far less certain. But reducing their emissions is more important than ever," The Breakthrough Institute, April 30, 2024.

5 K. Asher, Che Green et al. "Study of Current and Former Vegetarians and Vegans," Humane Research Council, Faunalytics, December 2014.

6 Anthony Crimarco, Sparkle Springfield, Christina Petlura, et al., "A Randomized Crossover Trial on the Effect of Plant-based Compared with Animal-based Meat on Trimethylamine-N-Oxide and Cardiovascular Disease Risk Factors in Generally Healthy Adults: Study with Appetizing Plantfood—Meat Eating Alternative Trial (SWAP-MEAT)." *The American Journal of Clinical Nutrition* 112 no. 5 (2020); 1188–1199.

7 Stephan van Vliet, James R. Bain, Michael J. Muehlbauer, et al., "A metabolomics comparison of plant-based meat and grass-fed meat indicates large nutritional differences despite comparable Nutrition Facts panels," *Sci Rep* 11, 13828 (2021).

8 Leo Horrigan, Robert S. Lawrence, and Polly Walker., "How Sustainable Agriculture Can Address the Environmental and Human Health Harms of Industrial Agriculture." *Environmental Health Perspectives* 110, 5 (2002): 445–56.

9   "New USDA Data Shows Nearly 50% Increase in U.S. Factory Farmed Animals in 20 Years," Food and Water Watch, February 13, 2024.

10 JoAnn Burkholder, Bob Libra, et al., "Impacts of Waste from Concentrated Animal Feeding Operations on Water Quality," *Environmental Health Perspectives* 115, 2 (February 2007): 308–312.

11 Nicole Goodkind, "Meet the Four Meat Empires Biden Says are Unreasonably Jacking Up Prices for Americans," *Fortune*, January 8, 2022.

12 John McCracken, "Small Meat Processors Say USDA Measures Don't Address Consolidated Industry's Root Problems," *Investigative Midwest*, updated November 30, 2023.

13 H. Roger Segelken, "Simple change in cattle diets could cut E. coli infection," *Cornell Chronicle*, September 8, 1998.

14 Marina Bolotnikova and Kenny Torrella, "9 Charts That Show US Factory Farming is Even Bigger Than You Realize," *Vox*, February 26, 2024.

15 Ellen K. Silbergeld, *Chickenizing Farms and Food: How Industrial Meat Production Endangers Workers, Animals, and Consumers* (Baltimore: Johns Hopkins University Press, 2016).

16 Christopher Flavelle, Somini Sengupta, Mira Rojanasakul, "How America's Diet is Feeding the Groundwater Crisis," *The New York Times*, December 24, 2023.

17 Since I reported this chapter Cannan has begun working with another livestock farm in the Hudson Valley, though she still serves as a consultant for Kinderhook Farm.

CHAPTER 6

1   Naomi Hirahara, Geraldine Knatz, *Terminal Island: Lost Communities on America's Edge*, (Los Angeles: Angel City Press, 2024), 125, 151.

2   Toshiro Izumi, "Terminal Island Life History Project," interview with Charlie Hamasaki. Online Archive of California.

3   William Atlas et al., "Indigenous Systems of Management for Culturally and Ecologically Resilient Pacific Salmon (*Oncorhynchus spp.*) Fisheries, *BioScience*, 71, no. 2, (February 2021): 186–204.

4   "Working the Line," *From Tides to Tins*, Gulf of Georgia Cannery Society.

5   Paul Greenberg, "The Expansion of Global Fishing," Earth Journalism Network, April 18, 2014.

6   Joseph Gough, Erin James-abra, "History of Commercial Fisheries," *The Canadian Encyclopedia*, August 12, 2013, updated July 23, 2015.

7   Ibid.

8   Eric J. Pedersen, Patrick L. Thompson et al., "Signatures of the Collapse and Incipient Recovery of an Overexploited Marine Ecosystem," *Royal Society Open Science*, 4:170215, July 5, 2017.

9   B.K.K.K. Jinadasa, Christopher Elliott et al., "A Review of the Presence of Formaldehyde in Fish and Seafood," *Food Control* 136 (June 2022).

10   Kathryn Saducas, Caroline Slootwed, "Is the Answer to Land-Based Agriculture Found in the Ocean?" World Economic Forum: Food and Water, February 10, 2022.

11   Bren Smith, *Eat Like a Fish: My Adventures as a Fisherman Turned Restorative Farmer* (New York, Alfred A. Knopf, 2019), 115.

12   Alexandra Talty, "The Promise and Possible Pitfalls of American Kelp Farming," *Civil Eats*, June 27, 2024.

13   Ibid.

14   Harrison Charo Karisa, Christopher Ian Brett, "Unlocking the Potential of the Seaweed Sector for Sustainable Growth," World Bank Blogs, August 16, 2023.

15   Christine Hall, "AKUA Lands $3.2M to Turn Kelp Into Burgers," *TechCrunch*, November 5, 2021.

16   Stephen T. Garnett et al., "A Spatial Overview of the Global Importance of Indigenous Lands for Conservation, *Nature Sustainability*, 1, (July 2018): 369–374.

CHAPTER 7

1   Andrew Gunsul, "Mesoamerican Cultures and Their Histories: Cacao and Chocolate," University of Oregon, Edublogs, Spring 2010.

2   Clair Lanaud, Hélène Vignes et al., "A Revisited History of Cacao Domestication in Pre-Columbian Times Revealed by Archaeogenomic Approaches," *Sci Rep* 14, 2972, March 7, 2024.

3   "When Money Grew on Trees," Cornell University Library, online exhibits, *Chocolate: Food of the Gods*.

4   Eline Poelmans, Johan Swinnen "A Brief Economic History of Chocolate," in Mara P. Squicciarini, Johan Swinnen, eds. *The Economics of Chocolate* (Oxford, Oxford University Press, online edition, Oxford Academic), March 2016.

5   Antonie Fountain, "Cocoa Barometer 2022," Voice Network, Nieuwe Kazernelaan, Netherlands.

6   "Cargill at a Glance," webpage (Home/About Cargill/Cargill at a Glance).

7   "Living Income in Cocoa," Wageningen University & Research, Wageningen, Netherlands, November 17, 2021.

8   "What is Racial Capitalism?" American Medical Association: *Health Equity*, November 10, 2021.

9   Antonie Fountain, "Cocoa Barometer 2022," Voice Network, Nieuwe Kazernelaan, Netherlands.

10   Matt Reynolds, "The World's Broken Food System Costs $12.7 Trillion a Year," *Wired*, November 6, 2023.

11   Claire Lanaud et al, "A Revisited History of Cacao Domestication in Pre-Columbian Times Revealed by Aarchaeogenomic Approaches," *Sci Rep* 14, 2972 (2024).

12   Tracy Barnett, Hernán Vilchez, "The Arhuacos: A Message from the Mamos, the Prophets of the Sierra Nevada," Pulitzer Center, November 2, 2021.

13   "The Guatemala Genocide Case," The Center for Justice and Accountability, 2009.

14   "History of Polk County," Polk County Historical Association, Bartow, Florida.

15   "Comparing Apalachee, Timucua, and Calusa Settlements at the Time of European Exploration," adapted from Florida Department of State website by Mound House education staff, July 27, 2020.

16   The school itself is a product of the exploitation of labor in the original "banana republics" of Honduras and Guatemala; it was founded in 1941 by Samuel Zemurray, president of the United Fruit Company, who made his fortune in the banana trade, organized a successful coup to overthrow the Honduran president, and in 1912 installed one who would treat his business interests in the country more favorably. In 1953, faced with a democratically elected government that threatened to expropriate some of his vast land holding in Honduras for redistribution to peasants, he launched a successful propaganda campaign that led to a CIA-led coup. Zemurray went on to become a major philanthropist, the Zamorano Pan-American Agricultural School being among one of many institutions that benefited from his legacy-repairing largesse.

17   Cooperative and Fair Trade expert Jonathan Rosenthal notes that this is a key feature of ethical direct trade systems, often achieved by working with nonprofit finance organizations such as Massachusetts-based Root Capital, UK-based Shared Interest, or ethical banks and/or funds.

18   Indigenous smallholder farmers in remote areas untouched by the Green Revolution

are much better positioned to adopt the latest organic practices. Converting from low input and passive organic to certified organic can mean an increase in yields and quality, while commercial Green Revolution–style farmers find it more difficult and costly to convert.

19 Paul Hicks, "Scandal of the C-Price," Coffeelands, Catholic Relief Services, September 13, 2018.

20 "2022 List of Goods Produced by Child Labor or Forced Labor," Bureau of International Labor Affairs, U.S. Department of Labor, September 2022, Washington, D.C.

21 Julie Hjerl Hansen, "Bitter Coffee II," Danwatch, 2016, Copenhagen, Denmark.

CHAPTER 8

1 Rick Nelson, "Sioux Chef Sean Sherman's New Minneapolis Restaurant Owamni Will Blend the Past and Future," *The Minneapolis Star Tribune*, June 4, 2021.

2 Stefanie Ellis, "Owamni: A (R)evolution of Indigenous Foods," "World's Table," BBC, September 28, 2022.

3 Jane Lamm Carroll, "Engineering the Falls: The Corps of Engineers' Role at St. Anthony Falls," U.S. Army Corps of Engineers, St. Paul District website, October 27, 2015.

4 Lauren Asprooth, University of Wisconsin, Madison et al., "Drivers and Deterrents of Small Grain Adoption in the Upper Midwest," Michael Fields Agricultural Institute, September 2023.

5 Vincent F. Garry et al., "Birth defects, season of conception, and sex of children born to pesticide applicators living in the Red River Valley of Minnesota, USA." *Environmental Health Perspectives*, Vol. 110, Issue suppl 3, 441–449.

6 Alice Feiring, *Natural Wine for the People: What It is, Where to Find It, How to Love It* (Emeryville, California, Ten Speed Press, 2019), 24.

7 "Production Volume of Mezcal in Mexico from 2011 to 2022," Statista 2024.

8 "How Many Agaves Does It Take to Make a Bottle of Mezcal," "Agave Road Trip" podcast, February 10, 2021.

9 Rowan Jacobson, "The Last Days of Mezcal: Can the World's Most Beautiful Spirit Survive Its Boom?" *Bloomberg Business Week*, February 26, 2024.

10 Ryan Nebeker, "The Sustainability Challenges that Threaten the Agave Industry," foodprint.org, December 4, 2020, last updated November 9, 2023.

11 "Cofece Sanctions the Mexican Regulatory Council for the Quality of Mezcal with Over 4 Million Pesos for Harming Mezcal Producers," Mexico Federal Economic Competition Commission (Cofece), June 27, 2024.

12 David Yetman, "Ejidos, Land Sales, and Free Trade in Northwest Mexico: Will Globalization Affect the Commons? *American Studies*, 41, no. 2/3 (Summer/ Fall 2000): pp. 211–234 "Globalization, Transnationalism, and The End of the American Century."

13 Caroline Hatchett, "The Philippine Influence in Mexican Mezcal Making," liquor. com, April 27, 2023.

CHAPTER 9

1 Paulina Jenney, "A Guide to Seed Intellectual Property Rights," Organic Seed Alliance, June 30, 2023, adapted from "Keeping What You Sow: Intellectual Property Rights for Plant Breeders and Seed Growers," submitted May 2022 to the University of Montana.

2 Dee Laninga, "The Story of Seeds: Our Collective Legacy, Our Stolen Birthright," Farm Action, November 10, 2022.

3 Kristina Hubbard, "Seed Privatization and the Path Toward Equitable Exchange," Organic Seed Alliance, March 2023.

4 Robert Lee and Tristan Ahtone, "Land-Grab Universities: Expropriated Indigenous Land is the Foundation of the Land Grant University System," *High Country News*, March 30, 2020.

5 Howard, Philip H. 2009. "Visualizing Consolidation in the Global Seed Industry: 1996–2008," *Sustainability* 1, no. 4,: 1266–1287.

6 Keith Fuglie and James M. MacDonald, "Expanded Intellectual Property Protections for Crop Seeds Increase Innovation and Market Power for Companies," USDA Economic Research Service, Feature: Crops, August 28, 2023.

7 Paulina Jenney, "A Guide to Seed Intellectual Property Rights," Organic Seed Alliance, June 30, 2023, adapted from "Keeping What You Sow: Intellectual Property Rights for Plant Breeders and Seed Growers," submitted May 2022 to the University of Montana.

8 Kristina Kiki Hubbard, "The Sobering Details Behind the Latest Seed Monopoly Chart," *Civil Eats*, January 11, 2019.

9 Paulina Jenney, "A Guide to Seed Intellectual Property Rights: Can I Get Sued for Growing Patented Seeds," Organic Seed Alliance, June 30, 2023, adapted from "Keeping What You Sow: Intellectual Property Rights for Plant Breeders and Seed

Growers," submitted May 2022 to the University of Montana.

10   "Monsanto and Terminator Seeds," *Open Case Studies*, The University of British Columbia, February 8, 2021.

11   "What's the Controversy over 'Terminator Seeds,'" Genetic Literacy Project. Copyright 2012 - 2025.

12   Rose White, "What is Jalapeñogate? Gardeners Surprised by Mystery Pepper Harvest," MLive.com, August 4, 2023.

13   "Indigenous Peoples," *Social Sustainability and Inclusion*, World Bank Group, April 6, 2023.

14   David Zotigh, "Native Perspectives on the 40th Anniversary of the American Indian Religious Freedom Act," *Smithsonian*, November 30, 2018.

EPILOGUE

1   Karen Perry Stillerman, "What a Second Trump Administration Means for Food and Farmers, *The Equation, Union of Concerned Scientists*, November 6, 2024.

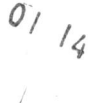

RESOURCES

Black Farmer Fund—New York, NY

New Communities Land Trust—Albany, GA

Hope Well Wine—Hopewell, OR

Iliamma Fish Company—Bristol Bay, AK

Rhody Wild Sea Gardens—Portsmouth, RI

Taza Chocolate—Somerville, MA

Ethos Coffee Roaster—Lakeland, FL

Cà Pháo Farm and the California Grain Campaign—Uriah, Mendocino
County / Sebastopol, Second Generation Seeds—El Sobrante, Contra
Costa County, CA

Zinacantán mezcal—San Diego La Mesa Tochimiltzingo, Atlixco Valley,
Mexico

Castronovo Chocolate—Stuart, FL

Stonington Kelp Company—Stonington, CT

North Country Creamery—Keeseville, NY

Chaseholm Far—Pine Plain, NY

Full Belly Farm—Capa Valley, CA

Maine Grains—Skowhegan, ME

Motherdough Mill and Bakery—Toronto, CAN

Black Yard Farm Collective—Argyre, NY

Jubilee Justices Farm—Alexandria, LA

Federation of Southern Cooperatives—across the South

GrowNYC—New York, New York

Artisan Grain Collaborative—across the Midwest

Baker's Field Flour & Bread—Minneapolis, MN

Veritable Vegetable—San Francisco, CA

Chaseholm Farm—Pine Plain, NY

Corse Farm Dairy—Whittingham, VT

Kinderhook Farm—Valatie, NY

La Salumina—Hurleyville, NY

Founder Pla Organic Fish Market—Bangkok, Thailand

Rhody Wild Sea Gardens—Portsmouth, RI

Amevive Wine—Santa Ynez Valley, Santa Barbara, CA